Getting to the Core of Writing

Essential Lessons for Every Sixth Grade Student

Richard Gentry, Ph.D.
Jan McNeel, M.A.Ed.
Vickie Wallace-Nesler, M.A.Ed.

SHELL EDUCATION

M000122093

Publishing Credits

Dona Herweck Rice, *Editor-in-Chief*; Robin Erickson, *Production Director*;
Lee Aucoin, *Creative Director*; Timothy J. Bradley, *Illustration Manager*;
Sara Johnson, M.S.Ed., *Senior Editor*; Christine Dugan, *Editor*;
Jennifer Kim, M.A.Ed., *Associate Education Editor*; Leah Quillian, *Assistant Editor*;
Grace Alba, *Designer*; Corinne Burton, *M.A.Ed., Publisher*

Standards

© 2004 Mid-continent Research for Education and Learning (McREL)
© 2007 Teachers of English to Speakers of Other Languages, Inc. (TESOL)
© 2010 National Governors Association Center for Best Practices and Council of Chief State School Officers (CCSS)

Shell Education
5301 Oceanus Drive
Huntington Beach, CA 92649-1030
http://www.shelleducation.com
ISBN 978-1-4258-0920-1
© 2013 Shell Educational Publishing, Inc.

Table of Contents

Table of Contents *(cont.)*

The Importance of Writing

In recent years, many school districts and teachers referred to writing as the "Neglected R" and viewed reading as the path to literacy success. Today, as research has revealed more information about the fundamental connection between reading success and writing competency, we are realizing that the road to literacy is a two-way street (Graham and Hebert 2010). While working as literacy consultants, we encountered numerous, capable teachers struggling with the complexity of implementing rigorous writing instruction. We wrote this book to enable all teachers to implement a successful writing program with a high degree of teaching competency. The success enjoyed by many of the teachers using the materials in this book has relieved frustrations, rejuvenated careers, and rekindled enthusiasm for teaching.

This book was written to fulfill two major objectives. The first objective involves motivating teachers to value and incorporate writing instruction as an essential element of literacy development. It should help them implement best practices and simplify the planning of writing instruction. New writing standards have been applied by education leaders at every level. Ultimately, the responsibility for implementing these standards is placed on the classroom teacher. Historically, the lack of emphasis on writing instruction in teacher education programs has left teachers feeling woefully unprepared to teach students to write, particularly at a level which meets the expectations of the standards for writing. The burden of this responsibility and feelings of inadequacy have left both experienced and novice teachers feeling empty-handed and unprepared.

Since 2010, most states have adopted the Common Core State Standards (CCSS), which are designed to provide teachers and parents with a clear understanding of what students are expected to learn. Since the CCSS are newly adopted, many teachers have not received professional development to become familiar with the standards nor have they received resources for their instruction, particularly in the area of writing. Therefore, the second objective of this book is to assist teachers in becoming familiar with these standards for writing and provide resources to support the implementation of these standards in their classrooms. *Getting to the Core of Writing* provides lessons outlining four key areas of writing: Text Types and Purposes, Production and Distribution of Writing, Research, and Range of Writing. It offers suggestions to meet those standards in instruction during Writer's Workshop. It also addresses how speaking and listening standards are easily practiced by engaging students in an interactive lesson format.

It is no secret that students become better writers by writing every day. This book contains the foundational structure and best practices that will guide teachers as they establish a daily Writer's Workshop that includes consistent, structured instruction to engage students in the writing process. Beyond that, a flexible pacing guide is provided to aid in planning writing instruction.

It is our hope that this book provides teachers with all the tools needed to inspire and equip young writers in today's classrooms.

—Richard, Jan, and Vickie

Traits of Quality Writing

The traits of quality writing continue to gain recognition as the language of successful writers. Educators at the Northwest Regional Educational Laboratory, now Education Northwest, searched for an accurate, reliable method of measuring student writing performance. Six attributes of good writing are identified in *Seeing with New Eyes* (Spandel 2005). These characteristics are used to inform and guide writing instruction:

- **Ideas** are the heart of the message, the content of the piece, and the main theme.

- **Sentence fluency** is the rhythm and flow of the language, the sound of word patterns, and the way in which the writing plays to the ear, not just to the eye.

- **Organization** is the internal structure, the thread of central meaning, and the logical and sometimes intriguing pattern of ideas within a piece of writing.

- **Word choice** is the use of rich, colorful, and precise language that moves and enlightens the reader.

- **Voice** is the heart and soul, the magic, and the wit, along with the feeling and conviction of the individual writer that emerge through the words.

- **Conventions** are how the writer uses mechanical correctness in the piece—spelling, paragraphing, grammar and usage, punctuation, and capitalization.

Knowing and understanding the traits of quality writing supports teachers, students, and parents in thinking about writing and understanding what makes for writing success. Even in the early grades, students can communicate and recognize the characteristics of quality writing. The works of Ruth Culham (2008) and Vicki Spandel (2008) emphasize the value and benefits of using these traits to provide a common language—"a writer's vocabulary for thinking, speaking, and working like writers" (Spandel 2008, 7)—to enrich instruction and assessment in any classroom.

The value and importance of using this trait language in writing instruction is well supported by research (Gentry 2006). It is particularly important when working with students in the early grades to provide instructional tools to support students' different learning styles. In *Getting to the Core of Writing*, the traits are personified through student-friendly characters. Each of the characters represents a different writing trait, and collectively they are referred to as the Traits Team (traitsteam.pdf). Students are introduced to the individual team members through the mini-lessons. The Traits Team becomes a valuable tool for a Writer's Workshop experience. A more detailed description and poster of each Traits Team member is provided in the introduction to each trait section.

The Reading and Writing Connection

Students' writing abilities often shift in third through sixth grade as student readers make a giant cognitive leap from learning to read to reading to learn. Students have likely advanced through all five phases of beginning reading and writing development, attaining a degree of independence as both readers and writers by the time they enter third grade.

In some ways, reading advances faster than writing, and the complexity of writing is accentuated during third through sixth grade. It becomes apparent that writing is more demanding and, in some ways, harder than reading for third, fourth, fifth, and sixth graders. For example, fourth graders can read fairly complex novels, but they would not be able to write novels at that same level of complexity. In the words of writing expert Ralph Fletcher, "Reading is up here and writing is down there. Probably the smartest fourth grader in the country cannot write a novel" (Fletcher 2000).

One expectation of the reading and writing connection in third through sixth grade is that students gain facility in reading a book like a writer (Yates 1995). During this period, students likely begin viewing writing more from the author's perspective, bringing structure and organization to pieces they create based on the reading they do and the study of literary authors' crafts.

In earlier grades, young writers often have a linear sense of writing; they follow a story map or a simple structure, such as *first*, *then*, *next*, and *last*, or *beginning*, *middle*, and *end*. Younger writers often move purposely straight through their composition in a step-by-step approach, rarely rereading or reflecting as they write. Rereading and reflecting as they move through a text becomes more important in the intermediate grades, helping students make

sense of what they have written (Gentry 2002). Not only do they read like a writer, the Common Core State Standards help them think like a writer.

Moving from Concrete to Abstract Thinking

Third-, fourth-, fifth-, and sixth-grade writing often mirrors how children think. Initially in this period of elementary school, students' writing can reflect thinking "limited to concrete phenomena and their own past experiences: that is, thinking is not abstract" (Bjorklund 1999). A third-grade writer following a clear-cut, step-by-step sequence may reflect thinking "limited to tangible facts and objects and not to hypotheses" (Bjorklund 1999). During third grade through sixth grade, students will learn to shift back and forth during drafting to survey the piece from both the reader's and writer's perspective. This includes responding to varying demands of audience, purpose, task, and genre, often guided by the Common Core State Standards and based on a rich array of appropriate models for writing.

The Reading and Writing Connection *(cont.)*

As third- through sixth-grade writers mature, they begin to reflect on their own thinking, pausing and rereading to see how the piece they have crafted sounds or discovering alternative routes for a story plot or other written presentation. They are more likely to begin to consider the reader before putting words down on paper. They gain greater mastery of paragraphing, revising, and editing.

Towards the end of elementary school, writers are much more likely "to introspect about their own thought processes, and generally, can think abstractly" (Bjorklund 1999, 62). Moving from the constraints of story mapping or events in their immediate experience, they advance in ability to critique, consider the impact of specific details, choose just the right word, cite specific textual evidence to support their views, and make other appropriate choices for their writing. They demonstrate both deductive and inductive reasoning, moving from the general to the specific or moving from specific observations to broad generalizations, respectively. Their understanding of components and conventions of the writing process grows, and with the support of the Common Core State Standards, their writing becomes more sophisticated, moving along the grade-by-grade continuum that will eventually lead to college- and career-readiness.

As students move through third through sixth grade, the reading and writing connection likely changes them as thinkers, helping them develop abilities to assimilate information into abstract schemes, question their own thinking, test their own hypotheses, and develop deeper levels of knowledge and thinking (Mann 2002).

The Reading and Writing Connection *(cont.)*

Basic Common Core Goals for Writers

Students engage in a rich array of literature as models for writing.
Students continue to develop the ability to write both fiction and nonfiction.
Students' writing ties into a comprehensive, content-rich curriculum.
Students demonstrate independence as writers appropriate for their grade level.
Students demonstrate strong content knowledge through writing.
Student writers respond to the varying demands of audience, task, purpose, and discipline.
Students' writing demonstrates ability to both comprehend and critique.
Student writers cite specific textual evidence in their writing to support their views.
Students consider the impact of specific words and details and make appropriate choices.
Students bring structure and organization to their own writing based on studies of the literary authors' crafts.
Students use technology to enhance their writing.

Adapted from "College and Career Readiness Standards for Reading, Writing, and Speaking and Listening" (Shanahan In Press).

The Purpose of Assessment

Assessment plays an integral role in writing instruction. It may occur at the district or state level to measure the student's ability to meet specific standards. Many classrooms include self-assessments where students use rubrics and checklists to score and reflect on their own work. Writing assessment can also take place informally as we sit and confer with writers, taking anecdotal notes. Maintaining student writing portfolios comprised of both spontaneous and directed writing provides assessment information of a student's writing development and performance over a specific time. No matter the type or form of assessment, it should enable you to determine students' strengths and weaknesses so you may revise your instruction to meet the needs of your writers.

> *Assessment must promote learning, not just measure it. When learners are well served, assessment becomes a learning experience that supports and improves instruction. The learners are not just the students but also the teachers, who learn something about their students.*
>
> —Regie Routman (1999, 559)

Monitoring students' writing over time provides valuable information about their growth and development. The samples, collected periodically throughout the year into student portfolios, reflect where the Writer's Workshop journey began and the student's ongoing progress and achievement relative to the instructional goals. Portfolios, along with your anecdotal notes, not only inform parents of their child's growth but also show students the variety of concepts and skills learned during Writer's Workshop.

In addition to ongoing classroom assessment, it is valuable to conduct benchmark assessments at the beginning, middle, and end of the year. The beginning of the year benchmark provides you with a baseline of data that represents the foundational skill level of the student writer. The middle and end of the year benchmarks show areas of achievement and needs as well as identify effective instructional strategies. *Getting to the Core of Writing* refers to these benchmarks as Benchmarks 1, 2, and 3, respectively. After each benchmark, it is important to analyze students' work using the grade-level rubric (pages 258–259; writingrubric.pdf) in order to identify the additional support needed for each student.

Collaborating with other teachers encourages targeted conversations about student work and helps build confidence as you become more knowledgeable in interpreting and evaluating student writing. Although *Getting to the Core of Writing* includes a Suggested Pacing Guide (pages 12–13; pacingguide. pdf) and a Year-at-a-Glance plan of instruction (yearataglance.pdf) that provide benchmark prompt suggestions, it is not a one-size-fits-all classroom writing map. Your assessments and observations provide essential information to guide instructional decisions designed to meet the needs of all of your students. For additional assessment resources, including benchmark support information, a rubric, a scoring guide, a classroom grouping mat, and scored student writing samples, see Appendix B (pages 256–267).

Planning Writing Instruction

Essential in any literacy development is planning and scheduling. *Getting to the Core of Writing* supports teachers as they learn and grow as writers along with their students while at the same time implementing Writer's Workshop. Growing requires nurturing like writing requires practice. The provided plan of instruction is based on the conviction that Writer's Workshop happens each and every day throughout the school year. Mini-lessons may be retaught when necessary. Some mini-lessons may require more than one day for students to fully grasp an understanding of the writing concept. Additionally, teachers proficient in writing instruction may select individual mini-lessons and teach them in an order that meets the specific needs of their students.

When writing is shared consistently and enthusiastically, students learn, love, and choose to write. As always, instruction must also be guided by the developmental needs of the students as revealed through their daily writing. The structure provided by Writer's Workshop and the lessons in this book allow both students and teachers to recognize themselves as successful writers. Once the routines of Writer's Workshop are in place, it is much easier for the teacher to focus on a quality daily writing time. Things become so routine that teachers will find themselves feeling motivated and passionate about writing instruction instead of overwhelmed.

The pacing guide found on pages 12–13 provides a suggested sequence for when to teach the lessons in this book. It serves as a guide for consistent practice in the writing process and incorporates the traits of quality writing. It is suggested that some lessons be taught more than once throughout the year.

When this occurs, if desired, the content of the student writing pieces can be modified slightly to provide students with opportunities to practice writing opinion-, informative-explanatory-, and narrative-based texts. By doing this, students get to write different genres in formats that are familiar to them. For example, in Ideas Lesson 1, students can change the content about which they brainstorm to create an opinion piece on why dogs are the best pet, a narrative on their summer vacation, and an informative piece on the types of plants around the school.

Planning Writing Instruction (cont.)

Suggested Pacing Guide

Month	Lesson
August/September	• Managing WW Lesson 1 (page 35) • Managing WW Lesson 2 (page 38) • **Administer Benchmark 1:** What if you were to explore your favorite place and find something extraordinary? What if it were a magic lamp? What would you do? Write an interesting story and tell about the experience. • Managing WW Lesson 3 (page 41) • Managing WW Lesson 4 (page 50) • Managing WW Lesson 5 (page 52) • Managing WW Lesson 6 (page 58) • Ideas Lesson 1 (page 77) • Organization Lesson 1 (page 127) • Managing WW Lesson 7 (page 62) • Managing WW Lesson 8 (page 65) • Conventions Lesson 1 (page 219) • Ideas Lesson 2 (page 80) • Sentence Fluency Lesson 1 (page 103) • Organization Lesson 2 (page 130) • Conventions Lesson 2 (page 224) • Sentence Fluency Lesson 2 (page 107) • Word Choice Lesson 1 (page 169)

Month	Lesson
October	• Review Managing WW Lessons 1–8 as needed • Managing WW Lesson 9 (page 68) • Managing WW Lesson 10 (page 71) • Ideas Lesson 3 (page 83) • Sentence Fluency Lesson 3 (page 110) • Word Choice Lesson 2 (page 174) • Ideas Lesson 4 (page 86) • Organization Lesson 3 (page 134) • Voice Lesson 1 (page 201) • Organization Lesson 4 (page 137) • Conventions Lesson 3 (page 227) • Conventions Lesson 4 (page 231) • Ideas Lesson 2 (page 80)

Month	Lesson
November	• Review Managing WW Lessons 1–10 as needed • Ideas Lesson 5 (page 89) • Organization Lesson 5 (page 140) • Sentence Fluency Lesson 4 (page 113) • Voice Lesson 2 (page 204) • Conventions Lesson 5 (page 234) • Word Choice Lesson 3 (page 177) • Sentence Fluency Lesson 1 (page 103) • Organization Lesson 3 (page 134) • Organization Lesson 4 (page 137) • Conventions Lesson 6 (page 237) • Ideas Lesson 2 (page 80)

Month	Lesson
December	• Review Managing WW Lessons 1–10 as needed • Ideas Lesson 6 (page 92) • Voice Lesson 3 (page 207) • Word Choice Lesson 4 (page 182) • Organization Lesson 6 (page 143) • Sentence Fluency Lesson 5 (page 116) • Sentence Fluency Lesson 3 (page 110) • Conventions Lesson 7 (page 241) • Ideas Lesson 2 (page 80)

Planning Writing Instruction (cont.)

Suggested Pacing Guide (cont.)

Month	Lesson
January	• Review Managing WW Lessons 1–10 as needed • Ideas Lesson 7 (page 95) • Word Choice Lesson 5 (page 185) • Sentence Fluency Lesson 6 (page 119) • Conventions Lesson 1 (page 219) • Voice Lesson 4 (page 210) • Organization Lesson 7 (page 147) • Sentence Fluency Lesson 4 (page 113) • Word Choice Lesson 6 (page 190) • Conventions Lesson 8 (page 244) • Ideas Lesson 2 (page 80) • **Administer Benchmark 2:** The local Board of Education is considering approval of gardening projects on school sites to provide fresh fruit and vegetables for school breakfasts and lunches. Make a claim to the board members about school gardening and support your claim with details and evidence.

Month	Lesson
February	• Review Managing WW Lessons 1–10 as needed • Ideas Lesson 5 (page 89) • Sentence Fluency Lesson 7 (page 122) • Organization Lesson 8 (page 150) • Conventions Lesson 6 (page 237) • Voice Lesson 5 (page 213) • Organization Lesson 3 (page 134) • Organization Lesson 4 (page 137) • Conventions Lesson 3 (page 227) • Ideas Lesson 2 (page 80)

Month	Lesson
March	• Review Managing WW Lessons 1–10 as needed • Ideas Lesson 8 (page 98) • Sentence Fluency Lesson 1 (page 103) • Voice Lesson 3 (page 207) • Word Choice Lesson 4 (page 182) • Organization Lesson 9 (page 153) • Word Choice Lesson 3 (page 177) • Sentence Fluency Lesson 2 (page 107) • Conventions Lesson 4 (page 231) • Conventions Lesson 8 (page 244) • Ideas Lesson 2 (page 80)

Month	Lesson
April	• Review Managing WW Lessons 1–10 as needed • Ideas Lesson 7 (page 95) • Sentence Fluency Lesson 5 (page 116) • Sentence Fluency Lesson 6 (page 119) • Word Choice Lesson 2 (page 174) • Word Choice Lesson 5 (page 185) • Organization Lesson 10 (page 157) • Conventions Lesson 6 (page 237) • Conventions Lesson 5 (page 234) • Ideas Lesson 2 (page 80)

Month	Lesson
May	By this time of the year, students will have mastery of many concepts. And although you may have completed your state writing assessment, it is important to continue writer's workshop. Revisit mini-lessons based on students' needs and interests. **Administer Benchmark 3:** Your family members have many life experiences. Use your interview notes* to write an informative piece about specific information from past memories and experiences. Provide details, facts, and examples to support your writing. * Students were asked to interview family members prior to the benchmark.

Components of Writer's Workshop

Writer's Workshop entails common characteristics that are essential to developing enthusiastic and successful student writers (Graves 1994, 2003; Fletcher and Portalupi 2001; Calkins 1994; Calkins, Hartman, and White 2005; Ray 2001; Ray and Cleaveland 2004; Gentry 2000, 2004, 2010). The guidelines that follow have been time-tested by years of classroom practice and collaboration with master writing teachers. The framework of this structure includes the following: the mini-lesson, writing practice time, and sharing time.

The Mini-Lesson

The mini-lesson is 5–15 minutes in length and begins the workshop. It is an opportunity to review past learning, introduce new writing strategies through modeling, and engage students in practicing those strategies through oral rehearsal. Each mini-lesson is focused on one specific topic that both addresses the needs of writers and reflects these skills as practiced by real authors. The mini-lesson is always energetic and challenges students to participate while building their confidence as writers. Students gather in a common area and become part of a comfortable, safe environment that provides guidance and encouragement.

In the appropriate mini-lessons, introduce the Traits Team poster as a visual reminder for students of the writing traits. The Traits Team includes *Ida, Idea Creator* (page 76); *Simon, Sentence Builder* (page 102); *Owen, Organization Conductor* (page 126); *Wally, Word Choice Detective* (page 168); *Val and Van, Voice* (page 200); and *Callie, Super Conventions Checker* (page 218). These characters work as a team to show students that good writing is not built one skill at a time but with a team of strategies.

Writing Practice Time

During the 15–30 minute writing practice, students apply the skill, strategy, or craft taught in the mini-lesson. This part of the lesson gives students practice necessary in becoming proficient writers as they compose a message to share with a reader. Simultaneously, the teacher helps individual students or small groups of students compose through conferencing. These conferences provide teachers the opportunity to praise students for applying a strategy, followed by a short teaching point. Teachers document observations in a Conferring Notebook to be used for evaluating students' progress, planning new instruction, and meeting with parents. An important part of the writing practice time is the *Spotlight Strategy*. It briefly calls attention to one or two students each day by spotlighting their work, especially when attempting the focus skill presented in the mini-lesson.

Sharing Time

The 5–15 minutes of sharing echoes the mini-lesson across Writer's Workshop and provides an additional opportunity for student talk time. At the end of the writing practice time, students are invited to spend several minutes sharing with partners, in small groups, or individually in the Author's Chair. Teachers select students to share based on their observations during writing time. A variety of sharing methods is used to promote motivation and excitement. At the end of Writer's Workshop, homework suggestions are made to help students follow up on the mini-lesson ideas. Homework can be shared on the next workshop day.

Implementing the Lessons

Each lesson supports teachers in their writing instruction and encourages students to write like published authors. Consistent language builds a commonality between students as well as across grade levels. Talking about writers, studying other writers, and practicing the craft of writing give students the gift of being authors. While the focus of the lesson may change each day, the lesson routine remains constant. Building routines in any instruction yields smooth transitions between activities and fewer opportunities for distractions. Some mini-lessons may be taught daily while others might be explored across several days. Several mini-lessons can easily be adapted to multiple themes and various pieces of literature, including those listed in the Common Core State Standards Suggested Works. It is important to consider the specific developmental levels and needs of the students. The lesson format provides structure, support, and a framework for instruction for the busy classroom teacher.

Using consistent language during each section of Writer's Workshop is one structure that students will recognize and that will be helpful for smooth transitions. Suggested language for each section of Writer's Workshop is provided in the lessons. Each Writer's Workshop lesson includes the following sections:

- Think About Writing
- Teach
- Engage
- Apply
- Write/Conference
- Spotlight Strategy
- Share
- Homework

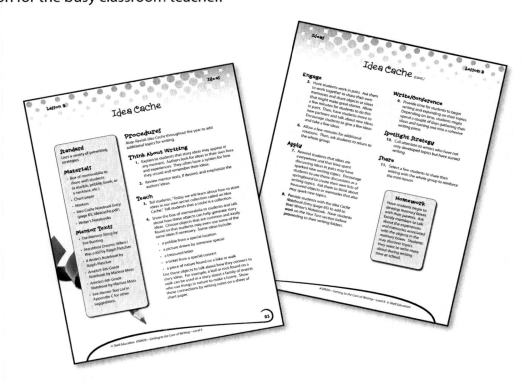

Implementing the Lessons (cont.)

Think About Writing—Students reconnect to past mini-lessons and teachers make authentic connections between reading and writing.

Procedures and **Notes**—Special information and teaching tips, followed by the explicit directions for teaching the lesson.

Standards and **Materials**—Indicates the areas of focus for the lesson and all materials needed.

Mentor Texts—Published writing that contains explicit and strong examples of the concepts addressed in the lesson. Use the recommended mentor text as a read-aloud during your reading block or quickly review it during Writer's Workshop. During the writing block, focus on small samples of text that match the mini-lesson skill. Recommended mentor texts are suggested as part of each lesson. Alternative suggestions can be found in Appendix C or on the Teacher Resource CD (mentortextlist.pdf).

Teach—Supports students through demonstration and modeling to help elevate their level of writing.

Lesson 3 — Ideas

Idea Cache

Standard
Uses a variety of prewriting strategies

Materials
- Box of memorabilia to share with students (a marble, pebble, book, or a necklace, etc.)
- Chart paper
- Markers
- *Idea Cache Notebook Entry* (page 85; ideacache.pdf)
- Writer's Notebooks

Mentor Texts
- *The Memory String* by Eve Bunting
- *Marshfield Dreams: When I Was a Kid* by Ralph Fletcher
- *A Writer's Notebook* by Ralph Fletcher
- *Amelia's 5th-Grade Notebook* by Marissa Moss
- *Amelia's 6th-Grade Notebook* by Marissa Moss
- See *Mentor Text List* in Appendix C for other suggestions

Procedures
Note: Revisit *Idea Cache* throughout the year to add additional topics for writing.

Think About Writing
1. Explain to students that story ideas may appear at any moment. Authors look for ideas in their own lives and experiences. They often have a system for how they record and remember their ideas.
2. Review mentor texts, if desired, and emphasize the authors' ideas.

Teach
3. Tell students, "Today we will learn about how to store ideas in our own secret collection called an Idea Cache." Tell students that a *cache* is a collection.
4. Show the box of memorabilia to students and talk about how these objects can help generate story ideas. Choose objects that are common and easily found so that students may even use some of the same ideas if necessary. Some ideas include:
   - a pebble from a special location
   - a picture drawn by someone special
   - a treasured letter
   - a ticket from a special concert
   - a piece of nature found on a hike or walk
   Use these objects to talk about how they connect to story ideas. For example, a leaf or rock found on a walk can be used in a story about a family of insects who use things in nature to make a home. Show these connections by writing notes on a sheet of chart paper.

© Shell Education #50920—Getting to the Core of Writing—Level 6 — 83

Implementing the Lessons *(cont.)*

Engage—Students will talk to each other about what they will apply in their writing. Talk time is short, intense, and focused. The teacher monitors, observes, and offers supportive comments.

Write/Conference—Students have essential, independent practice time. The teacher confers with students in one-on-one or small-group settings.

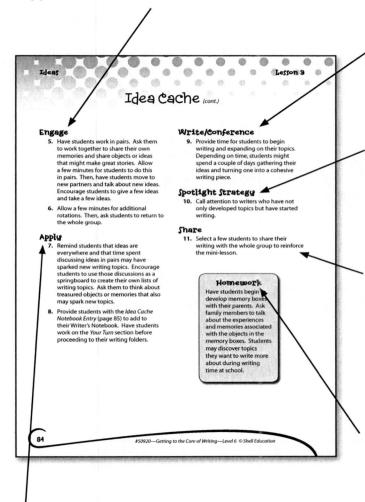

Spotlight Strategy—The teacher points out students' efforts and successes, emphasizing a skill or specific task to further student understanding.

Share—Students converse, explain, question, and give feedback to their groups or partners and share portions of their writing relating to the day's mini-lesson focus.

Homework—Students observe, notice, discuss, and collect important information at home and with their families that can then be used in their writings.

Apply—Students will practice what was taught in the mini-lesson, develop independence, and take ownership of their writing. The teacher restates the mini-lesson concept to solidify it for students.

Implementing Writer's Workshop

Writer's Workshop-at-a-Glance

This chart provides an at-a-glance overview of the Writer's Workshop format provided in *Getting to the Core of Writing*. It can be a helpful tool to use when planning instruction.

Component	Time	Description
Mini Lesson	5–15 minutes	Lesson plan subsections include: • Think About Writing • Teach • Engage • Apply

Writing Practice	15–30 minutes	Lesson plan subsections include:
		• Write/Conference
		  • Praise accomplishments
		  • Make a teaching point
		  • Use Conference Log
		• Spotlight Strategies

Sharing	5–15 minutes	Lesson plan subsections include:
		• Share
		  • Whole/small group
		  • Partners
		  • Compliment and comment
		• Homework

The Writing Conference

Writing conferences are most successful when they occur as a conversation between two writers who are simply talking about writing. It is a time to value students as writers, to differentiate instruction, to teach new strategies, and to gather information for forming instructional decisions. Anderson (2000) notes that a conference conversation basically includes two parts: conversation based upon the student's current writing and conversation based on what will help him or her become a better writer. Katie Wood Ray (2001) and Lucy Calkins, Amanda Hartman, and Zoe White (2003) tell us conferring is hard! It is one part of the day that is a bit unknown. When conferring one-on-one with writers, there is no script—no specific plan developed prior to the meeting. That is a strong deterrent that can keep many teachers from stepping into the conferring role during Writer's Workshop.

Following Calkins, Hartman, and White's dictum, "Conferring is the heart of Writer's Workshop" (2003, VIII), and the sharing of information in conference conversation over the development of a specific writing piece is the very heart of teaching writing. Although difficult at times, especially at first, even the smallest conversation lets your students know you are interested in them as writers and helps nudge them forward in their writing development. Just as students become better writers by writing, you will only become better at conferring by conferring. The sincerity with which you approach this task will not only affect your students' writing future but also your sense of accomplishment as a teacher.

Although the content of the conference conversation is unknown, the conference structure is predictable. The four phases of a conference structure are:

1. Observe
2. Praise
3. Guide
4. Connect

First, study to determine what the writer knows, what the writer is trying to do, and what the writer needs to learn. Next, provide praise. Then, develop a teaching point and guide and encourage the writer to practice that teaching point. Lastly, stress the importance of using what was learned in future writing. For a more detailed explanation of each phase, see pages 253–255 in Appendix A.

The Writing Conference (cont.)

Included in Appendix A and on the Teacher Resource CD are additional resources dedicated to the subject of conferring with students.

- **Essential Materials**—Use this list to assemble a "toolkit" of items you can carry with you as you conference with students (page 248).

- **Mini-Lesson Log**—Keep a record of the mini-lessons taught to serve as a reminder of writing strategies and crafts students have been exposed to during whole-group instruction (page 250).

- **Conference Log**—This conference form serves as a good starting point and makes it easy to view your entire class at one glance. It is a simple summary of the conference listing the name, date, praise, and teaching point. See pages 253–255 in Appendix A for more information on conferring steps. Some teachers prefer a separate conference page for each student as they become more familiar with the conferring process (page 251).

- **Conference Countdown**—This page lists simple reminders of salient points to consider during writing conferences (page 252).

When you take the time to have a conversation, you are sending a message that you care enough to listen and communicate. With so much emphasis on testing achievement, it is important to stay committed to teaching the writer and not just the work of the writer. Carl Anderson (2000) tells us that student efforts and achievements are most likely not due to the questions we ask, the feedback we give, or our teaching. He states, "In the end, the success of a conference often rests on the extent to which students sense we are genuinely interested in them as writers—and as individuals."

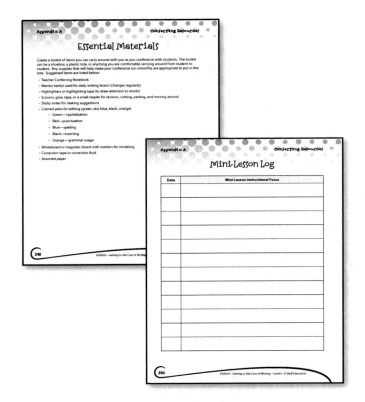

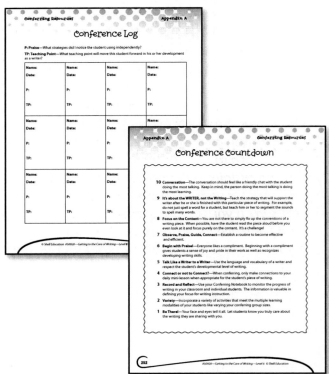

The Writer's Notebook

The Writer's Notebook can be a writer's best friend, always at his or her side to help out. It is personalized, customized, and interactive. Students can refer back to any mini-lesson taught during the year in Writer's Workshop to refresh their memories or find a tip for moving forward. The Writer's Notebook is like a friend, giving student writers a helping hand when they need guidance or are struggling with a writing skill. Consider this scenario:

The student's pencil taps incessantly on his desk. He's stuck. He can't think of how to begin an informational piece following a jumpstart mini-lesson in Writer's Workshop. The teacher observes the problem, stops by his desk and asks, "How's your writing going?" The student's response is quick and to the point. "Not so good! I don't have anything to write about." Writer's Notebook to the rescue! The teacher invites the student to return to lessons presented months ago, with notebook entries to gather ideas for writing. As the student moves his finger down his customized expert list, his facial expression completely changes from confusion to a brilliant smile. "I've got it," he exclaims with relief. "It's in my list. I know a lot about model volcanoes." "Then off you go!" the teacher replies with a smile.

The notebook is intended as a resource that student writers revisit to dig deeper, gather old ideas, or return to an anthology of mini-lessons taught throughout the year. Previous lessons are readily available and students can return to any lesson at a moment's notice for support. The left side of the notebook holds a glued-in notebook entry sheet designed to help the student with a skill or strategy connected to the writing traits and coordinated to a daily mini lesson. The right side of the notebook is used for individual or partner practice of the specific skill or strategy that was taught. Students move from their Writer's Notebook to writing pieces in their writing folders and apply the notebook entry skills or strategies on their essays, stories, and compositions.

Here are some tips for creating Writer's Notebooks and using them with your students:

- Use inexpensive, well-constructed composition notebooks if possible; however, you may also use spiral-bound notebooks or three-ring binders. Aimee Buckner (2005) tells us to select notebooks that match our style of teaching, the space and time available, and the management of the notebooks. There are a variety of brands available that are often on sale during back-to-school season.

- Encourage students to decorate and personalize their notebooks. This activity can be done in class or you may provide directions and make this a student-and-parent activity for a home connection. Personalizing the notebook with pictures, words, and phrases develops ideas for writing projects. (See page 280 in Appendix D for a sample home connections letter.)

- Store notebooks in a location accessible to students, such as small baskets on desks or shelves. If the Writer's Notebooks are easily available, students are more apt to use them as a writing resource.

The Writer's Notebook (cont.)

- Copy and cut notebook entry sheets in advance. Notebook entries are easily cut with a paper cutter and are then readily available for students to glue into their notebooks.

- Deliver specific instructions on adding notebook entries. Have materials available so students can add a few dots of glue and have the sheet in the notebook quickly. Develop expectations and routines to save valuable writing time.

- Set up a Table of Contents and create chapter sections:

  1. Managing Writer's Workshop: 10 pages
  2. Ideas: 15 pages
  3. Sentence Fluency: 15 pages
  4. Organization: 15 pages
  5. Word Choice: 15 pages
  6. Voice: 5 Pages
  7. Conventions: 15 pages
  8. Assessment: 5 pages

- Have students number the chapters using flags for ease of management. When teaching a lesson, your prompt should be simple, such as, "Turn to Chapter 4— Organization." Extra pages may be included in each chapter to give teachers the prerogative to add additional lesson ideas for any chapter.

Students react positively to the use of the Writer's Notebook. Ralph Fletcher (1996), author and educational consultant, states, "…the most important tool I use: my writer's notebook. Keeping a writer's notebook is one of the best ways I know of living a writing kind of life." That is exactly the desired response from students as well.

Top 10 Tips for Creating Successful Writers

1. **Schedule Writer's Workshop Daily.** Scheduling Writer's Workshop daily grants valuable, necessary time for students to practice and grow as writers.

2. **Establish and Commit to Routines.** Life is good when everyone knows what to do and when to do it. Take the time to establish foundational routines that will impact your Writer's Workshop throughout the year. Revisit Managing Writer's Workshop lessons as the need arises.

3. **Model, Model, Model!** Modeling gives direct instruction while scaffolding for writers. Use these steps to model specific skills and behaviors with students (*I* is the teacher and *you* is the student) (Pearson and Gallagher 1983):

   - I do, you watch
   - I do, you help
   - You do, I help
   - You do, I watch

4. **Read, Read, Read!** Reading a variety of texts through the eyes of a writer exposes students to the craft of the author and encourages students to explore new avenues of writing.

5. **Display and Celebrate!** Walking down the hallway in a school setting, you can usually get a good idea of the writing that is going on in each classroom. The more students write, the more comfortable they become, and they will want to show off their work. Celebrate student writing and recognize students as writers.

6. **Confer Weekly.** This is your opportunity to learn about each student's writing development. Encourage, guide, and listen.

7. **Share, Share, Share!** Students love to share everything. Sharing during Writer's Workshop enhances their sense of importance as writers.

8. **Involve and Inform Parents.** Writing is an automatic means of connecting with parents. Wall displays of writing samples show parents how you value their child's writing effort. Hold an Author's Tea and invite parents so they can see first-hand the important writing of their child.

9. **Be Flexible and Reflect.** A well-planned lesson may fall flat. So, go back to the drawing board and ask yourself, "Why?" "What happened?" How can you reteach to make the right connections for students? Take time to reflect on your teaching and student learning.

10. **Set High Expectations.** Be specific with your expectations and articulate clearly what you would like the students to accomplish. Believe in your students' abilities and challenge them to succeed. Every student can be an author.

Correlation to Standards

Shell Education is committed to producing educational materials that are research- and standards-based. In this effort, we have correlated all of our products to the academic standards of all 50 United States, the District of Columbia, the Department of Defense Dependent Schools, and all Canadian provinces. We have also correlated to the **Common Core State Standards**.

How To Find Standards Correlations

To print a customized correlation report of this product for your state, visit our website at **http://www.shelleducation.com** and follow the on-screen directions. If you require assistance in printing correlation reports, please contact Customer Service at 1-877-777-3450.

Purpose and Intent of Standards

Legislation mandates that all states adopt academic standards that identify the skills students will learn in kindergarten through grade twelve. Many states also have standards for Pre-K. This same legislation sets requirements to ensure the standards are detailed and comprehensive.

Standards are designed to focus instruction and guide adoption of curricula. Standards are statements that describe the criteria necessary for students to meet specific academic goals. They define the knowledge, skills, and content students should acquire at each level. Standards are also used to develop standardized tests to evaluate students' academic progress. Teachers are required to demonstrate how their lessons meet state standards. State standards are used in the development of all of our products, so educators can be assured they meet the academic requirements of each state.

McREL Compendium

We use the Mid-continent Research for Education and Learning (McREL) Compendium to create standards correlations. Each year, McREL analyzes state standards and revises the compendium. By following this procedure, McREL is able to produce a general compilation of national standards. Each lesson in this product is based on one or more McREL standard. The chart on pages 25–27 and on the Teacher Resource CD (standards.pdf) lists each standard taught in this product and the page number(s) for the corresponding lesson(s).

TESOL Standards

The lessons in this book promote English language development for English language learners. The standards listed on the Teacher Resource CD (standards.pdf) support the language objectives presented throughout the lessons.

Common Core State Standards

The lessons in this book are aligned to the Common Core State Standards (CCSS). The standards on pages 28–30 and on the Teacher Resource CD (standards.pdf) support the objectives presented throughout the lessons.

Correlation to Standards (cont.)

McREL Standards

Standard	Lesson
Understands the structure of Writer's Workshop	Our Group Meeting (page 38); The Writing Folder (page 41); The Writer's Notebook (page 50); Organizing the Writer's Notebook (page 52); Sharing (page 58); Turn and Talk (page 62); Guidelines for Writer's Workshop (page 65); Teacher and Peer Conferences (page 68); The Five-Step Writing Process (page 71)
Prewriting: Uses a variety of prewriting strategies	My Top Ten Ideas (page 77); Stinky Tennis Shoes Trip (page 80); Idea Cache (page 83); Ideas from A to Z (page 86); I Saw It in a Book (page 89); My Declarations (page 92); It's My Choice (page 95); I Question, Question, Question (page 98); Prewriting with the Knuckle Planner (page 134); Organizing Thinking for Expository Writing (page 150); Building Vocabulary Webs (page 182)
Drafting and Revising: Uses a variety of strategies to draft and revise written work	Playing with Sentence Patterns (page 103); Double Trouble with Compound Elements (page 107); The Long and Short of It (page 110); Sentence Stretch and Scramble (page 113); SOS! Semicolons Offer Style (page 116); Adding Details (page 119); Let's Make It Clear! (page 122); Drafting with the Knuckle Planner (page 137); Reeling In and Wrapping Up (page 140); It's Newsworthy (page 143); It's All About Me! (page 147); Researching from A to D (page 153); A Poetry Collage (page 157)
Editing and Publishing: Uses a variety of strategies to edit written work	Time to Edit! (page 244)
Uses content, style, and structure appropriate for specific audiences and purposes	I Saw It in a Book (page 89); It's Newsworthy (page 143); The Voice of R.A.F.T. (page 207); A Writer's Toolbox for Voice (page 213)

Correlation to Standards (cont.)

McREL Standards (cont.)

Standard	Lesson
Writes expository compositions	Organizing Thinking for Expository Writing (page 150)
Writes compositions about autobiographical incidents	It's All About Me! (page 147)
Uses descriptive language that clarifies and enhances ideas	Playing with Poetry (page 127); A Poetry Collage (page 157); Simple to Sophisticated Synonyms (page 169); Using Your Senses to Show, Don't Tell (page 174); Just a Figure of Speech (page 185); The Power of Connotation (page 190); I Know How You Feel (page 201); Voice Reflections (page 204); If I Were A... (page 210)
Uses paragraph form in writing	The Stacker Paragraph (page 130)
Uses a variety of sentence structures to expand and embed ideas	Playing with Sentence Patterns (page 103); Double Trouble with Compound Elements (page 107); The Long and Short of It (page 110); Sentence Stretch and Scramble (page 113); Let's Make It Clear! (page 122)
Uses explicit transitional devices	Shifting Ideas with Transition Signals (page 177)
Uses pronouns in written compositions	Presenting SOP Pronouns (page 234)
Uses prepositions in written compositions	Adding Details (page 119)
Uses conventions of spelling in written compositions	Exploring Etymology (page 195); Commonly Misspelled Words (page 219); The Sensational Six (page 227); The CUPS Challenge (page 237); What's the Difference? (page 241)
Uses conventions of capitalization in written compositions	Boot Camp Caps Chant (page 231); The CUPS Challenge (page 237)

Correlation to Standards (cont.)

McREL Standards (cont.)

Standard	Lesson
Uses conventions of punctuation in written compositions	SOS! Semicolons Offer Style (page 116); Punctuation Partners (page 224); The CUPS Challenge (page 237)
Uses a variety of resource materials to gather information for research topics	Researching from A to D (page 153)
Writes research papers	Researching from A to D (page 153)
Uses appropriate methods to cite and document reference sources	Researching from A to D (page 153)
Contributes to group discussions	All lessons
Responds to questions and comments	All lessons
Listens to classmates and adults	All lessons
Uses level-appropriate vocabulary in speech	All lessons
Listens for specific information in spoken texts	All lessons

Correlation to Standards (cont.)

Common Core State Standards

The purpose of the Common Core State Standards is to guarantee that all students are prepared for college and career literacy as they leave high school. These standards indicate that all students need the ability to write logical opinions and informational texts with sound reasoning to support their findings. *Getting to the Core of Writing* provides the fundamental writing skills to support students in their continued growth as writers, thus enabling them to enjoy continued success as the challenges presented by the curriculum become increasingly complex.

The structure of Writer's Workshop and the lessons in this book address the Common Core State Standards for **writing**. They also address **speaking and listening** standards, which are the building blocks of written language, through the Engage and Share components of the lesson. Due to the reciprocal nature of reading and writing, *Getting to the Core of Writing* naturally meets many of the Common Core State Standards for **reading** and for **language** as well. The standards below can also be found on the Teacher Resource CD (standards.pdf).

Standard	Lesson
Writing: Text Types and Purposes, W.6.1.	My Declarations (page 92)
Writing: Text Types and Purposes, W.6.2.	It's Newsworthy (page 143); Organizing Thinking for Expository Writing (page 150); Researching from A to D (page 153)
Writing: Text Types and Purposes, W.6.3.	Playing with Sentence Patterns (page 103); Double Trouble with Compound Elements (page 107); Reeling In and Wrapping Up (page 140); It's All About Me! (page 147); Shifting Ideas with Transition Signals (page 177)
Writing: Production and Distribution of Writing, W.6.4.	All lessons in Ideas (pages 77–98); All lessons in Sentence Fluency (pages 103–122); All lessons in Organization (pages 127–157); All lessons in Word Choice (pages 169–195); All lessons in Voice (pages 201–213); All lessons in Conventions (pages 219–244)

Correlation to Standards (cont.)

Common Core State Standards (cont.)

Standard	Lesson
Writing: Production and Distribution of Writing, W.6.5.	All lessons in Ideas (pages 77–98); All lessons in Sentence Fluency (pages 103–122); All lessons in Organization (pages 127–157); All lessons in Word Choice (pages 169–195); All lessons in Voice (pages 201–213); All lessons in Conventions (pages 219–244)
Writing: Research to Build and Present Knowledge, W.6.7.	Researching from A to D (page 153)
Writing: Research to Build and Present Knowledge, W.6.8.	Researching from A to D (page 153)
Writing: Research to Build and Present Knowledge, W.6.9.	Researching from A to D (page 153); I Know How You Feel (page 201); Voice Reflections (page 204); If I Were A... (page 210)
Writing: Range of Writing, W.6.10.	All lessons
Speaking and Listening: Comprehension and Collaboration, SL.6.1.	All lessons
Speaking and Listening: Presentation of Knowledge and Ideas, SL.6.6.	All lessons
Language: Conventions of Standard English, L.6.1.	Sentence Stretch and Scramble (page 113); Presenting SOP Pronouns (page 234)

Correlation to Standards (cont.)

Common Core State Standards (cont.)

Standard	Lesson
Language: Conventions of Standard English, L.6.2.	SOS! Semicolons Offer Style (page 116); Commonly Misspelled Words (page 219); Punctuation Partners (page 224); The Sensational Six (page 227); Boot Camp Caps Chant (page 231); The CUPS Challenge (page 237); Time to Edit! (page 244)
Language: Knowledge of Language, L6.3.	All lessons
Language: Vocabulary Acquisition and Use, L.6.4.	Exploring Etymology (page 195); What's the Difference? (page 241)
Language: Vocabulary Acquisition and Use, L.6.5.	Simple to Sophisticated Synonyms (page 169); Shifting Ideas with Transition Signals (page 177); Just a Figure of Speech (page 185); The Power of Connotation (page 190)
Language: Vocabulary Acquisition and Use, L.6.6.	All lessons

Acknowledgments

We stand on the shoulders of national and world-renowned teachers of teachers-of-writing, such as our friend the late Donald Graves, Lucy Calkins, Ralph Fletcher, Donald Murray, Vicki Spandel, Ruth Culham, Katie Wood Ray, Carl Anderson, Charles Temple, Jean Gillet, Stephanie Harvey, Debbie Miller, Regie Routman, Marissa Moss, Steve Graham, and Connie Hebert to name a few, as well as educators at Northwest Regional Educational Laboratory. Thank you. We are also truly grateful to the faculty at Auckland University, workshop leaders, and experiences with the teachers in New Zealand some 20 years ago who got us started.

While writing this series and in the past, there were frequent chats about writing and words of wisdom from Dona Rice, Sara Johnson, Jean Mann, Lois Bridges, and Tim Rasinski. Scores of teachers who read our manuscripts, praised our work, gave us confidence, and adjusted our missteps. We could not have succeeded without two super editors, Dona and Sara, and the great staff at Teacher Created Materials/Shell Education.

We attribute much of what's good about our series to teachers who invited us into their classrooms. Over all the years that went into this project, there are too many people to list separately, but here's a sampling: Thank you to all the teachers and districts who allowed us to visit and model in your classrooms, try our materials, and listen to your insights as we refined our writing instruction. A special thank you to the teachers at Fayette, Logan, Mingo, Pocahontas, Upshur, Wood, Wirt, and Harrison County Schools. We owe special gratitude to French Creek Elementary, Mt. Hope Elementary, and Nutter Fort Elementary teachers. We can't forget the "Writing Teachers Club": Debbie Gaston, Tammy Musil, Judy McGinnis, Jenna Williams, Cheryl Bramble, Karen Vandergrift, Barb Compton, Whitney Fowler, and Jennifer Rome, who spent countless hours learning, questioning, and sharing ideas. "You really need to write a book," you said, and your words have made that happen. You and many others inspired us, including the WC Department of Teaching and Learning (especially Angel, Karen, Lesley, Marcia, Matt, M.C., and Wendy). We can't forget Jean Pearcy, Miles 744, the talented teachers of the West Clermont Schools, the 4 Bs (Bailey, Bergen, Blythe, and Brynne), Candy, Mrs. Hendel, the lab rats (Becky, Mary, Mike, Sally, Sharon, and Vera), and the littlest singers at CHPC. Last but not least, a special thank you to Rick and Ro Jensen, Bill McIntyre, and Carolyn Meigs for years of support, and to Dawna Vecchio, Loria Reid, Terry Morrison, Laura Trent, Jeanie Bennett, Millie Shelton, Therese E., and Kathy Snyder for listening, cheering, and celebrating!

Many thanks to administrators who provided opportunities, leadership, and support for teachers as they explored the implementation of writing workshop and applied new teaching strategies: superintendents Beverly Kingery, Susan Collins, director Kay Devono, principals Allen Gorrell, Frank Marino, Joann Gilbert, Pattae Kinney, Jody Decker, Vickie Luchuck, Jody Johnson, and Wilma Dale. We owe many thanks to WVDE Cadre for continuous professional development—you brought us together.

We owe immense gratitude for having been blessed with the company of children who have graced us with their writing, creativity, and wisdom. Thank you to hundreds of children who have shared marvelous writing and insight.

Finally, for never-ending patience, love and support we thank our families: Clint, Luke, and Lindsay; Lanty, Jamey, John, Charlie, Jacki, Jeffrey; and Bill. You all are the best!

About the Authors

Richard Gentry, Ph.D., is nationally recognized for his work in spelling, phase theory, beginning reading and writing, and teaching literacy in elementary school. A former university professor and elementary school teacher, his most recent book is *Raising Confident Readers: How to Teach Your Child to Read and Write—From Baby to Age 7*. Other books include topics such as beginning reading and writing, assessment, and spelling. He also blogs for *Psychology Today* magazine. Richard has spoken at state and national conferences and has provided teachers with inspiring strategies to use in their classroom.

Jan McNeel, M.A.Ed., is a forty-year veteran of education and leader of staff development throughout West Virginia and Maryland. Formerly a Reading First Cadre Member for the West Virginia Department of Education and Title I classroom and Reading Recovery teacher, Jan consults with schools and districts across the state. Jan's studies of literacy acquisition at the Auckland University in New Zealand serve as the foundation of her expertise in reading and writing. Her practical strategies and useful ideas are designed to make reading and writing connections that are teacher-friendly and easy to implement. She has won awards for her excellent work as a master teacher and has presented her work in early literacy at state, regional, and national conferences.

Vickie Wallace-Nesler, M.A.Ed., has been in education for 30 years as an itinerant, Title I, and regular classroom teacher. Through her current work as a Literacy Coach for grades K–5, conference presenter, and literacy consultant, Vickie brings true insight into the "real world" of educators and their challenges. That experience, along with Master's degrees in both Elementary Education and Reading, National Board certification in Early and Middle Literacy for Reading and Language Arts, and studies at The Teachers College Reading and Writing Project at Columbia University, drive her passion for helping all teachers and students develop a love for learning.

Managing Writer's Workshop

Writer's Workshop begins on the first day of school and is taught every day thereafter. Establishing routines is critical to developing a successful, productive writing time. Therefore, Managing Writer's Workshop lessons should be focused on early in the year and revisited when necessary. The mini-lessons require time and repetition to develop automaticity during Writer's Workshop. A wide range of topics can be addressed during these mini-lessons. Repeat mini-lessons as needed, especially on the topics of guidelines for Writer's Workshop and having students share their writing with partners. These two particular lessons will be crucial to having Writer's Workshop run smoothly and successfully for the rest of the year. Ensure students are responding to those lessons in the ways you want them to, or spend additional time teaching and modeling. Observe your class to find the needs of your particular students. Lessons in this section include:

Components of Writer's Workshop

Standard

Understands the structure of Writer's Workshop

Materials

- Model writing folder
- Model Writer's Notebook
- *Components of Writer's Workshop Anchor Chart* (page 37; writersworkshop.pdf)

Mentor Texts

- *A Writer's Notebook* by Ralph Fletcher
- *Amelia's Notebook* by Marissa Moss
- See *Mentor Text List* in Appendix C for other suggestions.

Procedures

Note: Create a model writing folder and Writer's Notebook to share with students. After students create their own notebooks (Managing Writer's Workshop Lesson 4), review the Components of Writer's Workshop and have students add the notebook entry to the Organization section of their Writer's Notebook.

Think About Writing

1. Introduce the concept of Writer's Workshop to students. For example, "During this time, we will explore and practice becoming writers. We will meet together, practice writing, and share our writing with each other. This time will be called Writer's Workshop. We will follow procedures so everyone knows what is expected at each point during our Writer's Workshop time."

2. Read quotes from the mentor texts by Ralph Fletcher and Marissa Moss, if desired.

Teach

3. Tell students, "Today I will show you the schedule we will use during Writer's Workshop so you can use your writing time wisely."

4. Explain that there will always be three components to the writing schedule.

   - "We will have a daily group meeting where we pull together as a community of writers to get information. This is called a mini-lesson."

   - "You will have time to write quietly about an idea or an experience in your life. While you write, I will meet with you to talk about your writing projects."

   - "We will come back together to share our thoughts, ideas, successes, or concerns."

Components of Writer's Workshop *(cont.)*

5. Tell students that they will have a short homework assignment each night that requires them to think about writing, talk to their families about writing, or make observations.

Engage

6. Display the *Components of Writer's Workshop Anchor Chart* (page 37). Review the three components of Writer's Workshop by naming each part: mini-lesson, student writing time, and sharing. Then have students repeat each part in turn.

Apply

7. Remind students that the three components of Writer's Workshop will help them become accomplished writers. Practice making transitions by moving students to where they will be located for each component of Writer's Workshop. For example, students may be sitting in a circle during the mini-lesson, at their desks for writing, or meeting with a partner, triad, or quad for sharing.

8. Tell students that today will be a free-write day where the writing topic is their choice; however, they must be writing for the entire time.

Write/Conference

9. Provide time for students to write. Do not conference today. Practice moving students through the schedule to help them internalize your management system. Then, practice sustained writing time.

Spotlight Strategy

10. Spotlight students who know exactly how to move to each designated area without the loss of one moment of writing time. A suggestion is to use a small flashlight, which can be shined on students to spotlight them. Remember to provide lots of praise during these introductory days of Writer's Workshop.

Share

11. Ask students to meet with partners to name and explain the focus of the three components of Writer's Workshop. Provide approximately two minutes for students to share. Choose one or two students who clearly understood the idea and have them share with the whole group.

Homework

Ask students to write the three components of Writer's Workshop on a sheet of paper and share it with their parents.

Components of Writer's Workshop Anchor Chart

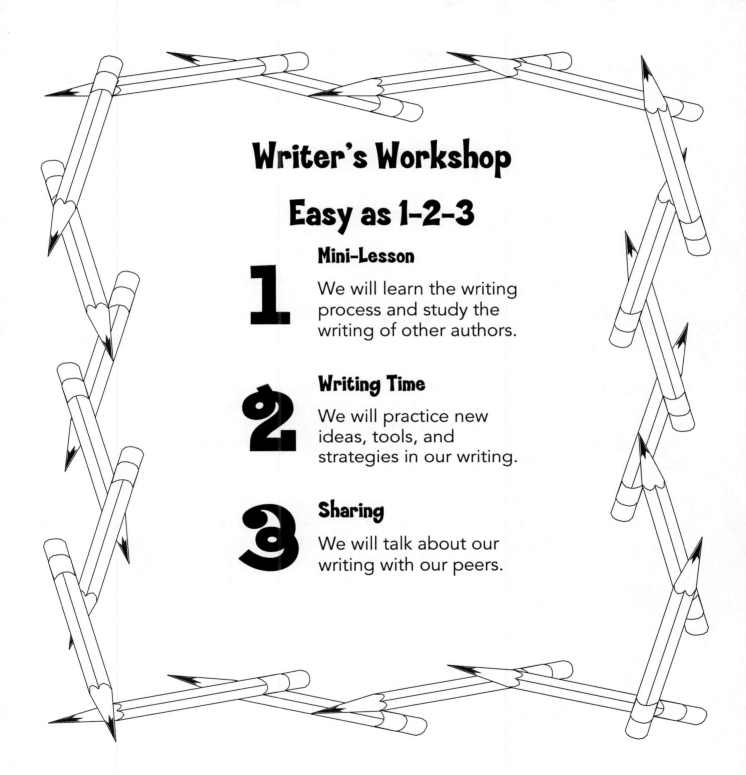

Writer's Workshop

Easy as 1-2-3

1 Mini-Lesson

We will learn the writing process and study the writing of other authors.

2 Writing Time

We will practice new ideas, tools, and strategies in our writing.

3 Sharing

We will talk about our writing with our peers.

Our Group Meeting

Standard

Understands the structure of Writer's Workshop

Materials

- *Sample Looks Like, Sounds Like, Feels Like Anchor Chart* (page 40; lookssoundsfeelschart.pdf)
- Chart paper
- Markers

Mentor Texts

- *A Writer's Notebook* by Ralph Fletcher
- *Amelia's Notebook* by Marissa Moss
- See *Mentor Text List* in Appendix C for other suggestions.

Procedures

Note: Decide on an area in your room or desk formation that will serve as a meeting place. You will need to repeat this lesson until the procedure is in place. Build solid routines. To build excitement, share your Writer's Notebook and folder in preparation for future lessons.

Think About Writing

1. Explain to students that today they will begin building an understanding of what a community of writers looks like, sounds like, and feels like.

2. Share from mentor texts, if desired.

Teach

3. Tell students, "Today I will show you how to work in Writer's Workshop with minimal noise and no confusion."

4. Model where and how to sit during the mini-lesson component of Writer's Workshop. You may wish to begin at a student's desk to show students exactly what they will do when they get ready for a mini-lesson. Then have students emulate what you modeled. Practice moving students several times. Throughout modeling and practicing, provide plenty of praise to students. It is important to draw attention to expected behaviors through praise and recognition. Repeat this same procedure for the other components of Writer's Workshop on subsequent days.

5. Using a sheet of chart paper, begin an anchor chart to record students' observations of what Writer's Workshop will look like, sound like, and feel like. Add to the anchor chart over the next several days as students become familiar with the routines. Use the *Sample Looks Like, Sounds Like, Feels Like Anchor Chart* (page 40) to help guide students as they add information to the chart your class creates.

Our Group Meeting *(cont.)*

Engage

6. Have students tell partners how to move to the community meeting area for mini-lessons.

Apply

7. Remind students that it is important to move quickly to the meeting area so that precious instructional time is not lost. Tell students that today will be a free-write day.

Write/Conference

8. Provide students with paper and have them write for seven minutes. As students work, observe and rotate among them to solve problems. Procedures must be solidly in place to get students moving toward independence in Writer's Workshop.

Spotlight Strategy

9. Spotlight students who moved quickly and quietly to and from the meeting area and began to transition into free-writing. Remember to provide lots of praise during these early days of Writer's Workshop.

Share

10. Have students meet with partners and share what they wrote today. Provide approximately two minutes for students to share. Choose one or two students who clearly understand the idea and have them share with the whole group.

Homework

Ask students to think about how important it is to move quickly and quietly during Writer's Workshop. Have students write two reasons why having this routine in place will help them as they work.

Sample Looks Like, Sounds Like, Feels Like Anchor Chart

Our Writer's Workshop...

Looks Like	Sounds Like	Feels Like

• Pencils, all supplies ready • Journals/folders/notebooks • Mentor texts available • Anchor charts • Author's chair • Partners/small groups • Smiling faces • Writing tool kits • Student engagement • Vocabulary list • Writing prompts • Turn and talk • Productive • Organized • Writing • Busy	• Buzz, hum, beehive • Two-inch voices • Conversation/oral language • Quiet during thinking and teaching phase • "Hum" when sharing with partners, triads, quads • Busy • Students making decisions • Learning is happening • Questioning • Writing is individualized/differentiated	• Comfortable, natural, happy • Nonthreatening, risk taking • Purposeful • Successful • Confident • Excited • Relaxed • Proud • Comfortable sharing thoughts • "I can" attitude

The Writing Folder

Standard

Understands the structure of Writer's Workshop

Materials

- Two-pocket folders with fasteners
- Red and green dot stickers
- *Student Mini-Lesson Log* (page 43; minilessonlog2.pdf)
- Reference inserts:

  Fry Sight Word List (pages 44–45; frywordlist.pdf)

  Short and Long Vowel Charts (pages 46–47; shortlongvowelcharts.pdf)

  Vowel Teams Chart (pages 48–49; vowelteamschart.pdf)
- Protective sleeves
- Model writing folder

Mentor Texts

- *A Writer's Notebook* by Ralph Fletcher
- *Amelia's Notebook* by Marissa Moss
- See *Mentor Text List* in Appendix C for other suggestions.

Procedures

Note: Implement this lesson over several days. It is important to model and explain how each reference insert can serve as a helpful tool for student writing projects. If not explicitly taught, students will not recognize the value and usefulness of these resources.

Think About Writing

1. Explain to students that they will organize a folder to hold their writing projects for this school year. Tell students that they will keep records of mini-lessons, and at the end of each month, they will clean their folders. Writing projects they want to save will go into their writing folders, and drafts not wanted will be stapled with the *Student Mini-Lesson Log* (page 43) and taken home for their personal records.

2. Review mentor texts, if desired.

Teach

3. Tell students, "Today I will show you how to organize your writing folder."

4. Distribute folders, red and green dot stickers, the *Student Mini-Lesson Log*, and the reference inserts, which are listed in the materials. Use the following steps to help students set up their writing folders:

   - Have students place a green dot sticker on the inside, left pocket. Explain that this will hold writing projects that are still in progress and the *Student Mini-Lesson Log* for keeping records of what they are learning. Have them record notes about each mini-lesson on the mini-lesson log on subsequent days.

   - Have students place a red dot sticker on the inside, right pocket. Explain that this pocket will hold all the writing pieces that are finished. These will be taken home or stored at school to show students' growth as writers.

The Writing Folder *(cont.)*

- Tell students that the reference inserts you have given them are important tools to help them in their writing. Show students how to put the reference inserts into protective sleeves and fasten them in the writing folders.

- Share what a completed writing folder looks like.

Engage

5. Have students explain to partners the different parts of the writing folder and what each is for. Provide approximately two minutes for students to share.

Apply

6. Review with students the importance of having a personalized and organized writing folder. Provide students time to decorate their writing folders. Tell students that when they are finished, they should take out a sheet of paper and free-write.

Write/Conference

7. Allow time for students to work on their writing folders, depending on the developmental levels of your students.

Spotlight Strategy

8. Spotlight students that are following directions, sustaining themselves, and practicing organizational strategies.

Share

9. No sharing time today.

Homework

Ask students to think about all of the things that happen in their lives that would make good stories. Have students make a list of three things they would like to write about. Tell students to be ready to start writing tomorrow.

Name:_____

Student Mini-Lesson Log

Date	I am learning to . . .	I can use this strategy in my writing.

Fry Sight Word List

First 100

a	before	get	I	me	out	there	when
about	boy	give	if	much	put	they	which
after	but	go	in	my	said	this	who
again	by	good	is	new	see	three	will
all	can	had	it	no	she	to	with
an	come	has	just	not	so	two	work
and	day	have	know	of	some	up	would
any	did	he	like	old	take	us	you
are	do	her	little	on	that	very	your
as	down	here	long	one	the	was	
at	eat	him	make	or	there	we	
be	four	his	man	other	them	were	
been	from	how	many	our	then	what	

Second 100

also	box	five	leave	name	pretty	stand	use
am	bring	found	left	near	ran	such	want
another	call	four	let	never	read	sure	way
away	came	friend	live	next	red	tell	where
back	color	girl	look	night	right	than	while
ball	could	got	made	only	run	these	white
because	dear	hand	may	open	saw	thing	wish
best	each	high	men	over	say	think	why
better	ear	home	more	own	school	too	year
big	end	house	morning	people	seem	tree	
black	far	into	most	play	shall	under	
book	find	kind	mother	please	should	until	
both	first	last	must	present	soon	upon	

Third 100

along	clothes	eyes	green	letter	ride	small	walk
always	coat	face	grow	longer	round	start	warm
anything	cold	fall	hat	light	same	stop	wash
around	cut	fast	happy	love	sat	ten	water
ask	didn't	fat	hard	money	second	thank	woman
ate	does	fine	head	myself	set	third	write
bed	dog	fire	hear	now	seven	those	yellow
brown	don't	fly	help	o'clock	show	though	yes
buy	door	food	hold	off	sing	today	yesterday
car	dress	full	hope	once	sister	took	
carry	early	funny	hot	order	sit	town	
clean	eight	gave	jump	pair	six	try	
close	every	goes	keep	part	sleep	turn	

Fry Sight Word List (cont.)

Fourth 100

across	covered	field	however	north	red	stand	upon
against	cried	figure	hundred	notice	remember	step	usually
area	didn't	fire	I'll	numeral	rock	sun	voice
become	dog	fish	king	order	room	sure	vowel
best	door	five	knew	passed	seen	table	war
better	draw	friends	listen	pattern	several	today	waves
birds	during	ground	low	piece	ship	told	whole
black	early	happened	map	plan	short	top	wind
body	easy	heard	mark	problem	since	toward	wood
certain	ever	himself	measure	products	sing	town	
cold	fall	hold	money	pulled	slowly	travel	
color	farm	horse	morning	questions	south	true	
complete	fast	hours	music	reached	space	unit	

Fifth 100

able	built	deep	front	island	pair	shown	thousands
ago	cannot	done	full	known	person	six	understand
am	carefully	dry	game	language	plane	size	verb
among	check	English	gave	less	power	special	wait
ball	circle	equation	government	machine	produce	stars	warm
base	class	explain	green	material	quickly	stay	week
became	clear	fact	half	minutes	ran	stood	wheels
behind	common	feel	heat	note	rest	street	yes
boat	contain	filled	heavy	nothing	road	strong	yet
box	correct	finally	hot	noun	round	surface	
bring	course	fine	inches	object	rule	system	
brought	dark	fly	include	ocean	scientists	ten	
building	decided	force	inside	oh	shape	though	

Sixth 100

anything	dance	Europe	instruments	mind	ready	soft	weather
arms	describe	exercise	interest	months	reason	square	west
beautiful	developed	farmers	job	moon	record	store	whether
believe	difference	felt	kept	paint	region	subject	wide
beside	direction	finished	lay	paragraph	represent	suddenly	wild
bill	discovered	flowers	legs	past	return	sum	window
blue	distance	forest	length	perhaps	root	summer	winter
brother	divided	general	love	picked	sat	syllables	wish
can't	drive	glass	main	present	shall	teacher	written
cause	drop	gone	matter	probably	sign	test	
cells	edge	happy	meet	race	simple	third	
center	eggs	heart	members	rain	sit	train	
clothes	energy	held	million	raised	sky	wall	

Short and Long Vowel Charts

Short Vowels				
a	e	i	o	u
ant	exercise	igloo	octagon	umbrella
map	leg	fish	mop	duck
Other words: pattern, exactly, accent, baggage, pancake, hamstring	**Other words:** method, attend, elephant, website, tennis, penny	**Other words:** district, inherit, consider, captive, pillow, himself	**Other words:** opportunity, positive, opposite, knot, raindrop, pottery	**Other words:** utterly, upper, custody, lucky, puppy, bumper

Short and Long Vowel Charts (cont.)

Long Vowels				
a	e	i	o	u
acorn	**e**asel	**i**cicle	**o**val	**u**niform
t**a**ble	g**e**nie	b**i**ke	gl**o**be	c**u**be
Other words: **a**cre l**a**bor v**a**cation **A**sia destin**a**tion sl**a**very	**Other words:** f**ee**ble th**e**me cr**e**ase **e**lectric spl**ee**n **e**quator	**Other words:** **i**tem **i**deal emp**i**re t**i**ghtrope v**i**olin sp**i**ne	**Other words:** vide**o** d**o**nate **o**ppose gh**o**st marshmall**ow** domin**o**	**Other words:** **u**nited contrib**u**te bea**u**tiful cost**u**me sal**u**te f**u**migate

Vowel Teams Chart

CVCe	CVCe	CVCe	CVCe	ai
c**a**v**e**	k**i**t**e**	n**o**s**e**	m**u**l**e**	r**ai**n
beh**a**v**e**	disg**u**i**se**	opp**o**s**e**	conf**u**s**e**	compl**ai**n
mist**a**k**e**	emp**i**r**e**	p**o**s**e**	disp**u**t**e**	det**ai**n
r**a**v**e**	requ**i**r**e**	dev**o**t**e**	acc**u**s**e**	obt**ai**n
ay	**ea**	**ee**	**oa**	**oe**
h**ay**	**ea**gle	ch**ee**se	b**oa**t	t**oe**
displ**ay**	le**a**gue	ind**ee**d	l**oa**ves	f**oe**
p**ay**able	me**a**ger	f**ee**ble	appr**oa**ch	w**oe**ful
rep**ay**ment	b**ea**gle	sl**ee**t	fl**oa**t	d**oe**
ie	**ue**	**au**	**aw**	**ew**
t**ie**	gl**ue**	s**au**ce	h**aw**k	n**ew**s
d**ie**t	tiss**ue**	**au**thor	y**aw**n	cr**ew**
bel**ie**	resc**ue**	s**au**sage	dr**aw**ing	scr**ew**
qu**ie**t	T**ue**sday	**au**tomatic	**aw**kward	ren**ew**

#50920—Getting to the Core of Writing—Level 6 © Shell Education

Vowel Teams Chart (cont.)

oi	oy	ou	ow	oo
oil	t**oy**s	h**ou**se	c**ow**	m**oo**n
b**oi**led	**oy**ster	bl**ou**se	p**ow**er	r**oo**ster
app**oi**nt	conv**oy**	l**ou**se	dr**ow**sy	pr**oo**f
an**oi**nt	empl**oy**	b**ou**ncer	cr**ow**n	ch**oo**se

ar	ur	ir	or	er
guit**ar**	t**ur**tle	sk**ir**t	h**or**n	flow**er**
h**ar**bor	f**ur**tive	d**ir**ty	**or**nament	powd**er**
c**ar**bon	c**ur**tain	c**ir**cular	m**or**ning	chowd**er**
gramm**ar**	c**ur**few	conf**ir**m	**or**der	own**er**

The Writer's Notebook

Standard

Understands the structure of Writer's Workshop

Materials

- Model Writer's Notebook
- Composition, spiral, or 3-ring notebooks
- Scissors
- Glue
- Materials and photos for decorating

Mentor Texts

- *A Writer's Notebook* by Ralph Fletcher
- *Amelia's Notebook* by Marissa Moss
- See *Mentor Text List* in Appendix C for other suggestions.

Procedures

Note: The Writer's Notebook will be the foundation of the lessons that will follow. Give students the opportunity to decorate, love, and personalize their notebooks. Create a feeling of excitement and allow the time needed to send them on this exciting journey. Allow students the time to collect mementos from home or have magazines available for them to cut and paste to decorate their notebooks. Cover the notebooks with contact paper to help preserve them.

Think About Writing

1. Explain to students that today they will be thinking and talking about how writers use a special Writer's Notebook. Tell them that just like authors Ralph Fletcher or Marissa Moss, the contents of their Writer's Notebooks is going to be unique.

2. Review mentor texts, if desired, and emphasize the use of a notebook. For example, in *Amelia's Notebook*, Amelia writes and draws her feelings about a number of her life experiences.

Teach

3. Tell students, "Today I will show you how to create your own Writer's Notebook." Share your model Writer's Notebook with students. Tell students why you selected the items on your cover, emphasizing how the items generate ideas for writing.

4. Explain to students that a Writer's Notebook is filled with special ideas and thoughts about an author's observations and experiences. Tell students that you will give them information to add to their notebooks that will help them as they write.

The Writer's Notebook (cont.)

Engage

5. Have students tell partners how they plan to personalize their Writer's Notebook. Listen in on conversations, making anecdotal notes. Select several students to share their thoughts and point out brilliant comments.

Apply

6. Distribute blank notebooks and materials to students. Review with students that their notebooks will be the place to keep ideas and strategies for writing. Explain that each notebook will be unique as they work to personalize them.

Write/Conference

7. Provide materials and time for students to personalize their Writer's Notebook. Be available to assist, problem solve, and observe. No conferring today.

Spotlight Strategy

8. Spotlight students who have begun personalizing their notebooks.

Share

9. Have students meet with a new partner and share how their special Writer's Notebook is progressing. Through observations, select one or two students to share with the whole group.

Homework

Ask students to tell their parents about how they are personalizing their Writer's Notebook. Ask students to bring a few mementos or pictures to add to the covers of their notebooks.

Organizing the Writer's Notebook

Standard
Understands the structure of Writer's Workshop

Materials
- *Traits of Writing Notebook Entry* (page 54; traitswriting.pdf)
- Chart paper
- Markers
- Writer's Notebooks
- Glue
- *Traits Team Mini Posters* (pages 55–57; traitsteamposters.pdf)

Mentor Texts
- *A Writer's Notebook* by Ralph Fletcher
- *Amelia's Notebook* by Marissa Moss
- Books by favorite authors, such as Eve Bunting, Patricia Polacco, Cynthia Rylant, etc.
- See *Mentor Text List* in Appendix C for other suggestions.

Procedures
Note: Notebook entries are always glued on the left side of the notebook and skills are practiced on the right. The notebook is arranged into sections as described in Step 4 below.

Think About Writing
1. Remind students that the class has been establishing Writer's Workshop routines and creating personal Writer's Notebooks.

2. Review mentor texts, if desired. Authors often integrate all the writing traits in their stories.

Teach
3. Tell students, "Today I will show you each of the writing traits and how we will use them to organize our Writer's Notebooks." Explain that there are six very important keys to writing success, called the *traits of writing*. Display the *Traits of Writing Notebook Entry* (page 54). Briefly explain each trait to students: Ideas, Sentence Fluency, Organization, Word Choice, Voice, and Conventions.

4. Share how to organize the Writer's Notebook as you develop a classroom anchor chart on a sheet of chart paper with the following information:

    Table of Contents

    Chapter 1: Managing Writer's Workshop (10 pages)

    Chapter 2: Ideas (15 pages)

    Chapter 3: Sentence Fluency (15 pages)

    Chapter 4: Organization (15 pages)

    Chapter 5: Word Choice (15 pages)

    Chapter 6: Voice (5 pages)

    Chapter 7: Conventions (15 pages)

    Chapter 8: Assessment (5 pages)

Organizing the Writer's Notebook (cont.)

5. Have students copy the Table of Contents into the front of their notebooks.

6. Model how to glue the *Traits of Writing Notebook Entry* on the first page of the Managing Writer's Workshop section of the notebook. Show students how to count the appropriate number of blank pages in each section and glue the *Traits Team Mini Posters* (pages 55–57) on the first page of each section of the Writer's Notebook.

Engage

7. Have students talk with partners about the traits of writing and how they are essential in developing quality writing. Listen to conversations, making anecdotal notes. Have a few groups share out their thoughts. Point out brilliant comments and notice positive behaviors and knowledge.

Apply

8. Remind students that the traits of writing will help them be successful as they begin to develop their own stories. Tell students that today they will divide their Writer's Notebook into sections for each writing trait.

Write/Conference

9. Provide time for students to divide their Writer's Notebook into sections by gluing the *Traits Team Mini Posters* into the notebook. Remind students to use the anchor chart as a guide so they will have the appropriate number of blank pages in each section.

Spotlight Strategy

10. Spotlight students who have organized their notebooks neatly and carefully.

Share

11. Have students meet with partners to share their Writer's Notebook. Choose one or two students who clearly understand the idea and have them share with the whole group.

Homework
Ask students to share what they learned about the traits of writing with their families. Challenge students to remember all six traits and to make a list.

Traits of Writing Notebook Entry

Traits of Writing

Ideas are the main topic and details that tell the writer's message. They are the heart ♥ of the story.

Sentence Fluency is the rhythm and flow of your words.

Organization includes the structure of the writing—beginning, middle, end, and more.

Word Choice is using just the right word in your writing.

Voice allows the reader to know the writer—it creates personality.

Conventions are needed to make our writing readable: CUPS—**C**apitalization, **U**sage, **P**unctuation, and **S**pelling!

Traits Team Mini Posters

Ida
Idea Creator

What is my writing about?

✔ Did I narrow and focus my topic?

✔ Did I gather background knowledge for my topic?

✔ Did I provide rich details, examples, reasons, and facts?

✔ Are details specific and related?

✔ Did I present ideas in an interesting/original way?

© Shell Education

#50920—Getting to the Core of Writing—Level 6

76

Simon
Sentence Builder

What kinds of sentences will I use?

✔ Did I use a variety of sentence patterns (simple, compound, complex)?

✔ Did I use a variety of sentence beginnings?

✔ Did I include a variety of sentence lengths?

✔ Are my sentences musical and rhythmic?

© Shell Education

#50920—Getting to the Core of Writing—Level 6

102

Traits Team Mini Posters *(cont.)*

Owen
Organization Conductor

How do I plan my writing?

✔ Did I organize and prioritize my thinking?

✔ Did I include an inviting beginning?

✔ Did I organize my thoughts in a logical sequence?

✔ Did I use appropriate transition words and phrases to make connections?

✔ Did I provide an adequate conclusion statement?

© Shell Education

#50920—Getting to the Core of Writing—Level 6

126

Wally
Word Choice Detective

What words will paint a picture for my reader?

✔ Did I use purposeful words?

✔ Did I use interesting yet appropriate word selections?

✔ Did I use precise nouns, verbs, and adjectives that evoke images?

✔ Did I use figurative language when necessary?

© Shell Education

#50920—Getting to the Core of Writing—Level 6

168

Traits Team Mini Posters *(cont.)*

Val and Van Voice

What is the purpose of my writing?

✔ Did I express myself with my own originality?

✔ Did I convey the purpose of my writing?

✔ Did I recognize and connect with my audience?

✔ Did I sound honest and confident in my position?

200

Callie Super Conventions Checker

How do I edit my paper?

✔ Did I check for capitalization and punctuation?

✔ Did I use the correct grammar?

✔ Did I spell words conventionally ?

✔ Did I reread for accuracy?

✔ Is my draft ready for publishing?

21B

Sharing

Standard

Understands the structure of Writer's Workshop

Materials

- *Compliment and Comment Cards* (page 61; complicommentcards.pdf)
- Anchor chart created in Managing Writer's Workshop Lesson 2
- *Sharing Notebook Entry* (page 60; sharing.pdf)
- Writer's Notebooks
- Glue

Mentor Texts

- *A Writer's Notebook* by Ralph Fletcher
- *Amelia's Notebook* by Marissa Moss
- See *Mentor Text List* in Appendix C for other suggestions.

Procedures

Note: You may need to repeat this lesson until procedures are consistent and automatic. Sharing can take place in the meeting area or at student desks, depending on the personalities in your class.

Think About Writing

1. Review with students that they have been learning the expected behaviors to manage themselves during Writer's Workshop.

2. Explain that another component of Writer's Workshop is sharing. Remind students that sharing is the last part of Writer's Workshop and will take place after students have had an opportunity to write.

Teach

3. Tell students, "Today I will show you how to meet with classmates to share." Tell students that sharing can take place in several different group situations. Remind them that they will need to use this time productively.

4. Explain to students that when you say, "Meet with a partner," they should each find a partner by the time you count to five. Model this group formation. Then, ask students to practice. Use this procedure to practice forming other groups of three called *triads* and groups of four called *quads*.

5. Remind students that sharing time will be short and is not an opportunity to read an entire writing piece. Reinforce that students should share their best example on the topic of the mini-lesson that day.

Sharing *(cont.)*

6. Share the *Compliment and Comment Cards* (page 61) with students. Explicitly model how to use these cards to compliment and comment on students' work.

7. Revisit the anchor chart created in Managing Writer's Workshop Lesson 2 and add student insights about what Writer's Workshop looks like, sounds like, and feels like.

Engage

8. Have students meet with partners and share what they learned about sharing today. Then, ask students to move into quads and share in a larger group. Provide lots of praise as students work to form the various groups.

Apply

9. Remind students that sharing gives them opportunities to have conversations with others about their writing work. Provide students with the *Sharing Notebook Entry* (page 60) and have them paste the entry into their Writer's Notebook. Distribute the *Compliment and Comment Cards* and have students store them in their writing folders.

10. Tell students that today they should either work on a piece of writing from their folders or begin a new piece.

Write/Conference

11. Provide time for students to write. All students write every day, even when mini-lessons are on managing Writer's Workshop. As students work, rotate among them to assist those who are having a difficult time getting started.

Spotlight Strategy

12. It will not be necessary to spotlight students until the end of Writer's Workshop during the sharing component.

Share

13. Tell students that they will practice the procedures for sharing. Remind them to use the *Compliment and Comment Cards*. First, have students meet with partners. Allow students to share their writing for one minute.

14. Repeat Step 13, this time having students meet in quads. Finally, have students meet in triads. Provide praise for students who are moving to form groups and share quickly.

Homework

Ask students to think about how to meet with partners, triads, and quads. Have students tell their parents the kind of compliments they might give to a friend about his or her writing.

Sharing Notebook Entry

Compliments and Comments

Compliments

A **compliment** is something you like about your partner's writing.

- I like the way you…
- Your details made me feel…
- The order of your writing really…
- Your sentences have…
- You used words that…

Comments

A **comment** is a positive statement that will improve your partner's writing.

- Can you say more about…?
- I am confused about the order because…
- Your sentences are…
- You might use a variety of words, such as…

#50920—Getting to the Core of Writing—Level 6 © Shell Education

Compliment and Comment Cards

Directions: Cut out the cards to distribute to students. Have them use the sentence stems to compliment and make suggestions about their partner's writing.

Compliment

Tell your partner what you like about his or her writing.

"I like the way you…"

"Your details make me…"

"Your sentences have…"

Compliment

Tell your partner what you like about his or her writing.

"I like the way you…"

"Your details make me…"

"Your sentences have…"

Comment

Make a suggestion that will help your partner improve his or her writing.

"Can you say more about…?"

"I am confused about the order because…"

"You might use a variety of words, such as…"

Comment

Make a suggestion that will help your partner improve his or her writing.

"Can you say more about…?"

"I am confused about the order because…"

"You might use a variety of words, such as…"

Turn and Talk

Standard

Understands the structure of Writer's Workshop

Materials

- Anchor chart created in Managing Writer's Workshop Lesson 2
- *Turn and Talk Notebook Entry* (page 64; turntalk.pdf)
- Writer's Notebooks

Mentor Texts

- *Swimmy* by Leo Lionni
- *Nothing Ever Happens on 90th Street* by Roni Schotter
- See *Mentor Text List* in Appendix C for other suggestions.

Procedures

Note: Teachers may assign writing partners that have been carefully selected based on language acquisition, or have students select their own partners. The collective personality of your class should guide your decision. You will need to repeat this lesson until the procedure is in place. Students will glue the notebook entry on the left side of the notebook. Students can reflect and write their thoughts on the right side.

Think About Writing

1. Tell students that they are getting the routines and procedures of Writer's Workshop in place. Remind students that it is important that they have a way to talk to others about mini-lessons and the writing that they do.

2. Review mentor texts, if desired.

Teach

3. Tell students, "Today I will show you how to have conversations with partners." Explain to students that when you say, "Turn and Talk," that is a signal for them to immediately turn to the person who is nearby and quickly follow directions on the discussion topic. Tell students to use a "two-inch voice"—a quiet voice that can only be heard two inches away. Explicitly model for students what this will look like, then have students practice.

4. Revisit the anchor chart created in Managing Writer's Workshop Lesson 2 to add student insights into what Writer's Workshop looks like, sounds like, and feels like.

Engage

5. Remind students that they practiced how to *Turn and Talk*. Ask students to talk with partners about how they will be expected to conduct themselves as they talk with other students.

Turn and Talk *(cont.)*

Apply

6. Provide students with the *Turn and Talk Notebook Entry* (page 64) to add to their Writer's Notebook. Remind students to follow the guidelines established today when they talk with peers. Encourage students to work on a piece of writing from their folders or begin a new piece of writing as they work today.

Write/Conference

7. Provide time for students to write. Continue to have quick roving conferences until the management of Writer's Workshop is solid and successful. Provide praise to your student writers.

Spotlight Strategy

8. No spotlight strategy today. Celebrating is done through the sharing component instead.

Share

9. Have students meet with partners to share their writing. Provide students approximately two minutes to share what they think about the value of sharing time.

Homework

Ask students to think about how sharing with other students energizes their writing ideas. Also, have them think about how important it is to show respect for every writer in the room by using a two-inch voice during Writer's Workshop.

Turn and Talk Notebook Entry

Turn and Talk

Remember to...

make eye contact with your partner

find your partner quickly

use a soft, two-inch voice

ask questions to clarify thinking

stick to the writing topic

make sure each person has a turn to talk

give only compliments— no put-downs

give a compliment when needed

Guidelines for Writer's Workshop

Standard

Understands the structure of Writer's Workshop

Materials

- *Guidelines for Writer's Workshop Notebook Entry* (page 67; guidelineswritersws.pdf)
- Chart paper
- Markers
- Writer's Notebooks
- Anchor chart created in Managing Writer's Workshop Lesson 1

Mentor Texts

- *A Writer's Notebook* by Ralph Fletcher
- *Amelia's Notebook* by Marissa Moss
- See *Mentor Text List* in Appendix C for other suggestions.

Procedures

Note: You will need to repeat this lesson many times until procedures are in place. Adjust the guidelines to meet the needs of your class.

Think About Writing

1. Explain to students that getting Writer's Workshop routines in place creates order and efficiency in the classroom.

2. Review mentor texts, if desired. You may also want to begin reading literature from your favorite authors to begin exploring mentor texts.

Teach

3. Tell students, "Today I will show you the guidelines for Writer's Workshop and what you need to be doing to make efficient use of the time scheduled for writing." Explain that after each daily mini-lesson, students will be expected to systematically follow some guidelines.

4. Model and explain the ideas listed on the *Guidelines for Writer's Workshop Notebook Entry* (page 67). Record each idea on a sheet of chart paper as it is discussed with students. Display the anchor chart in the room and refer to it often until students effortlessly follow the guidelines.

Engage

5. Have students turn to partners to review the guidelines for Writer's Workshop. Encourage students to use the anchor chart to guide their discussions.

Guidelines for Writer's Workshop *(cont.)*

Apply

6. Encourage students to think about how the guidelines for writing will help them spend their time more efficiently. Provide students with the *Guidelines for Writer's Workshop Notebook Entry* to add to their Writer's Notebook. Encourage students to work on a piece of writing from their folders or begin a new piece as they write today.

Write/Conference

7. Provide time for students to write. There should be no conferencing about writing until procedures are firmly in place. Begin to increase the amount of sustained writing time according to the developmental levels of your students.

Spotlight Strategy

8. Spotlight a student who immediately gets to work on his or her writing. For example, "Trevor did something brilliant. He went to his seat and immediately started to write in his Writer's Notebook."

Share

9. Have students meet with partners to share what they wrote today. Provide approximately two minutes for students to share. Choose one or two students and have them share with the whole group.

10. Do a group reflection on how the guidelines will help students become better writers. Continue to add to the anchor chart created in Managing Writer's Workshop Lesson 1.

Homework

Ask students to think about the guidelines introduced today. Have them write two sentences to explain how knowing what is expected of them will make them more disciplined writers.

Guidelines for Writer's Workshop Notebook Entry

Guidelines for Writer's Workshop

- You must always be writing or sketching in your Writer's Notebook, or working on a piece of writing for your writing folder.

- Always include the date of your work.

- Keep your drafts in your writing folder.

- Work quietly so that everyone can do their best thinking.

- Write on every other line when drafting.

- Request a conference when you are ready for a final draft.

- Use a soft, two-inch voice.

- Use your best handwriting or the computer on a final draft.

- Record what you have learned as a writer when you have completed a project.

Remember...

A writer's work is never done!

Teacher and Peer Conferences

Standard
Understands the structure of Writer's Workshop

Materials
- *Peer Conference Notebook Entry* (page 70; peerconference.pdf)
- Chart paper
- Markers
- Anchor chart created in Managing Writer's Workshop Lesson 2
- *Compliment and Comment Cards* (page 61; complicommentcards.pdf)
- Writing folder
- Writer's Notebooks

Mentor Texts
- *A Writer's Notebook* by Ralph Fletcher
- *Amelia's Notebook* by Marissa Moss
- See *Mentor Text List* in Appendix C for other suggestions.

Procedures

Note: You may assign writing partners or allow students to form partners on their own. The collective personality of your class should guide your decision. Repeat this lesson until the procedure is in place. Remind students that they should always glue the notebook entry on the left side of their Writer's Notebook.

Think About Writing

1. Explain to students that it is important to build teacher and peer conferencing into Writer's Workshop. Tell students that meeting with another person to share their writing is how they will get compliments and comments for improving their writing.

2. Review mentor texts, if desired.

Teach

3. Tell students, "Today I will show you how to meet with me or a partner in an assigned place in the room to review your writing."

4. Explain that getting feedback from another person is a great way to improve writing. Show students a designated area of the room for peer conferences. Explain to students how to sit with a partner so that they can read each other's work. Review how to give compliments and comments on writing. (See Managing Writer's Workshop Lesson 6.)

5. Review the questions on the *Peer Conference Notebook Entry* (page 70). Add each question to a sheet of chart paper and discuss each one. Model what a teacher conference will look like with a student. Next, have students practice peer conferencing. Revisit the anchor chart created in Managing Writer's Workshop Lesson 2 and add student insights about what Writer's Workshop looks like, sounds like, and feels like.

#50920—*Getting to the Core of Writing—Level 6* © Shell Education

Teacher and Peer Conferences *(cont.)*

Engage

6. Have students meet with partners by the time you count to five. Provide lots of praise for students who quickly meet with partners. Remind students to use the *Compliment and Comment Cards* (page 61) in their writing folders to help them make appropriate comments about writing work.

Apply

7. Encourage students to schedule weekly conferences with peers or with you in order to get feedback on their writing work. Provide students with the *Peer Conference Notebook Entry* to add to their Writer's Notebook. Tell students that today they can work on drafting a new piece of writing or continue with something from their folder.

Write/Conference

8. Provide time for students to write. Select two students to move to the designated peer conferencing area of your room and assist them in providing feedback to each other. Continue to select pairs of students to peer conference, paying close attention to the conferencing partners.

Spotlight Strategy

9. Spotlight a student who is revising his or her work based on a peer conference. For example, "Allison is doing something important. She is working on one small detail that was suggested by her partner to improve the quality of her writing."

Share

10. Have students *Turn and Talk* with partners about how providing compliments and comments during conferences will support their writing.

Homework

Ask students to think about the procedures for meeting with a peer to conference. Have students write one compliment and one comment they could give to a partner about his or her writing.

Peer Conference Notebook Entry

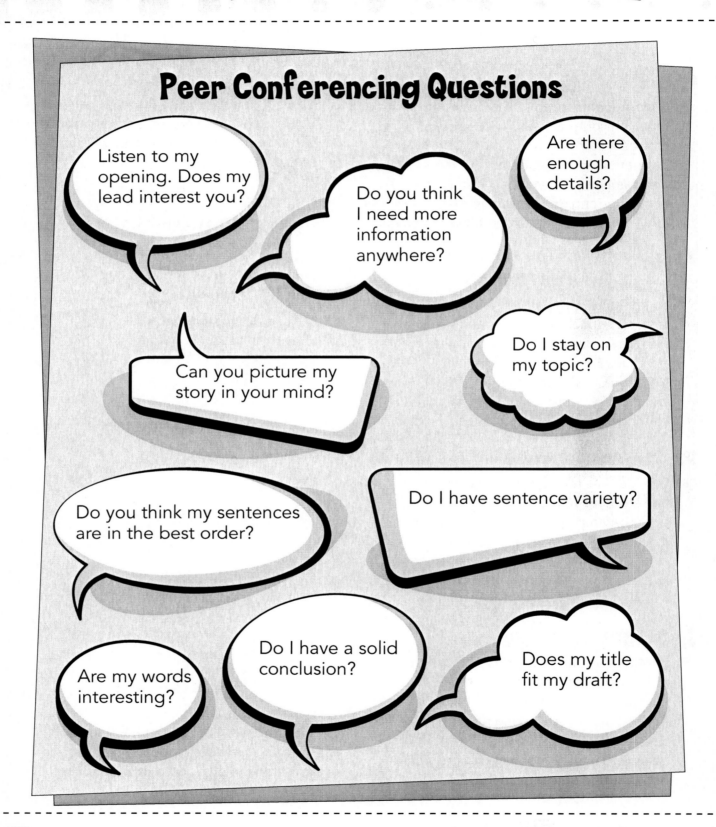

The Five-Step Writing Process

Standard

Understands the structure of Writer's Workshop

Materials

- *The Five-Step Writing Process Notebook Entry* (page 73; fivestepprocess.pdf)
- Chart paper
- Markers
- Writer's Notebooks
- Index cards
- Writing samples *(optional)*

Mentor Texts

- *Amelia's Notebook* by Marissa Moss
- *The Sloppy Copy Slipup* by DyAnne DiSalvo
- *Look at My Book: How Kids Can Write & Illustrate Terrific Books* by Loreen Leedy
- See *Mentor Text List* in Appendix C for other suggestions.

Procedures

Note: Refer to the five-step writing process (prewriting, drafting, revising, editing, and publishing) as students work through the writing process on numerous projects throughout the year.

Think About Writing

1. Remind students that they have been developing their writing by using a variety of ideas and talking about how authors write. Explain that writing can be separated into simple steps that make the process more manageable. These simple steps will help them improve their finished writing.

2. Review mentor texts, if desired.

Teach

3. Tell students, "Today I will show you each step of the Five-Step Writing Process to help you become better writers."

4. Record each step from *The Five-Step Writing Process Notebook Entry* (page 73) onto a sheet of chart paper. Discuss each step with students as you write it. If possible, display student work samples that show each step of the process. For example, for prewriting, you could show a graphic organizer.

Engage

5. Have students talk with partners to name and briefly discuss the steps of the writing process. Students may refer to the anchor chart, if necessary. Provide approximately two or three minutes of talk time.

The Five-Step Writing Process *(cont.)*

Apply

6. Remind students to use the steps of the writing process to make their writing the best it can be. Provide students with *The Five-Step Writing Process Notebook Entry* to add to their Writer's Notebook. Today, students can revise or edit an existing writing piece or begin with a new idea.

Write/Conference

7. Provide students time to write. Prepare index cards with the five steps of the writing process. Gather a small group at a table to reteach the steps as needed. Explain and clarify each step. Use concrete samples to demonstrate. Allow four or five minutes to reteach. Then begin to rotate around the room and individually confer.

Spotlight Strategy

8. Spotlight a student who is using an idea from a draft in his or her writing. For example, "Writers, you rock! Notice how Daniel is capturing a moment from an experience in his draft." Echo your thinking from the mini-lesson strategy.

Share

9. Have students share their writing with partners. Provide approximately two minutes for students to talk.

Homework

Ask students to think about how the Five-Step Writing Process can help their writing.

The Five-Step Writing Process Notebook Entry

The Five-Step Writing Process

1 **Prewriting:**
Think about your topic:
brainstorm and plan

2 **Drafting:**
Write your thoughts on paper:
rough copy

3 **Revising:**
Reread, rethink, and refine:
check organization and add
details and interesting words

4 **Editing:**
Review and correct:
   Capitalization
   Usage
   Punctuation
   Spelling

5 **Publishing:**
Complete the final copy and
share your writing with others

Ideas

Thinking, Thinking, Thinking!

Ideas are the heart of writing. The purpose of this section is to help students generate ideas for writing. The mini-lessons assist students in exploring the ideas of authors through mentor texts and in discovering unique writing ideas in their own lives. Through individually created lists, students will collect plenty of ideas so that when they begin to write, they are not at a loss for topics. Students are encouraged to keep their ideas in their writing folders so the ideas are readily at hand. Lessons in this section include the following:

- Lesson 1: My Top Ten Ideas (page 77)
- Lesson 2: Stinky Tennis Shoes Trip (page 80)
- Lesson 3: Idea Cache (page 83)
- Lesson 4: Ideas from A to Z (page 86)
- Lesson 5: I Saw It in a Book (page 89)
- Lesson 6: My Declarations (page 92)
- Lesson 7: It's My Choice (page 95)
- Lesson 8: I Question, Question, Question (page 98)

The *Ida, Idea Creator* poster (page 76) can be displayed in the room to provide a visual reminder for students that ideas is one of the traits of writing. You may wish to introduce this poster during the first lesson on ideas. Then, refer to the poster when teaching other lessons on ideas to refresh students' memories and provide them with questions to help hone their writing topics.

Ida
Idea Creator

What is my writing about?

❧ Did I narrow and focus my topic?

❧ Did I gather background knowledge for my topic?

❧ Did I provide rich details, examples, reasons, and facts?

❧ Are details specific and related?

❧ Did I present ideas in an interesting/original way?

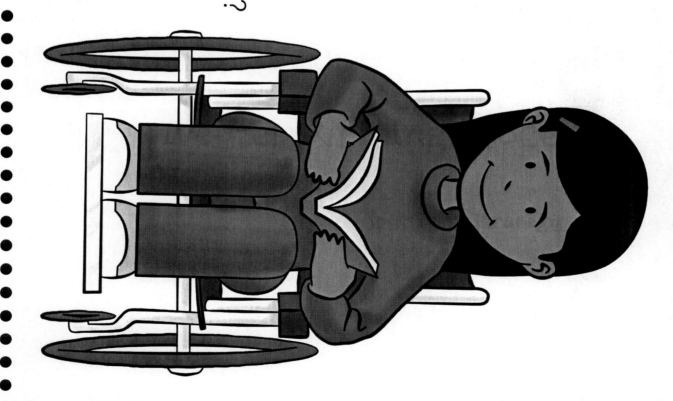

My Top Ten Ideas

Standard
Uses a variety of prewriting strategies

Materials
- Chart paper
- Markers
- *My Top Ten Ideas Notebook Entry* (page 79; topten.pdf)
- Writer's Notebooks

Mentor Texts
- *Written Anything Good Lately?* by Susan Allen
- *Top 10 of Everything 2012* by Caroline Ash
- See *Mentor Text List* in Appendix C for other suggestions.

Procedures

Think About Writing

1. Explain that writers often make lists of topic ideas before they begin writing. These lists allow writers to put their ideas on paper, move them around, erase them, and add to them.

2. Students can list topic ideas for writing short stories, long novels, poetry, and informational or opinion/ argumentative pieces to express their views.

3. Review mentor texts, if desired, and emphasize the authors' ideas. Remind students that authors make lists to collect their ideas for writing topics.

Teach

4. Tell students, "Today I will show you how to create lists of ideas that include your Top Ten ideas." Explain that they may have seen Top Ten lists in other places. Discuss examples of these lists, such as Top Ten basketball teams, Top Ten songs, Top Ten movies, Top Ten healthy foods, etc.

5. Tell students that they are going to be writing lists and ranking ideas from 1 to 10, with the most important idea being first on the list. Remind students that their lists may be used for writing.

6. Write the title *Top Ten Writing Ideas* on a sheet of chart paper. Think aloud as you develop your list. Use the following guiding questions as you develop your list:

   - What am I most interested in writing about in an informational text?

   - What has happened to me that would make an interesting narrative topic?

   - What topic do I have a strong opinion about and would work well for writing an opinion piece?

   - What experience in my past could be described in a poem?

My Top Ten Ideas *(cont.)*

7. Remind students that their lists can change as they add, move, or delete items as they rank the topics.

Engage

8. Divide the class into groups of five students. Explain that students will sit in a circle and each student will share two writing ideas to be included on a Top Ten list. Then, have students *Turn and Talk* to share and compare how they might prioritize the topics on the list.

9. Talk with students about the importance of getting writing ideas from other writers. Tell the class that many authors share their topic lists and get feedback from peers.

Apply

10. Tell students that the small group brainstorming session may help them write ideas on their own Top Ten lists. Provide students with the *My Top Ten Ideas Notebook Entry* (page 79) to add to their Writer's Notebook. Have students work on the *Your Turn* section before proceeding to their writing folders.

Write/Conference

11. Provide time for students to work. As they begin to make their lists, move around the room and help students who need inspiration or guidance.

Spotlight Strategy

12. Spotlight students who are working hard to list and prioritize their writing ideas.

Share

13. Select a couple of students to share their top three writing ideas on their lists. Have them share with the whole group to reinforce the mini-lesson.

Homework
Ask students to share with their families how they are learning to make lists of writing topics. Have students talk with family members and try to come up with an alternative Top Ten list.

My Top Ten Ideas Notebook Entry

My Top Ten Ideas

Authors keep lists of writing **ideas** so they can return to them over and over, again and again. Many writers write about their own personal experiences or topics they want to learn more about.

1. Surviving four tornadoes (narrative)

2. Facts about storms and tornadoes (informative)

3. You should read books by my favorite author (argumentative)

4. New York! New York! (informative/narrative/ argumentative)

5. Making popcorn balls with Auntie SudieBell (narrative)

6. Traveling in Europe (informative/narrative)

7. Mountaineer Football! The best fans! (argumentative)

8. Wondering why I'm allergic to bees (narrative)

9. Finding out why I was allergic to bees (informative)

10. Being a finalist in the Spelling Bee (narrative)

Your Turn:

What are your Top Ten ideas? Think about your experiences as well as those topics you want to learn more about.

Stinky Tennis Shoes Trip

Standard
Uses a variety of prewriting strategies

Materials
- Picture or photograph of a pair of old tennis shoes (used and well-traveled)
- Chart paper
- Markers
- *Stinky Tennis Shoes Trip Notebook Entry* (page 82; stinkyshoes.pdf)
- Writer's Notebooks

Mentor Texts
- *Those Shoes* by Maribeth Boelts
- See Mentor Text List in Appendix C for other suggestions.

Procedures
Note: Story ideas can be found in the most unusual places. Using the idea of a well-worn pair of tennis shoes and where they have traveled opens up a lot of interesting ideas for stories.

Think About Writing
1. Tell students that one of the goals of writing at this level is to be able to write well, even with different topics, formats, and genres. Explain to them that they will be using an object to help them consider different topics to write about descriptively.

2. Review mentor texts, if desired, and emphasize the authors' ideas. Remind students that authors get their ideas from all different kinds of places.

Teach
3. Tell students, "Today I will show you how you can use one image to help you make a list of writing ideas. Have you ever considered dirty, stinky tennis shoes and secret places where they might have gone? I'm going to be creative and remember every place that my worn tennis shoes have traveled."

4. Find a picture or a photograph of an old pair of tennis shoes and display it near a sheet of chart paper. Think aloud as you develop your own list of ideas. Help students see the importance of descriptive phrasing. Talk about the importance of using sensory language. Use the following guiding questions as you develop your list:

   - How do these shoes look or smell?
   - Who do you think wore these shoes? Where do you think this person traveled in these shoes?
   - How could these shoes be used in a story?
   - What descriptive phrases could be used in a story?

Stinky Tennis Shoes Trip *(cont.)*

Engage

5. Divide students into six groups. Ask each group to think deeply about places where tennis shoes might travel. Have students work quickly and quietly without disturbing other groups. Have groups record their ideas and keep them secret until they return to the whole group.

6. Allow a few minutes for small groups to gather information. Come back together as a whole class and ask each group to share a few of their ideas.

Apply

7. Remind students to include descriptive language as they write. Encourage them to include details that share how a place or object looks, feels, smells, tastes, and sounds. Provide students with the *Stinky Tennis Shoes Trip Notebook Entry* (page 82) to add to their Writer's Notebook. Have students work on the *Your Turn* section before proceeding to their writing folders.

Write/Conference

8. Provide time for students to generate their lists. Depending on the number of students who need assistance, you may confer individually or in small groups.

Spotlight Strategy

9. Spotlight students who are writing descriptive and detailed lists and recognize them for their efforts.

Share

10. Ask students to find partners. Encourage them to find a classmate who is wearing a similar type of shoe. In pairs, have students share at least three of their best ideas.

Homework

Ask students to look for well-worn shoes at home. Have them discuss the writing assignment with their parents and ask their parents to share real or imaginary ideas of where the shoes have traveled.

Stinky Tennis Shoes Trip Notebook Entry

Stinky Tennis Shoes Trip

Sometimes authors discover writing ideas in the most unusual places. Consider a pair of well-worn tennis shoes. Imagine the places they have traveled and the stories that the shoes can tell:

- into the garden to harvest vegetables

- down the lane running beside children

- down to the market to buy hot dogs

- down the street to pick up newspaper

- off to the stadium to watch football

- to the park to find worms, birds, and rocks

Your Turn:

If your tennis shoes could talk, what would they say about the places they have traveled? What have they explored? Write several ideas in your notebook. Then, choose an idea and begin a draft.

#50920—*Getting to the Core of Writing—Level 6* © Shell Education

Idea Cache

Standard
Uses a variety of prewriting strategies

Materials
- Box of memorabilia to share with students (a marble, pebble, book, or a necklace, etc.)
- Chart paper
- Markers
- *Idea Cache Notebook Entry* (page 85; ideacache.pdf)
- Writer's Notebooks

Mentor Texts
- *The Memory String* by Eve Bunting
- *Marshfield Dreams: When I Was a Kid* by Ralph Fletcher
- *A Writer's Notebook* by Ralph Fletcher
- *Amelia's 5th-Grade Notebook* by Marissa Moss
- *Amelia's 6th-Grade Notebook* by Marissa Moss
- See *Mentor Text List* in Appendix C for other suggestions.

Procedures
Note: Revisit *Idea Cache* throughout the year to add additional topics for writing.

Think About Writing
1. Explain to students that story ideas may appear at any moment. Authors look for ideas in their own lives and experiences. They often have a system for how they record and remember their ideas.

2. Review mentor texts, if desired, and emphasize the authors' ideas.

Teach
3. Tell students, "Today we will learn about how to store ideas in our own secret collection called an Idea Cache." Tell students that a *cache* is a collection.

4. Show the box of memorabilia to students and talk about how these objects can help generate story ideas. Choose objects that are common and easily found so that students may even use some of the same ideas if necessary. Some ideas include:

   - a pebble from a special location
   - a picture drawn by someone special
   - a treasured letter
   - a ticket from a special concert
   - a piece of nature found on a hike or walk

   Use these objects to talk about how they connect to story ideas. For example, a leaf or rock found on a walk can be used in a story about a family of insects who use things in nature to make a home. Show these connections by writing notes on a sheet of chart paper.

Idea Cache (cont.)

Engage

5. Have students work in pairs. Ask them to work together to share their own memories and share objects or ideas that might make great stories. Allow a few minutes for students to do this in pairs. Then, have students move to new partners and talk about new ideas. Encourage students to give a few ideas and take a few ideas.

6. Allow a few minutes for additional rotations. Then, ask students to return to the whole group.

Apply

7. Remind students that ideas are everywhere and that time spent discussing ideas in pairs may have sparked new writing topics. Encourage students to use those discussions as a springboard to create their own lists of writing topics. Ask them to think about treasured objects or memories that also may spark new topics.

8. Provide students with the *Idea Cache Notebook Entry* (page 85) to add to their Writer's Notebook. Have students work on the *Your Turn* section before proceeding to their writing folders.

Write/Conference

9. Provide time for students to begin writing and expanding on their topics. Depending on time, students might spend a couple of days gathering their ideas and turning one into a cohesive writing piece.

Spotlight Strategy

10. Call attention to writers who have not only developed topics but have started writing.

Share

11. Select a few students to share their writing with the whole group to reinforce the mini-lesson.

Homework

Have students begin to develop memory boxes with their parents. Ask family members to talk about the experiences and memories associated with the objects in the memory boxes. Students may discover topics they want to write more about during writing time at school.

Idea Cache Notebook Entry

Idea Cache

Authors collect ideas like many of us collect coins or rocks. They use the ideas to create topics for their writing. Sometimes real objects from collections can give us ideas for interesting stories.

What is in your **Idea Cache**? Each idea has a story just waiting to be told. Think about questions to generate details about the items in your collections. Ask questions, such as:

Who?   (Who gave it to you or who was with you?)

What?   (What is it? Use your five senses to describe it.)

Where?   (Where did it come from?)

When?   (When did you get it?)

Why?   (Why do you keep it? Why is it special?)

Your Turn:

Create an Idea Cache list in your Writer's Notebook. Select one idea and use questions to generate a few details. Write a paragraph using the information.

Ideas from A to Z

Procedures

Note: Use this lesson to generate writing ideas and introduce the ABC book format to students.

Think About Writing

1. Explain that coming up with topics for writing is a central goal of Writer's Workshop. Tell them that authors generate writing topics from their personal experiences, from people they love and admire, as well as from places they have visited or would like to visit some day. Authors also record topics and ideas that they want to learn about and explore so they may share information, concepts, and opinions. Tell students that they will be creating "Ideas from A to Z" to use in informative, opinion/argumentative, and narrative writing.

2. Review mentor texts, if desired, and emphasize the different ways authors organize their ideas.

Teach

3. Tell students, "Today I will show you how to make a list of topics that you are interested in for writing. The list will go from A to Z." Explain that organizing ideas helps authors keep track of them.

4. Tell students that an A to Z arrangement is one that they can identify and follow. Share that many books are organized this way. Alphabet books can be used to share information or to entertain. Explain that you will be modeling how to organize a list of alphabetical topics and include informative, opinion/argumentative, and narrative topics.

5. Use chart paper to write an A to Z list. Think aloud as you use the following questions to guide the topics:

   - What is special about where you live?
   - Do you think school uniforms should be required?
   - Think about a fictional place you would like to visit. What would you do there?

Ideas from A to Z (cont.)

- What does your family like to do together?

- What science or social studies topics do you find interesting?

Engage

6. Have students work in triads to brainstorm possible topics to include on an alphabet chart. Remind students that they will be writing opinion/ argumentative, informative, and narrative pieces and that their lists should reflect these three genres of writing. After a few minutes of planning time, ask students to return to the whole group.

Apply

7. Have students generate their own topics of interest to use in their writing. Provide students with the *Ideas from A to Z Notebook Entry* (page 88) to add to their Writer's Notebook. Have students work on the *Your Turn* section before proceeding to their writing folders.

Write/Conference

8. Provide time for students to write. If there are students who need individual guidance, create a small group so that they can generate ideas together. After working with a small instructional group, move around and confer individually with students.

Spotlight Strategy

9. Spotlight students who are demonstrating work ethic, motivation, and engagement.

Share

10. Have students meet back in triads. Have them each take turns sharing one of their most interesting ideas and why they chose that idea. Have students read over each list, reflect, focus, and share.

Homework

Have students share their lists with family members. They may ask family members to help them think of ideas that can be added to the Ideas from A to Z lists.

Ideas from A to Z Notebook Entry

Ideas from A to Z

Authors often get their writing topics from their own personal experiences. They may record topics and ideas that they want to learn about and explore so they may share information, concepts, and opinions. Here are a few topics to get you started:

Aa	Bb	Cc	Dd
animal habitats	bullying	China	deserts
Ee	Ff	Gg	Hh
environments	friendship	grandparents	healthy habits
Ii	Jj	Kk	Ll
iguanas	juggling	kites	lunar eclipse
Mm	Nn	Oo	Pp
migration	natural resources	Olympics	planets
Qq	Rr	Ss	Tt
quilts	Rembrandt	sailing	Texas
Uu	Vv	Ww	Xx
uniforms	vacations	Walt Disney	X-rays
Yy	Zz		
yo-yo	zodiac		

Your Turn:

Begin developing your Ideas from A to Z list for writing in your Writer's Notebook. Remember, you can revisit and add topics to this list throughout the year. Your topics should include ideas for informative, opinion/argumentative, and narrative writing.

#50920—Getting to the Core of Writing—Level 6 © Shell Education

I Saw It in a Book

Standards

- Uses a variety of prewriting strategies
- Uses content, style, and structure appropriate for specific audiences and purposes

Materials

- Chart paper
- Markers
- *I Saw It in a Book Notebook Entry* (page 91; sawit.pdf)
- Writer's Notebooks

Mentor Texts

Sample books representing a variety of genres:

- *The Table Where Rich People Sit* by Byrd Baylor
- *Dear Mr. Henshaw* by Beverly Cleary
- *Almost Gone: The World's Rarest Animals* by Steve Jenkins
- *Blizzard* by Jim Murphy
- *The Three Questions (Based on a story by Leo Tolstoy)* by Jon Muth
- See *Mentor Text List* in Appendix C for other suggestions.

Procedures

Note: It is important to tell students to "read like a writer" so they can mimic different styles and crafts of writing.

Think About Writing

1. Explain that authors often organize their ideas in a certain way in order to share a message with readers. Tell students that identifying this organization in books helps them to explore using that skill in their own writing. Students can study and identify the story elements authors use to develop narrative, informative, and opinion/argumentative writing.

2. Review mentor texts, if desired, and discuss the different text structures used.

Teach

3. Tell students that they are going to learn how to identify an author's genre and examine features of that type of text. Share some examples of writing genres (informative, opinion/argumentative, narrative) and discuss the characteristics of each.

4. List the different types of text structures on a sheet of chart paper. Include the following: Cause/Effect, Compare/Contrast, Chronological, Descriptive, Problem/Solution, Question/Answer, and Cyclical.

5. Use additional books and excerpts to share characteristics of informative, opinion/argumentative, and narrative writing. Discuss different text structures for each genre using familiar texts or literature from your Core Reading Program.

I Saw It in a Book (cont.)

Engage

6. Divide students into quads. Pass out a text to each group, and ask the groups to examine a text to determine the genre and text structure the author used. In their notebooks, have students record the topic idea, writing genre, and text structure they identified.

7. Ask small groups to share their information aloud so that other groups can also record the genre and text structures that were studied in their notebooks.

Apply

8. Rotate the provided texts around the room. Have students explore and examine the writings of other authors. Provide students with the *I Saw It in a Book Notebook Entry* (page 91) to add to their Writer's Notebook. Have students work on the *Your Turn* section before proceeding to their writing folders.

Write/Conference

9. Provide time for students to write. Once all students are engaged, rotate, conference, and make future plans.

Spotlight Strategy

10. Spotlight students who are able to make connections between text genres and structures and new topics for writing.

Share

11. Have students meet with partners to share topics of interest to be used in their writing. Then, have them determine what genre or text structure will be used.

Homework

Ask students to read different types of reading materials, such as a newspaper or magazine, with their families. Family members should read with students and help them notice different aspects of the reading material, such as opinion letters or weather reports in a newspaper.

I Saw It in a Book Notebook Entry

I Saw It in a Book

Authors develop their topics through different text **genres** and **structures**.

TEXT GENRES

Informative: Provides information to explain, inform, define

Opinion/Argumentative: Convinces someone to accept a point of view

Narrative: A story based on a real or imaginary event

TEXT STRUCTURES

Cause/Effect: Provides ideas and facts as a cause and the consequence(s) that occurred as a result

Compare/Contrast: Examines how two or more people, events, things, etc., are similar and/or different

Chronological: A sequence of events or steps to a procedure

Descriptive: Gives details, characteristics, features, and examples to provide a mental image for the reader

Problem/Solution: Tells a problem, shares one or more possible solutions

Question/Answer: Poses a question(s), provides an answer(s)

Cyclical: Begins with an event, includes a series of activities, and concludes with the initial event (circular ending)

Your Turn:

Explore and notice text topics, genres, and structures. Use the lines below to write about a topic idea that you saw in a book. Choose a text genre and structure and begin writing.

- Book Title: _____

- Topic: _____

- Text Genre: _____

- Text Structure: _____

- A Writing Topic: _____

My Declarations

Standards

- Uses a variety of prewriting strategies
- Writes persuasive compositions

Materials

- Chart paper
- Markers
- Sticky notes
- *My Declarations Notebook Entry* (page 94; mydeclarations.pdf)
- Writer's Notebooks

Mentor Texts

- *The American Story: 100 True Tales from American History* by Jennifer Armstrong
- *Give Me Liberty! The Story of the Declaration of Independence* by Russell Freedman
- *Children's Encyclopedia of American History* by David King
- See *Mentor Text List* in Appendix C for other suggestions.

Procedures

Note: Revisit *My Declarations* throughout the year to add additional topics for opinion/argumentative writing.

Think About Writing

1. Explain to students that making a declaration is a more formal way of stating what you believe, how things should be, or what you intend to do. Tell them that people can make declarations (intentions about a variety of subjects) in their writing. Interesting declarations might include the following topics: bullying, the use of video games, peer pressure, cell phone etiquette, access to social media, school uniforms, etc.

2. Review mentor texts, if desired, and emphasize the declarations made by the authors.

Teach

3. Tell students that they are going to work together to create a list of declarations that can be used as writing and discussion points. Explain that multiple declarations about the same issue may be contradictory. Many issues have good points on both sides of the argument.

4. Choose an issue or problem that is familiar and relevant to students in your class. Use a sheet of chart paper to record declarations and ideas that support them. The following are some examples:

   I believe that bullying is a serious problem.

   Supporting Ideas: students may harm themselves, causes stress, leads to depression and low self-esteem

   I believe that requiring school uniforms would reduce social competition and violence.

   Supporting Ideas: less money needed for clothing, reduce wear and tear on clothes, reduce parent/student arguments concerning appropriate clothing

#50920—Getting to the Core of Writing—Level 6 © Shell Education

My Declarations *(cont.)*

I believe that young students' access to social media should be limited.

<u>Supporting Ideas:</u> the wiring of the brain has not yet matured enough to make decisions about risky behaviors, safety issues, inappropriate and inaccurate information can harm reputations

Engage

5. Divide students into four groups and have them meet in the four corners of the room. Explain to students that their groups will meet to discuss their own personal declarations. Ask students to each finish the statement: *I believe* _____. Have students use sticky notes to contribute ideas to a group list.

Apply

6. Ask students to write and discuss ideas connected to their beliefs. Remind them to use supporting ideas to justify their thinking. Provide students with the *My Declarations Notebook Entry* (page 94) to add to their Writer's Notebook. Have students work on the *Your Turn* section before proceeding to their writing folders.

Write/Conference

7. Provide time for students to write. Be available to circulate, stop by desks to check in, observe any problem areas, and provide assistance.

Spotlight Strategy

8. Spotlight students who are working hard to write the supporting ideas. Praise these students for thinking about why they hold the beliefs they do.

Share

9. Ask students to sit in pairs and share their ideas. After a few minutes, have students rotate to another partner and share and listen to ideas. Allow a few minutes for one more rotation.

Homework

Ask students to talk with their parents about declarations and points of view. Have them share ideas about the topics and see if family members hold the same viewpoints or different ones.

My Declarations Notebook Entry

My Declarations

Authors often generate writing ideas from their personal beliefs and create stories to share those ideas with their readers.

A **declaration** is a statement of your beliefs or intentions about a specific subject. When stating a belief, also share reasons and points to consider. Read this example:

My declaration: In recent years, bullying has become an enormous problem in our society.

Supporting Ideas:

- Bullying often causes stress, drives students to harm themselves, leads to depression, and creates low self-esteem.

- Students often do not want to go to adults for help in a bullying situation, which allows the problem to continue on with no adult intervention.

Your Turn:

Create two declarations. Then, write down supporting ideas to consider for each topic.

#50920—Getting to the Core of Writing—Level 6 © Shell Education

It's My Choice

Standard

Uses a variety of prewriting strategies

Materials

- Various examples of texts: newspapers, magazines, poetry, brochures, advertisements, recipes, emails, etc.
- Music
- Chart paper
- Markers
- *It's My Choice Notebook Entry* (page 97; mychoice.pdf)
- Writer's Notebooks

Mentor Texts

- *A Poke in the I: A Collection of Concrete Poems* by Paul Janeczko
- *Our Solar System* by Seymour Simon
- *My Rotten Redheaded Older Brother* by Patricia Polacco
- *The ABCs of Habitats* by Bobbie Kalman
- *You Have to Write* by Janet S. Wong
- See *Mentor Text List* in Appendix C for other suggestions.

Procedures

Note: Allowing students a choice when writing promotes interest, responsibility, and independence. Although writing prompts are necessary and useful, give students a choice in their writing topics on a regular basis.

Think About Writing

1. Tell students that they are allowed to make choices every day in their lives. They may choose what to wear to school, what to read, how to celebrate a birthday, and many other things. Explain that making choices also requires sorting through information and options. This is true when students make choices about writing topics and writing materials.

2. Explain to students that they are exposed to varied printed materials both in school and at home. Learning to recognize and understand the many printed sources is easier if students have had opportunities to create various printed materials.

3. Review mentor texts, if desired, and discuss the characteristics of different text types.

Teach

4. Briefly show students different examples of printed material. Tell them, "I have a stack of material we will use to play a game called Musical Texts. We will pass examples of texts around the room until the music stops. You will then turn to a partner and discuss characteristics of the sample, with both of you having an opportunity for discussion."

5. Distribute the printed material and play music that turns off after a few seconds. Have students continue to discuss the characteristics of each type of text. Ask student pairs to vote quickly on each text type: a thumbs-up if a student is interested in trying to write that type of text and a thumbs-down if not interested.

It's My Choice *(cont.)*

Engage

6. Using a sheet of chart paper, quickly make a list as a group of all the types of writing materials that were observed. Place each student with a writing partner. Ask students to summarize their observations and make choices about which writing type to try for a writing exercise.

Apply

7. Remind students that it is important to have choices in writing. Provide students with the *It's My Choice Notebook Entry* (page 97) to add to their Writer's Notebook. Ask students to use their notebooks as a starting point for writing.

Write/Conference

8. Sometimes students have not been given ample opportunities to make choices and are unable to make decisions. If you notice that some are struggling, pull a small group together and generate ideas with them. Be certain that everyone is ready before you send them off to work. You may need to send them one at a time as they make their plans.

Spotlight Strategy

9. Call attention to students who have made great choices and used time wisely. Pay close attention to struggling students and be certain to include them in spotlighting.

Share

10. Ask students to reflect on what they have learned in this lesson and to share it in pairs. Allow a few student volunteers to share their ideas with the whole group.

Homework

Ask students to work with family members to observe as many types of writing at home as possible. Students can interview adult family members about the kinds of writing they do on a regular basis.

It's My Choice Notebook Entry

It's My Choice

Authors consider their audience, purpose, and format when planning writing projects. They may write to persuade, inform, or entertain, and may do each in a different form of writing like an editorial, an autobiography, or a comic strip.

Think about your topic, your audience, and the purpose of your writing. What form of writing will be most appropriate for your project? Consider a few ideas below and add other forms of writing as you explore texts.

ABC Book	Fable	Mystery	Scary Stories
Adventure	Fairy Tale	Myth	Science Fiction
Advertisement	Ghost Stories	Newsletter	Short Story
Autobiography	Greeting Card	Nonfiction	Song Lyrics
Biography	How-to Manual	Opinion	Speech
Book Review	Humorous Story	Personal Narrative	Sports Article
Brochure	Interview	Picture Book	Spy Story
Comic Strip	Invitation	Play	Thank You Note
Commercial	Jokes	Poetry	Tongue Twister
Diary	Journal Entry	Poster	Travel Brochure
Editorial	Letter	Realistic Fiction	TV News Report
Email	Magazine Article	Recipe	Twisted Fairy Tale
Essay	Movie Script	Report	Want Ad

Your Turn:

Consider topics for your writing. In your Writer's Notebook, write the topic, purpose, and format of writing you might consider for a writing project. There may be more than one form of writing listed!

I Question, Question, Question

Standard

Uses a variety of prewriting strategies

Materials

- Chart paper
- Markers
- *I Question, Question, Question Notebook Entry* (page 100; question.pdf)
- Writer's Notebooks

Mentor Texts

- *I Wonder Why Whales Sing and Other Questions About Sea Life* by Caroline Harris
- *The Three Questions (Based on a story by Leo Tolstoy)* by Jon Muth
- *Peeling the Onion* by Wendy Orr
- Excerpts from *Hatchet* by Gary Paulsen
- See *Mentor Text List* in Appendix C for other suggestions.

Procedures

Note: Although students are naturally curious, they still need to be taught how to ask questions that influence deep thinking. When students recognize that their questions have merit, they become more confident in their thinking.

Think About Writing

1. Tell students that when authors want to narrow topics, they ask questions. As a group, talk about a topic that is broad and would benefit from a more focused concept.

2. Review mentor texts, if desired, and emphasize the importance of asking questions to focus topics.

Teach

3. Tell students that they will work as a group to generate topics for possible writing projects. Then, the group will produce questions that might be asked about the topic to focus learning.

4. Remind students that asking questions while writing builds a deeper understanding of learning and fosters wonder and curiosity. Asking questions helps students generate and develop writing topics and ideas.

5. Model how to ask questions by reading a section of *Hachet,* or your personal selection. Use the text to generate a list of essential questions and write them on a sheet of chart paper. Build questions to develop a sense of wonder and curiosity. Have students think about questions the character was forced to ask and answer during that difficult experience.

I Question, Question, Question (cont.)

Engage

6. Divide the class into quads. Choose several topics that can be broken down into smaller sub-topics. Assign a topic to each group and ask each group to work together to formulate questions that could become writing topics. Social studies or science topics work well for this exercise.

Apply

7. Remind students that it helps to develop advanced thinking by asking deep questions about a topic of interest. Provide students with the *I Question, Question, Question Notebook Entry* (page 100) to add to their Writer's Notebook. Ask students to use their notebooks as a starting point for writing.

Write/Conference

8. Using blank paper, create a questioning cube to engage students with questions about *who, what, when, where, why,* and sentence stems, such as *I wonder who...* and *I wonder how....* Use the questioning cube with a small group of students who may need additional support. Generate topics and questions together as a group.

Spotlight Strategy

9. Spotlight students who are asking questions that help them to more deeply understand a topic. For example, "I'm noticing that Sofia is writing questions about endangered species that helps her think more about the human role in harming these animals. Good work!"

Share

10. Have students meet with partners to share their questions and topic ideas.

Homework

Ask students to share some of their topic ideas and questions with their families. Have students ask their families to help them think of a few more detailed questions about their topics.

I Question, Question, Question Notebook Entry

I Question, Question, Question

Authors ask **questions** to narrow the scope of a topic and develop a deeper understanding of ideas. They ask questions because they are curious, full of wonder, and want to learn about their topics and share that information with others. Many times one question leads to another question, which leads to another question.

Here are a few questions from the story *Hatchet* by Gary Paulsen.

Overall Topic: Survival

What supplies can I salvage from my crisis?

Will I need shelter? What resources do I need to build a shelter? Do I have the energy to build a shelter?

Do I have available resources needed to use as a signaling device? How do I use it? Where should I put it?

What resources can I utilize from my environment?

What about heat? Will it be necessary for me to build a fire? How do I build a fire? What resources do I need? Will the fire attract harmful animals?

How should I prepare myself to conserve and find available water? How do I know the water is pure?

Your Turn:

Consider topics for your own writing. In your Writer's Notebook, write the topic and generate questions. What are you curious about? What are your "I wonder" questions?

Sentence Fluency
Getting Started

Sentence fluency helps make writing interesting. It is a trait that allows writers to add interest to their writing. By changing the sentence length and where words are placed next to each other in the sentence, writers are able to help guide the reader through their work. Authors with good sentence fluency know the techniques needed to construct sentences that flow and have rhythm. The mini-lessons assist students in exploring parts of sentences, the ways sentences are built, and the ways to expand sentences to develop more interesting ideas. Lessons in this section include the following:

- Lesson 1: Playing with Sentence Patterns (page 103)
- Lesson 2: Double Trouble with Compound Elements (page 107)
- Lesson 3: The Long and Short of It (page 110)
- Lesson 4: Sentence Stretch and Scramble (page 113)
- Lesson 5: SOS! Semicolons Offer Style (page 116)
- Lesson 6: Adding Details (page 119)
- Lesson 7: Let's Make It Clear! (page 122)

The *Simon, Sentence Builder* poster (page 102) can be displayed in the room to provide a visual reminder for students that sentence fluency is one of the traits of writing. You may wish to introduce this poster during the first lesson on sentence fluency. Then, refer to the poster when teaching other lessons on sentence fluency to refresh students' memories and provide them with questions to help guide them as they create sentences.

Simon
Sentence Builder

What kinds of sentences will I use?

✔ Did I use a variety of sentence patterns (simple, compound, complex)?

✔ Did I use a variety of sentence beginnings?

✔ Did I include a variety of sentence lengths?

✔ Are my sentences musical and rhythmic?

Playing with Sentence Patterns

Standards

- Uses a variety of strategies to draft and revise written work
- Uses a variety of sentence structures to expand and embed ideas

Materials

- Chart paper
- Markers
- *Sentence Fragments* (page 106; sentencefragments.pdf)
- *Playing with Sentence Patterns Notebook Entry* (page 105; sentencepatterns.pdf)
- Writer's Notebooks

Mentor Texts

- *Twilight Comes Twice* by Ralph Fletcher
- *Under the Quilt of Night* by Deborah Hopkinson
- *An Angel for Solomon Singer* by Cynthia Rylant
- See *Mentor Text List* in Appendix C for other suggestions.

Procedures

Note: Writing great sentences requires clarity, proper sequencing, arrangements of parts of speech, and the proper use of punctuation to clearly depict the intention of the writer. Encourage students to try a variety of patterns.

Think About Writing

1. Tell students that sentence variety is key to clear and focused writing. Assure them that any writer can be successful with practice and application. Explain to them that they are going to study different sentence patterns and learn the reasons why sentence variety is so important.

2. Review mentor texts, if desired, and emphasize the variety of sentence patterns.

Teach

3. Tell students, "Today we will explore two different sentence patterns that can be used to begin a sentence." Use chart paper to display or write sentences using two sentence patterns. One sentence will begin with a prepositional phrase. The other sentence will begin with descriptive modifiers. Share additional examples from mentor texts.

4. Remind students that repeating the same words at the beginning of sentences can become boring and repetitive to their readers. Adding variety to how a sentence begins will improve the flow of the writing and engage the reader. As writers mimic and practice sentence patterns of other authors, they become confident in how to develop variety in sentence beginnings.

Playing with Sentence Patterns *(cont.)*

Engage

5. Have students form two circles, one inside the other. The students in the inner circle should face out and the students in the outer circle should face in. Distribute *Sentence Fragments* (page 106), one to each student. Have each student read his or her fragment aloud and the student facing opposite should complete the sentence in their Writer's Notebook. Partners should then switch roles. Encourage students to be creative and listen for the rhythm and flow of the sentence.

6. Next, have the circles rotate so everyone has a new partner to repeat the activity. Allow time for sentences to develop as you listen and monitor student discussions. Repeat the activity three or four times and share observations.

Apply

7. Provide students with the *Playing with Sentence Patterns Notebook Entry* (page 105) and have them practice writing different sentence patterns. Tell students that they will analyze and imitate sentence patterns to improve their own writing.

Write/Conference

8. As students move off to practice their writing, observe and note any confusion. Support students needing further assistance with more explicit instruction.

Spotlight Strategy

9. Spotlight students who are writing a variety of sentence patterns. For example, "You attempted this sentence pattern and it sounds great!"

Share

10. Have students meet with partners to share their best sentences. Ask students to listen for sentence variety.

Homework

Ask students to share what they have learned about sentence variety with their families. Have students work with family members to compose a sentence with a prepositional phrase and a sentence using a descriptive modifier in a noun fragment.

#50920—*Getting to the Core of Writing—Level 6* © Shell Education

Playing with Sentence Patterns Notebook Entry

Playing with Sentence Patterns

Authors use **variety** in how they begin their sentences to transition appropriately from sentence to sentence and to hold their readers' attention.

Learning a variety of sentence patterns to begin sentences will enhance your skills as an author. Explore sentence beginnings with the following two patterns:

Sentences that begin with a prepositional phrase:

Under the bridge,

During the game,

Out of the darkness,

Beneath the water,

Sentences that begin with a descriptive modifier:

The angry, young student…

A mischievous baby…

The pale morning mist…

The single deadliest tornado…

Your Turn:

Practice using the sentence patterns above. Draft three sentences beginning with prepositional phrases and three sentences beginning with descriptive modifiers. When you are finished, examine the sentences in your current writing project for sentence revisions.

Sentence Fragments

Directions: Have students create complete sentences using the sentence fragments below.

Prepositional Phrases	Descriptive Modifiers
At home in the dark,…	My beautiful dancing heart…
Along the roadside,…	Her fondest early memories…
In the misty clouds,…	The busy, quiet classroom…
As the swirling wind…	The shabby, wet puppy…
After I get an A in Math,…	The damp, misty morning…
Without my friend,…	Our wonderful friendship…
During the movie,…	The new early signs…
In the park,…	The rambling dialogue…
Before school,…	A slumbering baby cub…
Up in the sky,…	The dreary, rainy day…
By the side of the tree,…	Her early June retirement…
From the last rain,…	An angry young student…
Under the bridge,…	The mischievous baby
During the game,…	The single deadliest tornado…

Double Trouble with Compound Elements

Standards

- Uses a variety of strategies to draft and revise written work
- Uses a variety of sentence structures to expand and embed ideas

Materials

- Chart paper
- Markers
- Sticky notes
- *Double Trouble with Compound Elements Notebook Entry* (page 109; doubletrouble.pdf)
- Writer's Notebooks

Mentor Texts

- *Trouble Don't Last* by Shelley Pearsall
- *Owl Moon* by Jane Yolen
- *Esperanza Rising* by Pam Muñoz Ryan
- *Teammates* by Peter Golenbock
- See *Mentor Text List* in Appendix C for other suggestions.

Procedures

Note: The more that students can practice and plan when writing sentences, the more their overall writing skills improve.

Think About Writing

1. Explain to students that sentences may contain a single subject and verb, or a double subject and verb. By accurately combining sentences with compound elements, students can avoid repeating and creating sentences that lack style and tone.

2. Review mentor texts, if desired, and discuss how compound sentences give writing more variety.

Teach

3. Explain to the class that compound sentences may have two or more statements, two or more independent clauses, or even two or more subject-verb combinations. Tell students that when analyzing and practicing sentences, it is important to make certain that sentences make sense and flow together. Model examples of each sentence pattern based on student need.

Engage

4. Post four charts around the room with the following headings: *Compound Subject, Compound Verb, Compound Subject/Compound Verb,* and *Double Simple Sentence.* Explain each type of sentence and ask students to find examples in books they are reading or in their class textbooks. Have students write examples of each on sticky notes and post on the proper chart. Allow time for searching, talking, exploring, and crafting examples.

Double Trouble with Compound Elements *(cont.)*

Apply

5. Provide students with the *Double Trouble with Compound Elements Notebook Entry* (page 109) and have them practice writing different sentence patterns. Encourage students to draft sentences that are complete and concise.

Write/Conference

6. Rove and observe. Act as a facilitator during this time, and check in with as many students as possible.

Spotlight Strategy

7. Spotlight students who are using double trouble compound elements. For example, "Writers, your sentences are ranking right up there with the best. May I share a couple?"

Share

8. Have students meet with partners to share their best sentences.

Homework

Ask students to find examples of compound sentences in books or articles. Challenge them to find the four different kinds of compound elements: compound subject, compound verb, compound subject/ compound verb, and double simple sentences..

Double Trouble with Compound Elements

Authors create sentences with compound elements to create style and tone in writing projects.

Sentences may include **compound subjects**, **compound verbs**, or sometimes both a **compound subject** and a **compound verb**. A compound sentence may also include **double simple sentences**.

Compound subjects:

> <u>Josh and Luke</u> raced BMX bikes in the championship series.

Compound verbs:

> Calee <u>studied poetry and wrote limericks</u> every day after school.

Compound subject/compound verb:

> <u>Jackie and Jamey</u> <u>refurbish cabinets and give them as gifts</u>.

Double simple sentences:

> <u>Clint loves to eat Mexican food, but Lanty prefers Chinese.</u>
> <u>John walks to school with me, and I walk home with my best friend.</u>

Your Turn:

Create compound sentences using:

- Compound subjects
- Compound verbs
- Compound subject/double verb
- Double simple sentences

The Long and Short of It

Procedures

Note: To be proficient at writing, students need to be proficient at observing and analyzing an author's craft. You may wish to revisit this lesson throughout the year.

Think About Writing

1. Tell students that by studying the work of different authors and examining sentence structures, they are learning how to write interesting sentences. Explain that the goal is to have them write those sentences with automaticity in writing projects. Tell them that they will be working on using sentence patterns to develop a rhythmic flow to their writing by creating patterns of long and short sentences.

2. Review mentor texts, if desired, and discuss the effectiveness of using long and short sentences.

Teach

3. Tell students, "We will examine the use of long and short sentences. Authors use both to enhance meaning and vary sentence length. Incorporating sentence variety and length into writing is an important skill that makes a reader's experience more interesting and meaningful."

4. Choose a familiar example in literature or one from the mentor texts to model the use of varied sentence length. Read the sentences aloud and discuss how the author uses the lengths to add meaning, emphasis, tone, and rhythm to the message in the story. Use the following questions to guide your discussion:

   - How does this sentence length work for this idea?

   - Why would the author use a one-word sentence? What tone or emphasis does that create for the story?

   - How does the author include both short and long sentences?

The Long and Short of It (cont.)

5. Then, choose another example from a story that includes varied sentence length and write it on the board or a sheet of chart paper. Consider using *Lousy Rotten Stinkin' Grapes* by Margie Palatini:

   > *Fox eyed a bunch of tantalizing grapes hanging from a vine growing high on a tree.*
   >
   > *"Those juicy morsels are for me," he said with a grin.*
   >
   > *"No matter," said he. "I am sly. Clever. Smart. After all, I am a fox."*

6. Model for students how to use colored pencils or markers to underline longer sentences in green, medium-length sentences in yellow, and shorter sentences in red. Discuss how these sentences work together to strongly convey a mood and tone.

Engage

7. Assign students to small groups. Challenge them to find long and short sentences in excerpts from mentor texts, familiar literature, or from their Core Reading Program. Within the group, have students talk about how the author used different lengths of sentences to add meaning, emphasis, tone, and rhythm.

Apply

8. Provide students with *The Long and Short of It Notebook Entry* (page 112) and have them practice identifying sentence length in texts. Have them identify different sentence lengths and rewrite the sentences using colored pencils according to length.

Write/Conference

9. Plan an intervention and enrichment group to motivate, engage, and stimulate student writing. Use appropriate leveled reading material to locate sentences of varying length.

Spotlight Strategy

10. Spotlight students who are identifying sentences of different lengths. For example, "You are a master at finding short sentences that emphasize an important part of the story. Way to go, Jacob!"

Share

11. Give students time to each find one or two examples of sentence length that change the meaning or emphasis of the writing. Then, put students in triads to share those ideas.

Homework

Ask students to write long, short, and medium-length sentences that describe a recent family outing or celebration. Have them share their work with family members. Ask students to point out the variety of sentence lengths.

The Long and Short of It Notebook Entry

The Long and Short of It

Authors create a rhythmic flow to their writing by following patterns of long and short sentences.

Using a variety of **sentence lengths** adds energy and rhythm to your writing. Too many long sentences become repetitive and boring for the reader. Shorter sentences add tone and emphasis to important points. This example is from *Lousy Rotten Stinkin' Grapes* by Margie Palatini:

Fox eyed a bunch of tantalizing grapes hanging from a vine growing high on a tree.

"Those juicy morsels are for me," he said with a grin.

"No matter," said he. "I am sly. Clever. Smart. After all, I am a fox."

Your Turn:

Search for additional examples in a text you know. Select sentences with a variety of lengths and write them in your Writer's Notebook. Count the words in the sentences, and then underline longer sentences with green, medium-length sentences with yellow, and shorter sentences with red. Examine your writing for variety in sentence length and make revisions as needed.

Sentence Stretch and Scramble

Standards

- Uses a variety of strategies to draft and revise written work
- Uses a variety of sentence structures to expand and embed ideas

Materials

- Chart paper
- Markers
- *Sentence Stretch and Scramble Notebook Entry* (page 115; sentencestretch.pdf)
- Writer's Notebooks

Mentor Texts

- *Twilight Comes Twice* by Ralph Fletcher
- *Rosa* by Nikki Giovanni
- *The Twits* by Roald Dahl
- *The Bridge to Terabithia* by Katherine Paterson
- See *Mentor Text List* in Appendix C for other suggestions.

Procedures

Note: Playing games with parts of speech engages and encourages students in crafting sentences with variety and style.

Think About Writing

1. Tell students that they have been focusing on developing sentences with varied sentence structure and patterns to add style and tone to their writing. Explain to them that authors use a variety of tools to develop just the right sentence length, structure, and type in order to engage their readers. Recognizing parts of speech is another tool for developing strong sentences.

2. Review mentor texts, if desired, and discuss the parts of speech that enhance writing.

Teach

3. Tell students, "Today we will review using parts of speech to stretch interesting, meaningful sentences. This means that we will take our ideas and stretch them into a sentence with different parts of speech. Then, we will scramble those sentences to create variety in our writing."

4. Review the five main parts of speech: noun, verb, adverb, adjective, and prepositional phrase. Model how to include the different parts of speech to create sentences. Use a sheet of chart paper to write each part of speech, as well as an example. Then, put the five parts of speech together to stretch, or create, a complete sentence.

5. Next, demonstrate how to scramble parts of speech within a sentence to show sentence variations. Perhaps the prepositional phrase will come first or the adjective will modify the noun. Show students that scrambling a sentence can result in several different statements that mean the same thing.

Sentence Stretch and Scramble (cont.)

Engage

6. Display the *Sentence Stretch and Scramble Notebook Entry* (page 115). Tell students that they will work in quads to use parts of speech to stretch a sentence and then scramble the sentence to create variety using Steps 1–7 from the notebook entry. Explain that students must be ready to share their sentences.

7. Provide quads with words that are connected to current curriculum topics to use for the activity. Allow time for collaboration and have students return to the meeting area to share their sentences.

Apply

8. Provide students with the *Sentence Stretch and Scramble Notebook Entry* and have them practice stretching and scrambling words in a sentence independently. Encourage students to use parts of speech and sentence variety to make their writing more interesting.

9. Have students work on the *Your Turn* section and then turn to their own writing folders and select writing samples that need sentence improvement.

Write/Conference

10. Observe and support students needing additional help. Encourage more advanced students to develop more complex sentence structure. Note observations in your Conferring Notebook.

Spotlight Strategy

11. Select one or two students who clearly stretch and scramble sentences in their notebooks. Spotlight their efforts and encourage others to do the same.

Share

12. Have students work in pairs to share their best sentences. Have students rotate to new partners until you give a signal. Allow approximately three minutes for students to share.

Homework

Ask students to share how to stretch and scramble sentences with family members. Have students challenge family members to write the longest, funniest, silliest, or most descriptive sentences.

Sentence Stretch and Scramble Notebook Entry

Sentence Stretch and Scramble

Authors use a variety of tools to develop just the right sentence length, structure, and type in order to engage their readers. Recognizing and using **parts of speech** is another way to add to sentence variety.

Try these easy steps to stretch a sentence.

Step 1: Who or what is your sentence about? (noun) **the baby**

Step 2: What does it do? (verb) **cries**

Step 3: How or when? (adverb) **loudly**

Step 4: Describe it. (adjective) **The crabby baby**

Step 5: Tell where or when. (prepositional phrase) **when she is hungry**

Step 6: Create your complete sentence.

> **The crabby baby cries loudly when she is hungry.**

Step 7: Scramble your sentence to show possible variations.

> **When she is hungry, the crabby baby cries loudly.**

> **The crabby baby, when she is hungry, cries loudly.**

Your Turn:

Use these nouns or your own topics to practice developing Stretch and Scramble sentences. Then, examine your current writing projects and revise for sentence length and structure.

- elephant
- friend
- pancakes
- bird
- teacher
- storm

SOS! Semicolons Offer Style

Procedures

Note: Writers become competent in sentence writing when they practice reading and writing different sentence types.

Think About Writing

1. Explain to students that they have practiced different ways to write sentences that have meaning, are interesting, and fit with other sentences in their writing. Tell students that authors also use punctuation like the semicolon to add variety and sophistication to their writing.

2. Review mentor texts, if desired, and discuss the ways authors use commas and semicolons to pause.

Teach

3. Tell students that they are going to learn about how to use a semicolon correctly to write more interesting sentences. Explain that a sentence with two independent clauses can be combined with a coordinating conjunction and a comma, or a semicolon. Share the following on chart paper:

   Two independent clauses:

   > *It is nearly nine o'clock. We can't finish mowing the grass.*

   These can be combined with a coordinating conjunction and a comma or with a semicolon:

   > *It is nearly nine o'clock, and we can't finish mowing the grass.*

   > *It is nearly nine o'clock; we can't finish mowing the grass.*

4. To help students remember that semicolons provide sentences with style and variety, explain the acronym SOS: **S**emicolons **O**ffer **S**tyle.

SOS! Semicolons Offer Style (cont.)

5. Explain to students that either example is grammatically correct. The difference is the amount of emphasis the author wishes to place on the pause in the sentence. A semicolon is considered a strong pause, but not as strong as a period. A comma is considered a brief pause. It is important to read and reread writing aloud to listen for the sentence fluency.

Engage

6. Remind students that a semicolon is used in the place of a conjunction to join two simple sentences that are closely related. Put students into pairs. Ask them to stand shoulder to shoulder. Have the pairs start with the partner on the left who will state a simple sentence aloud. The partner on the right will make a simple sentence that closely relates to the first sentence. Then, together as a team, the pairs will write down the sentence, using a semicolon to combine the two simple sentences.

7. Give students time to repeat this exercise a few times. Then, have student pairs choose a favorite combined sentence to share with the group.

Apply

8. Provide students with the *SOS! Semicolons Offer Style Notebook Entry* (page 118) and have them practice identifying the independent clauses that are combined in different ways. Tell them to use their notebook entries as a guide to practice and repeat the pattern.

Write/Conference

9. Roam around the classroom, observe, comment, and praise students.

Spotlight Strategy

10. Give students a choice of which sentence they would like to be in the spotlight. For example, "Please select one sentence that you feel is worthy of our celebration. Raise your hand if you'd like a spotlight!" Select a few students to share.

Share

11. Allow time for students to share their findings in pairs.

Homework

Ask students to talk with family members about the use of semicolons. Have students explain that a semicolon takes the place of a comma and conjunction when joining two simple sentences. Then, have students write example sentences to share with their family and the class.

SOS! Semicolons Offer Style Notebook Entry

SOS! Semicolons Offer Style

Authors use punctuation, such as semicolons, to create variety and sophistication in their writing. Using a **semicolon** adds different phrasing, meaning, and flow to writing.

A semicolon is frequently used to connect two independent clauses and takes the place of a conjunction and a comma.

1. It is nearly nine o'clock, (brief pause) and we can't finish mowing the grass.

2. It is nearly nine o'clock; (moderate pause) we can't finish mowing the grass.

3. It is nearly nine o'clock. (complete pause) We can't finish mowing the grass.

Identify the independent clauses in each sentence.

1. Justin is going to Germany; he is studying their culture.

2. New York has a population density of 27,016 per square mile; Dallas, the 9th largest city, has a population density of 3,517.8 per square mile.

3. Tonight, I started doing my homework immediately after leaving the bus; my homework will be turned in on time.

Your Turn:

Create SOS sentences. Write two related independent clauses. In your Writer's Notebook, combine these clauses using a comma and conjunction, and then with a semicolon. Explore sentences in your current writing that may be combined with a semicolon.

Adding Details

Standards

- Uses a variety of strategies to draft and revise written work
- Uses prepositions in written compositions

Materials

- Chart paper
- Markers
- *Adding Details Notebook Entry* (page 121; addingdetails.pdf)
- Writer's Notebooks

Mentor Texts

- *Little Women* by Louisa M. Alcott
- *Thank You, Mr. Falker* by Patricia Polacco
- *Football in Action* by John Crossingham
- *Sky Boys: How They Built the Empire State Building* by Deborah Hopkinson
- See *Mentor Text List* in Appendix C for other suggestions.

Procedures

Note: More experience with and exposure to quality literature provides opportunities for students to hear, see, and explore many examples of sentence fluency.

Think About Writing

1. Tell students that they have practiced several sentence patterns and are becoming quite adept at using a variety of sentence structures. Explain to them that authors continually explore the written language of others to gather new ideas for their own writing. Understanding the construction of sentence structures and patterns can improve their confidence as writers.

2. Review mentor texts, if desired, and discuss how appositives and prepositional phrases add detail.

Teach

3. Tell students, "We will practice the use of phrases—appositive and prepositional—to add information and variety to our sentences." Share with students that appositives are nouns or noun phrases that identify or rename another noun. A prepositional phrase is a group of words that begins with a preposition and can tell how, when, or where something took place. Explain to students that using both types of phrases brings new sophistication to their sentence structures.

4. Write the following sentences on a sheet of chart paper. Point out the appositives and prepositional phrases in both. Discuss as a group how these parts make the sentences more interesting and varied than other sentences.

   The mountain, <u>Pike's Peak,</u> (*appositive*) stretched <u>into the sunset</u> (*prepositional phrase*).

Adding Details *(cont.)*

The girl's best friend, <u>the next door neighbor's daughter</u>, (*appositive*) played <u>in the falling raindrops</u> (*prepositional phrase*).

Engage

5. Have students *Turn and Talk* with partners or triads to orally create sentences with an appositive and a prepositional phrase to strengthen their writing. Provide students with sticky notes and have each pair and/or triad write a sentence to share with the group. Ask group members to provide support and encouragement to each other.

Apply

6. Provide students with the *Adding Details Notebook Entry* (page 121) and have them practice writing sentences with prepositional phrases and appositives. They can use the sentence starters provided or write their own. Have students work on the *Your Turn* section before proceeding to their writing folders. They can explore revisions in their own writing projects.

Write/Conference

7. Provide time for students to work. Scan the room to see if there is anyone who needs assistance getting started. When everyone is engaged, select a group to reteach the mini-lesson. Then, rotate around the room to have conferences with individual students or small groups.

Spotlight Strategy

8. Spotlight students who are using prepositional phrases and appositives in their writing. For example, "Listen to how Felix added these phrases to make his sentence sound much more interesting."

Share

9. Have students share their writing in pairs or small groups. Ask students to praise each sentence effort and give feedback to each group member.

Homework

Tell students to select three advertisements and listen to specific sentence patterns. Ask students to listen for examples of appositives and prepositional phrases.

Adding Details Notebook Entry

Adding Details

Authors continually explore the written language of others to gather new ideas for their own writing. Understanding and using phrases adds a dash of variety, energy, and pizzazz to sentences.

Appositives are nouns or noun phrases that identify, rename, or explain another noun.

A **prepositional phrase** is a group of words that begins with a preposition and can tell how, when, or where something took place.

Using both in your sentences provides details and adds variety in a text. For example:

The mountain, <u>Pike's Peak,</u> stretched <u>into the yawning sunset</u>.

A mischievous lad, <u>hiding in the bushes,</u> swiftly darted <u>between the buildings</u>.

Your Turn:

Use these sentence starters as a pattern to create your own stylistic sentences. You may use these or create your own.

The best team …

My favorite author …

The holiday season …

Let's Make It Clear!

Standards

- Uses a variety of strategies to draft and revise written work
- Uses a variety of sentence structures to expand and embed ideas

Materials

- Chart paper
- Markers
- *Let's Make It Clear! Notebook Entry* (page 124; makeitclear.pdf)
- Writer's Notebooks

Mentor Texts

- *Day of Tears* by Julius Lester
- *Harriet Tubman: Conductor on the Underground Railroad* by Ann Petry
- *Dragonwings* by Laurence Yep
- See *Mentor Text List* in Appendix C for other suggestions.

Procedures

Note: You may wish to provide students with a blank circle map (described below) to add their own notes as you model complex sentences. They can add these to their notebooks.

Think About Writing

1. Tell students that they have been studying sentence patterns to improve the style and sophistication of their writing projects. Explain to students that they will learn about how clauses can be used to add variety to their writing.

2. Review mentor texts, if desired, and emphasize the authors' use of independent and dependent clauses.

Teach

3. Explain to students that you are going to model how to use a circle map to gather information for creating complex sentences. On a sheet of chart paper, write *Complex Sentence* in a circle. Draw an outer circle that encompasses the inner circle. Draw a line that separates the top and bottom of the outer circle. See the *Let's Make It Clear! Notebook Entry* (page 124) for an example.

4. In the top half of the outer circle, write *Independent Clause*. Tell students that independent clauses can stand alone in a sentence. It is the main idea of the sentence. Share examples.

5. Next, move to the lower half of the outer circle and write *Dependent Clause*. Tell students dependent clauses cannot stand alone in a sentence and need support. They are not complete thoughts or ideas. A dependent clause also begins with a subordinating conjunction. Share examples.

6. Around the exterior of the outer circle, note the kinds of places where you might read or hear examples of complex sentences. Ask students to share their ideas to add to the circle map.

Let's Make It Clear! *(cont.)*

Engage

7. Tell students that they are going to work together to determine if clauses are independent or dependent. Read a few examples aloud and ask students to turn to a partner and share an answer and their reasoning.

Independent:

> *The ice cream melted and dripped down my elbow.*

> *The shark circled the surfboard.*

Dependent:

> *When I was six,…*

> *Because I forgot my ticket,…*

Challenge students to build a complex sentence using one of these clauses.

Apply

8. Provide students with the *Let's Make It Clear! Notebook Entry* and have them read the circle chart about independent and dependent clauses. Then, have them write their own complex sentences. Students should work on the *Your Turn* section before proceeding to their writing folders.

Write/Conference

9. While students are writing, take time to check in with two student groups: one intervention group and an enrichment group. Use your benchmark data to determine small-group instruction.

Spotlight Strategy

10. Spotlight students who are writing complex sentences with independent and dependent clauses. For example, "That sentence sounds so interesting. The two parts of the sentence work great together."

Share

11. Ask students to work in pairs and share their writing.

Homework
Ask students to listen to conversations around their home like words from their family members, television shows, video games, etc. Oral conversation is different from written communication. Ask students to listen for sentence patterns that they could use in their writing.

Let's Make It Clear! Notebook Entry

Let's Make It Clear!

A **complex sentence** includes an **independent clause** and a **dependent clause** introduced by a subordinating conjunction, such as *although* or *because*. Independent clauses are like "parents" and dependent clauses are like "children." The dependent clause depends on the parent clause.

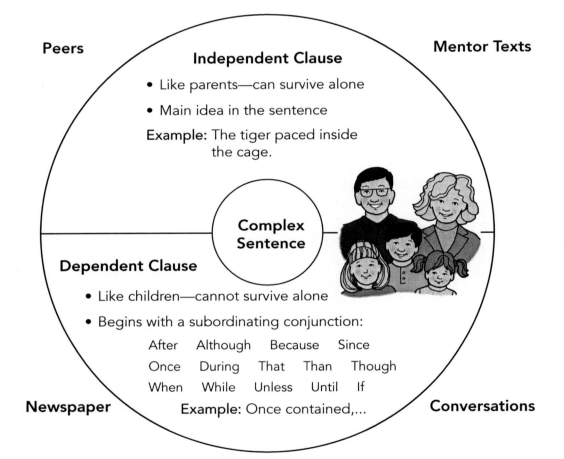

Peers

Mentor Texts

Independent Clause

- Like parents—can survive alone
- Main idea in the sentence

Example: The tiger paced inside the cage.

Complex Sentence

Dependent Clause

- Like children—cannot survive alone
- Begins with a subordinating conjunction:

After	Although	Because	Since
Once	During	That	Than	Though
When	While	Unless	Until	If

Newspaper

Example: Once contained,...

Conversations

Your Turn:

Create complex sentences with independent and dependent clauses. Search your writing projects, select sentences for revision, and record the revised sentences in your Writer's Notebook.

Organization
Linking the Pieces Together

Organization provides the structure of writing. It helps readers make connections from one idea to the next. Organization provides the skeletal support for the overall meaning of writing. The mini-lessons assist students to explore different types of writing and the ways they are organized. Lessons in this section include the following:

- Lesson 1: Playing with Poetry (page 127)
- Lesson 2: The Stacker Paragraph (page 130)
- Lesson 3: Prewriting with the Knuckle Planner (page 134)
- Lesson 4: Drafting with the Knuckle Planner (page 137)
- Lesson 5: Reeling In and Wrapping Up (page 140)
- Lesson 6: It's Newsworthy (page 143)
- Lesson 7: It's All About Me! (page 147)
- Lesson 8: Organizing Thinking for Expository Writing (page 150)
- Lesson 9: Researching from A to D (page 153)
- Lesson 10: A Poetry Collage (page 157)

The *Owen, Organization Conductor* poster (page 126) can be displayed in the room to provide a visual reminder for students that organization is one of the traits of writing. You may wish to introduce this poster during the first lesson on organization. Then, refer to the poster when teaching other lessons on organization to refresh students' memories and provide them with questions in order to guide them as they organize their writing.

Owen
Organization Conductor

How do I plan my writing?

❯ Did I organize and prioritize my thinking?

❯ Did I include an inviting beginning?

❯ Did I organize my thoughts in a logical sequence?

❯ Did I use appropriate transition words and phrases to make connections?

❯ Did I provide an adequate conclusion statement?

Playing with Poetry

Standard

Uses descriptive language that clarifies and enhances ideas

Materials

- Chart paper
- Markers
- *Playing with Poetry Notebook Entry* (page 129; playingpoetry.pdf)
- Writer's Notebooks

Mentor Texts

- *Giant Children* by Brod Bagert
- *School Fever* by Brod Bagert
- *A Kick in the Head: An Everyday Guide to Poetic Forms* by Paul Janeczko
- *Pizza, Pigs, and Poetry: How to Write a Poem* by Jack Prelutsky
- See *Mentor Text List* in Appendix C for other suggestions.

Procedures

Note: You may find it helpful to refer students to the *Poetry Cards* (pages 160–165) to first review elements of poetry. Immersing students in poetry is a way to get them active, involved, writing, and talking early in the year. Poetry can be free form, or various patterns can be used to scaffold writing. Creating couplets and quatrains using student names at the beginning of the year is also a fun activity.

Think About Writing

1. Tell students that reading and exploring poetry helps us listen, focus, and reflect on the world around us. Explain that they will be discussing how poetry is organized.

2. Review mentor texts, if desired, and point out the different forms of poetry.

Teach

3. Tell students that there are many different forms of poetry. Some poets write freestyle while others use patterns and arrangements of words to write poetry. Tell students that a *couplet* is made up of two lines about the same length and with a similar rhythm. Most couplets rhyme the last word of each line.

4. Tell students that a *quatrain* is a stanza or verse made up of four lines and can have different rhyme patterns. A simple pattern uses two couplets making an AABB poetry pattern, which means lines 1 and 2 rhyme and lines 3 and 4 rhyme.

5. As a group, discuss these two different poetry forms and characteristics. On a sheet of chart paper, write examples of couplets and quatrains to share with students. Model and emphasize the simplicity of the couplet by selecting two rhyming words and creating a simple couplet. Additionally, identify the quatrain's rhyme pattern and rhythm.

Playing with Poetry *(cont.)*

Engage

6. Have students work in pairs to write at least one couplet and one quatrain. Remind students to use the class chart for support. Allow approximately 10–15 minutes for writing before pulling the group back together to reflect, discuss, and share.

Apply

7. Provide students with the *Playing with Poetry Notebook Entry* (page 129) and have them practice writing couplets and quatrains. Explain that there is an example to read and study before writing. Have them complete the *Your Turn* section before proceeding to their writing folders and editing their own writing.

Write/Conference

8. Pull together a small group of reluctant writers and work on another example of a couplet or quatrain. Send your group off to work and begin to rove and confer.

Spotlight Strategy

9. Spotlight a student who has written a couplet or quatrain. For example, "What a great start! Just listen to this example of a couplet by Julia."

Share

10. Have students meet in pairs and work as peer editors. Students can read each other's writing and comment on the poetry structure and rhythm to the words.

Homework

Ask students to work on poetry by first thinking about something their family has in common. Have students teach their families the process for writing couplets as they create a couplet together.

Playing with Poetry Notebook Entry

Playing with Poetry

Authors are always observing and taking note of what they see and what they hear. Reading and exploring poetry helps us listen, focus, and reflect on the world around us.

"Computer Game Habitat" by Brod Bagert uses back-to-back **couplets** with the ABBA rhyme pattern.

Computer Game Habitat

If I were born a little fish,
I know exactly what I'd wish—
a sleek aquatic acrobat,
I'd want a water habitat.

If I were born a chimpanzee
I know what would be best for me—
of all the places, coast to coast,
the jungle's what I'd like the most.

If I were born a rattlesnake,
I wouldn't want a bellyache—
so for a home I would demand
a desert world of gentle sand.

But I was born a human child,
a little tame, a little wild,
The game-room is my favorite place,
It's where I wear my happy face.

The game-room? Yes! It's really true.
There's so much there for me to do.
A human-born computer brat,
the game-room is my habitat.

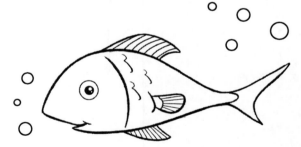

Your Turn:

Create your own couplet and quatrain poetry. Remember to consider topics that are interesting to you. Illustrate and publish for display.

The Stacker Paragraph

Standard
Uses paragraph form in writing

Materials
- Chart paper
- Colored markers
- *Sample Stacker Paragraph* (page 133; samplestacker.pdf)
- *The Stacker Paragraph Notebook Entry* (page 132; stackerparagraph.pdf)
- Writer's Notebooks

Mentor Texts
- Classroom textbooks
- Various newspaper articles and magazines
- See *Mentor Text List* in Appendix C for other suggestions.

Procedures

Note: Use this lesson to review the structure of paragraphs. Bear in mind that the organization of narrative writing differs from informative and opinion/argumentative writing.

Think About Writing

1. Explain to students that they will learn to organize their writing so readers can follow and visualize the piece of writing. Explain that having an organization plan for informative, opinion/argumentative, and narrative writing, and even poetry is a helpful skill.

2. Review mentor texts, if desired, and discuss how each text is organized.

Teach

3. Tell students that they will learn about writing stacker paragraphs. A stacker paragraph is loaded with details, yet packed tightly to flow from sentence to sentence. Review how paragraphs include groups of related sentences that relate to the same idea. They typically contain a main idea, transition signals, details that are full developed, and a summary sentence.

4. Draw a visual representation of the parts of a hamburger on chart paper. Show how this compares to a paragraph:

   - The bread represents the main idea and concluding statement holding the information together.

   - The meat, cheese, lettuce, tomatoes, and pickles represent the details.

   Continue explaining paragraph writing using the hamburger metaphor. It is important to stress how each element of a hamburger adds to its flavor, but adding chocolate syrup, although tasty, would probably not make the hamburger tastier. Equally important is pointing out that students have been exposed to paragraph writing lessons in previous grades, but now need to stack the paragraph and fill it with important information.

The Stacker Paragraph (cont.)

5. Model writing a stacker paragraph to demonstrate the process for students. Writing with students shows them that you are a writer too, and you understand the process they are undertaking. You can use the *Sample Stacker Paragraph* (page 133) or write a paragraph based on a more relevant topic.

Engage

6. Divide the class into groups. Place chart paper around the room, enough to accommodate the number of groups. Provide a colored marker at each chart. Each group should develop and write a main idea statement on their chart. Give ample time for students to discuss possibilities, and rotate to the next chart. Together, they must come up with a detail that supports the main idea statement and add it to the chart. Encourage detail and elaboration. Continue rotation until students have completed details and summary statements. Gather and discuss.

Apply

7. Provide students with *The Stacker Paragraph Notebook Entry* (page 132) and have them practice writing a group of sentences focused around a single idea or topic. Understanding the stacker paragraph will help them enhance their future writing projects.

Write/Conference

8. Rove and support students who need assistance. Take notes in your Conferring Notebook.

Spotlight Strategy

9. Spotlight the class for work ethic and focus. For example, "Good job for working so hard!"

Share

10. Have students circulate around the room and look at others' work.

Homework

Have students reteach what they learned about stacker paragraphs to their family members. Have them work together to write paragraphs about a recent family event or gathering.

The Stacker Paragraph Notebook Entry

The Stacker Paragraph

Practicing ways to organize your writing helps you become a proficient writer. **Paragraphs** should be structured so readers can follow along and visualize the author's message.

Use the Stacker Paragraph to organize your writing. Remember, a paragraph is a structured group of sentences focused around a single idea/topic.

Top Slice of Bread: Topic Sentence
- usually at the beginning of the sentence
- states the main idea

Ingredients: The Body
- sentences that support the topic sentence

Condiments: The Details
- related details by adding examples, descriptions, definitions, facts, reasons, and anecdotes
- transitions to connect thoughts

Bottom Slice of Bread: Concluding Sentence
- restates the main idea
- wraps up the points in the paragraph

Writing different types of paragraphs—informative, opinion/argumentative, narrative—requires different information just as we use different ingredients on a sandwich, hamburger, or hot dog.

Your Turn:

Write a Stacker Paragraph. Remember to add all the information to stack it with facts! Consider topics related to informative, opinion/argumentative, and narrative paragraphs. Challenge yourself to write one of each!

Sample Stacker Paragraph

Directions: Use the paragraph below to model for students how to write a paragraph, explaining how details are added to give more information to the paragraph while maintaining smooth flow.

The news reporters called it "the storm of the century"—cautioning the public to gather food, flashlights, warm clothing, and other essential supplies. The snowfall was fast and furious. No one expected it to cover an area from Cuba to Nova Scotia. The eastern half of the country came to a screeching halt that Saturday morning. Railways, airways, and roadways, including interstates, were closed to the public. Even huge snow plows were trapped in the depths of the heavy, wet snow as they were trying to clear roads for stranded motorists. What appeared to be a frosty white winter wonderland actually became a winter nightmare as snow mounded and bushes and trees became weighed down under the dense, wet snow. Three days of absolute silence! No TVs, no humming of engines, no Internet. Just dead silence!

Prewriting with the Knuckle Planner

Standard
Uses a variety of prewriting strategies

Materials
- *Prewriting with the Knuckle Planner Notebook Entry* (page 136; prewritingknuckle.pdf)
- Student writing samples (samples.doc)
- Writer's Notebooks

Mentor Texts
- *A Letter to Mrs. Roosevelt* by C. Coco De Young
- *Esperanza Rising* by Pam Muñoz Ryan
- *Roll of Thunder, Hear My Cry* by Mildred D. Taylor
- *The Watcher: Jane Goodall's Life with the Chimps* by Jeanette Winter
- See *Mentor Text List* in Appendix C for other suggestions.

Procedures
Note: The Knuckle Planner helps students organize their thinking, yet provides the freedom to determine the amount of information needed to complete writing projects, depending on students' writing levels.

Think About Writing
1. Tell students, "You have been brilliant in management, ideas, and sentences. You have wowed me! We will now begin to challenge ourselves to increase the quantity and improve the quality of our writing projects. Remember, you're writing to increase your confidence, to express how you feel, to show how you're learning, and to please yourself."

Teach
2. Tell students, "Today you are going to learn a new way to organize your writing called the Knuckle Planner. It uses your hand, which is always available, as a graphic organizer for an essay, story, or report."

3. Refer to the Knuckle Planner variations found on the *Prewriting with the Knuckle Planner Notebook Entry* (page 136) to model the prewriting process of organizing thoughts and ideas. Remember, this is a prewriting organizer and should only include words and phrases. Words and phrases become sentences during the drafting stage. Select topics to represent different genres and share with students across several days.

4. Locate an example of a paragraph that follows the Knuckle Planner organization. It may be found in a mentor text or in another familiar text. Share the paragraph. Talk with students about how this graphic organizer supports writing a well-written, clear, and concise paragraph. Share the sample Knuckle Planner and draft (samples.doc) with students to provide an additional example for support.

Prewriting with the Knuckle Planner (cont.)

Engage

5. Place students in groups. Ask groups to work together and develop a Knuckle Planner. They may choose a topic or you may assign one for them based on your current units of study. As a group, ask students to remind each other of the elements that should be included in the paragraph.

Apply

6. Provide students with the *Prewriting with the Knuckle Planner Notebook Entry* and have them write paragraphs using the Knuckle Planner. Encourage students to write different types of paragraphs so that you end up with a variety that can be compared and contrasted.

Write/Conference

7. Provide time for groups to write. Be available to roam, observe, make notes, and encourage. What instructional decisions need to be made before your next workshop session?

Spotlight Strategy

8. Spotlight a group that is working well together and collaborating on the writing. For example, "Group 2 is doing a great job of listening to each other and respecting everyone's ideas."

Share

9. Have students remain in their groups and reflect on and discuss how this plan may support their efforts in opinion/argumentative, informative, and narrative writing.

Homework

Have students make Knuckle Planners to write paragraphs about topics that come from their own family. They can be any type of paragraph but should have a personal connection for students.

Prewriting with the Knuckle Planner Notebook Entry

Prewriting with the Knuckle Planner

Study how to use the Knuckle Planner to write the different types of paragraphs described. Pay close attention to the order of information and the elements that are included in each type of paragraph.

Informational Text

Each FINGER TIP represents a main idea.

From the tip to the knuckle represents supporting sentences and details.

Topic
Hook
Main Idea

The THUMB: Wrap up
Restates the claim, summarizes reasons, and makes a final plea or statement.

Each FINGER TIP represents a reason.

From the tip to the knuckle represents examples and evidence:

- Uses quotes, facts, and research from important people/experts
- Relates urgency to take action
- Appeals to emotions

Topic
Hook
Claim

Argumentative/ Opinion Text

The THUMB: Wrap up
Restates the claim, summarizes reasons, and makes a final plea or statement.

Narrative Text

The PINKY and RING: The Events
Events occur and build up to the problem. There might even be a problem along the way.

The MIDDLE: The Dilemma
Something goes wrong or a mystery occurs.

Introduction
Characters
Setting

The POINTER: Resolution
The characters work together to solve the problem.

The THUMB: Conclusion
The problem is resolved and lessons learned.

Your Turn:

Use the Knuckle Planner to write your own paragraph. Choose whether to write an informational text, an opinion/argumentative text, or a narrative text.

Drafting with the Knuckle Planner

© Shell Education #50920—Getting to the Core of Writing—Level 6

Standard
Uses a variety of strategies to draft and revise written work

Materials
- Chart paper
- Markers
- Student writing samples (samples.doc)
- *Drafting with the Knuckle Planner Notebook Entry* (page 139; draftingknuckle.pdf)
- Writer's Notebooks

Mentor Texts
- *The Sloppy Copy Slipup* by DyAnne DiSalvo
- *Bearstone* by Will Hobbs
- *To Be A Slave* by Julius Lester
- *Baby* by Patricia MacLachlan
- See *Mentor Text List* in Appendix C for other suggestions.

Procedures
Note: This lesson should follow Organization Lesson 3. It addresses the next step in turning an idea and graphic organizer into an actual writing piece. If preparing students for high-stakes writing assessment, this planner can be used as a structured six paragraph essay. However, if prompts and organizational structure are required for assessment, the Knuckle Planner provides the necessary quantity of writing for high results.

Think About Writing
1. Tell students that they have learned to prewrite by organizing their thoughts and ideas for writing. Explain that now students will move to drafting. Drafting takes patience and hard work.

2. Review mentor texts, if desired, and emphasize the importance of drafting. Explain that authors write many drafts before they are satisfied with their work.

Teach
3. Tell students, "Today, you will learn how to use a Knuckle Planner to create a drafted copy." Remind students that drafted copies are not perfect and may contain some errors in spelling and grammar. Sentence patterns may need to be stretched and word choice may need to be improved. Reassure students that this draft will be a first draft.

4. Model the drafting process. Select a previous Knuckle Planner you have developed or use the model provided. You may also share the sample Knuckle Planner and draft (samples.doc). Work off of the graphic organizer, thinking aloud as you develop your draft on chart paper. Introductory hooks and conclusions can be addressed prior to drafting or during revision.

5. To provide additional support, follow up with a shared writing experience. Use the same process of working from a Knuckle Planner, but have students share the thinking and drafting.

Drafting with the Knuckle Planner *(cont.)*

Engage

6. Have students work in pairs to choose a Knuckle Planner and work together to write just the opening paragraph. Move around the classroom, providing support and praising effort and work ethic. Pull students back to a whole group to discuss, reflect, and question.

Apply

7. Provide students with the *Drafting with the Knuckle Planner Notebook Entry* (page 139) and have them organize their thoughts using a graphic organizer like the Knuckle Planner to create a draft.

Write/Conference

8. Selecting students for additional support is crucial to give them more individualized attention. Keep notes of observations in your Conferring Notebook.

Spotlight Strategy

9. Spotlight students who show extraordinary work ethic and planning. For example, "Maria has created a superb Knuckle Planner and a draft that is well organized. Smart writing work!"

Share

10. Have students meet in quads. Students should listen carefully to each group member question and compliment each other.

Homework

Have students make Knuckle Planners to write paragraphs about topics that come from their own family. Ask them to see what they notice around the house that might work for an opinion, informative, or narrative organizer. Have students bring their ideas to class the following day.

Drafting with the Knuckle Planner Notebook Entry

Drafting with the Knuckle Planner

Study this example of a Knuckle Planner that is ready for drafting. How would this writer begin to draft this topic?

Problem Solving

- violence is a problem-solving strategy
- violence solves problems

Values

- teaches violence as acceptable behavior
- strength, violence and aggression are valued

Desensitized

- overexposure to violence makes violent behavior the norm
- violence seems unreal or funny
- cartoon victims appear unharmed

Imitation

- learn violence through imitation
- heroes are violent role models

Children and Violence on Television

- children watch an average of 2 hours of television everyday
- negatively effects young children's behavior and beliefs

Summary

- violent television is harmful for children
- violence is learned and reflected in behavior

Your Turn:

Look at your own Knuckle Planner and decide how to get started with your topic. Use your Knuckle Planner to develop your draft. Remember, the more complete the planner, the stronger the writing.

Reeling In and Wrapping Up

Standard
Uses a variety of strategies to draft and revise written work

Materials
- *Reeling In and Wrapping Up Notebook Entry* (page 142; reelingin.pdf)
- Writer's Notebooks

Mentor Texts
- *Driver's Ed* by Caroline B. Cooney
- *Amelia's Notebook* by Marissa Moss
- *Smoky Mountain Rose: An Appalachian Cinderella* by Alan Schroeder
- *Tornadoes* by Seymour Simon
- See *Mentor Text List* in Appendix C for other suggestions.

Procedures
Note: Once students begin to understand that stories can be organized by including a beginning, middle, and end, it is time to explore how authors begin and end their stories. Be sure to study both fiction and nonfiction as a group.

Think About Writing
1. Ask students to think about how their favorite stories begin and end. Tell students that a story's beginning and ending are critical for reeling in the reader and then leaving them with a satisfying conclusion.

2. Review mentor texts, if desired. Encourage students to think about how authors they have read have approached story beginnings and endings. These examples can give students hints about how to do this well in their own writing.

Teach
3. Ask students to share examples of great openings—hooks, leads, and grabbers—as a way to get a reader interested in a story. Conversely, talk about how great stories have compelling endings. Authors hope that readers will be interested enough to finish reading a story. This is why writers must organize ideas so that interest continues through to the end.

4. Tell students that they will begin a collection of beginnings and endings—hooks, leads, grabbers, and conclusions. Use examples that students find, excerpts from mentor texts and from student writing. Discuss what makes a great story beginning and ending. How does an author reel in a reader? How does an author satisfy the reader in the end?

Reeling In and Wrapping Up *(cont.)*

Engage

5. Ask students to work in pairs to reflect on and review the purpose of having an interesting hook, lead, or grabber. Have students share their own writing and how they have incorporated strong beginnings or endings in their stories. How could they improve them? Ask pairs to give each other feedback.

Apply

6. Provide students with the *Reeling In and Wrapping Up Notebook Entry* (page 142) and have them read different examples of how stories begin and end in ways that grab a reader's attention. Students will begin a personal collection of memorable beginnings and endings.

Write/Conference

7. Select small groups to review, reteach, or enrich. Allow groups three minutes to look through books you have available to check for helpful examples of both beginnings and endings.

Spotlight Strategy

8. Spotlight students who are identifying examples of openings and excellent conclusions. For example, "Great job looking at the parts of a story and finding interesting starts and ends to stories. Smart work!"

Share

9. Have students work in pairs and share their work. Encourage students to be PALS—**P**raise, **A**sk, **L**ook, and **S**uggest. Allow a few minutes for students to share.

Homework

Ask students watch the evening news for news anchors who are excellent at grabbing the audience's attention and holding it through a commercial so that they will remain for "the rest of the story." Ask students to share examples the following day.

Reeling In and Wrapping Up Notebook Entry

Reeling In and Wrapping Up

Writers of all kinds must choose a way to grab a reader's attention.

Ways to Reel In: Ask a question, use a quotation, begin with an opinion, use onomatopoeia, use vivid descriptions for the character and setting, start with a mysterious fact, use dialogue, or give a brief anecdote.

Writers also have to know how to draw their stories to a close.

Ways to Wrap Up: Connect the beginning to the end, use a quote, use dialogue, share feelings, be humorous, state a challenge, or ask a question.

Examples of Beginnings	Examples of Endings
From *Sun, Stars & Planets* by Tom Stacy: The sun is a star, one of the billions in space. It is like a giant powerhouse—a glowing ball of hot gases, producing a vast amount of energy which streams out through space in waves of light and heat.	From *Tornadoes* by Seymour Simon: You don't have to worry too much in advance about tornadoes, but finding out when they are coming and knowing what to do is certain to help you if one strikes.
From *Number the Stars* by Lois Lowry: "I'll race you to the corner, Ellen!" Annemarie adjusted the thick leather pack on her back so that her schoolbooks balanced evenly. "Ready?" She looked at her best friend.	From *Fireflies* by Julie Brinckloe: I held the jar, dark and empty in my hands. The moonlight and the fireflies swam in my tears but I could feel myself smiling.

Your Turn:

Begin a collection of beginnings and endings for opinion/argumentative, informative, and narrative writing. Notice how the words reel you in or leave you feeling satisfied.

It's Newsworthy

Standards

- Uses a variety of strategies to draft and revise written work
- Uses content, style, and structure appropriate for specific audiences and purposes

Materials

- Newspaper articles and editorials
- Chart paper
- Markers
- *Prewriting Organizer* (page 146; organizer.pdf)
- *It's Newsworthy Notebook Entry* (page 145; newsworthy.pdf)
- Writer's Notebooks

Mentor Texts

- *America's Best Newspaper Writing* by Roy Clark and Christopher Scanlan
- *The Furry News: How to Make a Newspaper* by Loreen Leedy
- *Kids in Print: Publishing a School Newspaper* by Mark Levin
- See *Mentor Text List* in Appendix C for other suggestions.

Procedures

Note: Teach students to become familiar with newspaper sections. This lesson can be taught over several days.

Think About Writing

1. Tell students that journalists who write for newspapers have a responsibility to inform their readers through their writing. Remind them that there are newspaper sections that are opinion pieces. Therefore, it is important to distinguish between a standard newspaper article that gives information versus an editorial that shares a writer's opinion.

2. Review mentor texts, if desired, and have students distinguish between informative and opinion writing.

Teach

3. Tell students that they are going to examine different news articles to learn how to distinguish between informative and opinion writing. Ask students to summarize what these two styles of writing are and how they are organized.

4. As a group, read through two or three short articles and editorials to get a feel for style and characteristics. Divide students into groups to develop questions they may have related to writing informative articles and editorials.

5. On a sheet of chart paper, create a T-chart with the two headings: *Informative Writing* and *Opinion Writing*. Have students meet in groups and discuss similarities and differences. Have students share their responses. Add their ideas to the chart.

6. Generate a list of topics based on student suggestions and current events. Examples may include health education, cyber-bullying, dress codes, and alcohol or drug abuse. Assign students to a topic and tell them that they will have to decide whether their topic requires informative writing or opinion writing.

It's Newsworthy *(cont.)*

Engage

7. Distribute the *Prewriting Organizer* (page 146) to help students record their ideas on paper and get their thoughts in order. Divide students into groups to help each other through the drafting process. Over several days students should meet in groups to discuss each step of the writing process: generating questions, analyzing articles and editorials, creating and selecting topics, drafting, and editing.

Apply

8. Provide students with the *It's Newsworthy Notebook Entry* (page 145) and have them analyze how they will organize their ideas and make sure they are clear about their purpose for writing.

Write/Conference

9. Provide time for students to write. Be available as a facilitator and be ready to problem solve, make suggestions, and encourage. Make astute observations of writing behaviors in your Conferring Notebook.

Spotlight Strategy

10. Each day spotlight one or two students who connected specifically to the skill for that writing session.

Share

11. Have students check in and share their work with their group.

Homework

Ask students to sort through newspapers, magazines, and other resources at home to examine articles and editorials. Students can invite their parents to join in this work as well.

It's Newsworthy Notebook Entry

It's Newsworthy

Journalists have the responsibility to inform their readers through their writing. However, some newspaper writers write opinion pieces. A reader has to be able to distinguish between the two.

Article: Gives information

- Captures reader with opening sentence
- Gives concrete details
- Sometimes uses quotes from interviews
- May include illustrations
- Specifically answers questions: Who? What? When? Where? Why? How?
- May include charts and graphs
- Uses a formal style of writing
- Includes a concluding statement

Editorial: Gives point of view

- Captures reader with opening sentence
- Gives point of view
- Provides an understanding about a topic
- Generally relates to current events, recent happenings, economics, or political views, etc.
- Subjects need to address the targeted audience
- Requires asking questions
- Must research and find information
- Requires accurate and factual information to persuade
- Provides a concluding statement about the argument presented

Your Turn:

Draft an article or editorial. Your task is to decide how to inform the reader or to share your opinion. Use the *Prewriting Organizer* to plan your ideas.

Name:_____ Date:_____

Prewriting Organizer

Directions: Use the organizer below to record and organize your ideas.

Journalist: _____

Topic for Article: _____

Type of Publication: _____

Audience: _____

Purpose: Persuade—Inform—Entertain

Possible Sources: _____

Specific Vocabulary: _____

My Title: _____

My Hook/Lead: _____

Important Details/Points/Facts: _____

_____

Text features I will include to organize and create interest:

Headings	Subheadings	Separate Text Box	Bullets
Italics	Bold Font	All Caps	Underlining
Diagram/Chart	Captions/Labels	Quotations	Illustrations
Other:			

My Conclusion/Wrap-Up:

_____

_____

_____

It's All About Me!

Standards

- Uses a variety of strategies to draft and revise written work
- Writes compositions about autobiographical incidents

Materials

- *It's All About Me! Notebook Entry* (page 149; allaboutme.pdf)
- Writer's Notebooks

Mentor Texts

- *Through My Eyes: Ruby Bridges* by Ruby Bridges
- *Rosa Parks: My Story* by Rosa Parks and Jim Haskins
- *Helen Keller: The Story of My Life* by Helen Keller and Candace Ward
- See *Mentor Text List* in Appendix C for other suggestions.

Procedures

Note: Prior to the lesson, review Conventions Lesson 6 and discuss how to edit writing using CUPS. Also note that it is important to share autobiographical mentor texts to learn about the types of events, details, and organizational structures used by various authors. This project will develop across several days and may utilize technology and publishing tools.

Think About Writing

1. Tell students that their next project—organizing and developing their own autobiography—is a challenge and will provide an opportunity to learn about themselves and about each other.

2. Review mentor texts, if desired, and have students note important characteristics of autobiographies.

Teach

3. Review what an autobiography is and make sure that students know that it is the story of a person's life written by that person. What makes it unique is that no one has the knowledge to write the details and emotions of an autobiography except for the author. Model and share your own information and process with students. You are asking them to share their memories with you, so you must be willing to share yours with them.

4. Explain to students that they will use a chronological organizational structure called a *lifeline*. It is a list of memorable events in the order they occurred. Photographs add a lot of interest if students can access them for some events. Events might include family, activities (dance, sports), travel, school, historical events, or summer vacations/camps. Choose a few events from your own life to use as a model. Think aloud as you share why an event is important, describe the event, and give additional details about the event. Students should research and interview parents to gather additional information.

It's All About Me! *(cont.)*

5. Model for students how they will use a lifeline to organize their life stories. Use the Knuckle Planner to organize the most relevant and interesting events.

6. Model drafting paragraphs that are well-developed and pull the reader into the story of your life. The possibilities are endless for how students can publish their work.

Engage

7. Have students *Turn and Talk* with partners to share some events they will add to their lifelines. Tell them to explain why these events are memorable and should be shared with others.

Apply

8. Provide students with the *It's All About Me! Notebook Entry* (page 149) and have them follow the steps for the writing assignment.

Write/Conference

9. Be available to support students as they develop lifelines and autobiographies. Provide opportunities for small group work. This provides security and a safety net for students who are reluctant writers.

Spotlight Strategy

10. Recognize partners for teamwork and supporting each other in the process. For example, "You worked together and gave each other great feedback. Well done!"

Share

11. Invite students to present their published works to the class. Compliment each student for the hard work and focus that this assignment required.

Homework
Midway through this writing project, ask students to talk with their parents about memorable and significant events in their lives. Have students ask questions and gather details that can be added to the writing assignment.

It's All About Me!

An **autobiography** is the story of a person's life written by that person. What makes this writing unique is that no one has the knowledge to write the intricate details and emotions of an autobiography except for the author.

Your Turn:

Plan and write your own autobiography. You have experienced many special events in your lifetime up until now that will make an interesting read.

Step 1: Create a Lifeline

A lifeline is a list of memorable events in the order they occurred in your life. Events might include family, activities/hobbies, travel, school, historical events, or summer vacations/camps. Adding photographs makes the lifeline even more interesting. Label and date each event.

Step 2: Select and Organize

Use the Knuckle Planner to organize the most relevant and interesting events.

Step 3: Draft

Use the information from your Knuckle Planner to draft your autobiography. Remember to write paragraphs that are well-developed and reel in the reader.

Step 4: Revise

Work with a partner to check for organization and sequence, varied sentence structure, and interesting word choice.

Step 5: Edit

Work with a partner to CUPS your autobiography.

Step 6: Publish

Use the information to publish your autobiography. Select a style that best represents you and your personality. It may be a presentation of your life in a photo essay, a brochure, a PowerPoint, or even a fairy tale. The possibilities are endless!

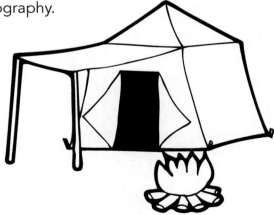

Organizing Thinking for Expository Writing

Standards

- Uses a variety of prewriting strategies
- Writes expository compositions

Materials

- Chart paper
- Markers
- Student writing samples (samples.doc)
- *Organizing Thinking for Expository Writing Notebook Entry* (page 152; expository.pdf)
- Writer's Notebooks

Mentor Texts

- *Hurricanes* and *Tornadoes* by Seymour Simon
- Nonfiction texts by Gail Gibbons, Seymour Simon, Bobbie Kalman, Aliki, Jim Arnosky, Loreen Leedy, and George Ancona
- See *Mentor Text List* in Appendix C for other suggestions.

Procedures

Note: This lesson (adapted from Betsy Rupp Fulwiler 2007) can be revisited throughout the school year as students continue to work on expository writing.

Think About Writing

1. Explain that it is sometimes necessary to follow a writing framework when learning a new organizational structure. Tell students they will use a writing framework to help them draft an expository text. Writing frameworks include partially completed sentences and specific transition words that eventually are removed or modified as the writer becomes more proficient.

Teach

2. Tell students that they will be working on an expository writing piece that is organized as a compare and contrast text. A framework will be used to compare/contrast numerous subjects.

3. Work with students to choose two topics. Use a sheet of chart paper to list similarities and differences using a Venn diagram. Complete the chart using information researched from mentor texts or content area texts. Explain to students that this is a framework that can be used to write constructed responses for scientific observations. Eventually, students will write in this form independently without the framework.

4. Share the sample framework (samples.doc) for an additional example and support.

Organizing Thinking for Expository Writing *(cont.)*

Engage

5. Move students into groups and have them read and discuss nonfiction information provided in the sample on tornadoes and hurricanes, or two other nonfiction topics of choice. Have them work with their groups to complete a Venn diagram. When students are finished, bring them back to a group meeting.

Apply

6. Provide students with the *Organizing Thinking for Expository Writing Notebook Entry* (page 152) to add to their Writer's Notebook. Have students research two topics to compare and contrast and then complete the *Your Turn* section before proceeding to their writing folders. They can work in pairs to complete the constructed response using the appropriate transition words.

Write/Conference

7. No conferring today. Help students by moving around, observing, and providing assistance as necessary.

Spotlight Strategy

8. Spotlight students who followed the writing framework. For example, "You did a great job of including transition words in your conclusion. Good work!"

Share

9. Take a few minutes for student pairs to share their work with the rest of the group.

Homework

Ask students to find a magazine or newspaper with informational text. Have them try this constructed response framework at home. Ask students to bring examples for group discussion.

Organizing Thinking for Expository Writing
Notebook Entry

Organizing Thinking for Expository Writing

Writing frameworks offer writers support. Frameworks can help writers become familiar with content area writing structures, such as compare and contrast, cause and effect, or chronological texts.

Your Turn:

Select and research two topics you wish to compare and contrast. Create a Venn diagram in your Writer's Notebook to record similarities and differences. Then, complete this writing framework to summarize your information.

Compare and Contrast Framework

_____ and _____ are similar because they _____.

They both _____. In addition, each _____.

_____ and _____ are different because _____.

Furthermore, they _____. For example, the _____,

but _____.

Circle the concluding transition that makes sense in your framework.

- In conclusion,
- To summarize,
- As a result,
- As shown above,

- In the final analysis,
- Consequently,
- To clarify,
- For this reason,

Researching from A to D

Procedures

Note: Creating a research report requires several days of study, research, reflection, mini-lessons, and time for collaboration and writing. Discuss Internet safety with students as they begin to do research.

Think About Writing

1. Tell students that they will explore another genre of writing: research writing. Explain that a research paper is based on information from a variety of sources. It informs the reader and explains factual information.

2. Review mentor texts, if desired, and emphasize the characteristics found in nonfiction texts, such as headings, subheadings, bold/italicized print, charts, and graphs.

Teach

3. Tell students, "Today, I will show you some basic steps to write a research report that you can use at any grade level and with any topic. Explain that it really is as simple as ABCD! **A**sk a question. **B**e a researcher. **C**omplete an outline. **D**raft your paper.

4. Model each step of writing a research report. The developmental writing level of students will determine the amount of information to include in your mini-lesson. Use *Narrowing the Topic* (page 156) as you work to help students through this process.

   - **A**sk a question. What do I want to know more about? Think about the topic, put it at the top of an inverted triangle, and then narrow it down.

   - **B**e a researcher. Gather information from at least three resources, such as books, periodicals, and credible Internet websites. Take notes using index cards, including the topic and facts about your topic. On one side of the card, write notes in your own words. On the other side of the card, include the bibliographic information.

Researching from A to D *(cont.)*

- **C**omplete an outline. The outline helps organize information and subtopics in a logical sequence. Sort index cards into subtopics to create paragraphs. Provide students with a sample to support.

- **D**raft your paper. Use your outline to develop your draft with:
  - a title page that includes the title, your name, class name, date submitted, photo, etc.
  - an introduction that includes the main idea of the report
  - a body that is divided into subsections related to the topic
  - a conclusion that restates the main idea
  - a bibliography that cites sources used in the report

5. Continue to model report writing through the entire process—revising, editing, and preparing a presentation of the research.

Engage

6. Allow students several minutes to talk in pairs about possible topics of interest for their papers. Gather students to share their ideas.

Apply

7. Remind students to create research papers that will be informational and easy for the reader to understand. Provide students with the *Researching from A to D Notebook Entry* (page 155) to add to their Writer's Notebook. Have students complete the *Your Turn* section before proceeding to their writing folders.

Write/Conference

8. No conferring today. Help students begin the process of gathering and narrowing topics.

Spotlight Strategy

9. Spotlight students who generated good topics for research. For example, "You must be proud of the topics you have generated today. Keep moving forward!"

Share

10. Allow time for students to share topics so that they can get ideas from others.

Homework
Have students watch the news for possible research project ideas. Ask students to be ready to add their ideas to their notebook entries tomorrow.

Researching from A to D Notebook Entry

Researching from A to D

A **research report** provides factual information and informs the reader about a specific topic.

Writing research reports includes basic steps that you can use with any report topic. Although it may sound challenging, it is really as simple as ABCD!

- **A**sk a question. What do I want to know more about? Think about the topic, put it at the top of an inverted triangle, and then narrow it down.

- **B**e a researcher. Gather information from at least three resources, such as books and credible Internet websites. Take notes using index cards: bibliographic information on one side of the card, your notes and quotes on the other. Remember, use your own words!

- **C**omplete an outline. The outline helps organize information and subtopics in a logical sequence. Sort note cards into subtopics to create paragraphs.

- **D**raft your paper. Include a title page, introduction, body (the largest, most informative section), conclusion, and bibliography.

Your Turn:

Use the ABCD steps to write your own research report. Choose from these general topics, or select one of your own. Remember to narrow them down.

- Inventors
- Musicians/Artists
- Nutrition
- Presidents
- Solar System

- States/Countries
- Animals
- Authors
- Environment
- Explorers

Narrowing the Topic

Sealife

Mammals of the Ocean

Whales

Orca

Additional Support for Taking Notes:

- First, give students five or six index cards. Use different colored index cards or markers for more support.

- Have students write one question on each card that they want to answer to learn about their topic (e.g., What do Orca whales eat?). For more support, provide categories/subheadings (e.g., Orca babies, food).

- Next, give students four or five additional cards of each color. Students will research to find information that answers each question and write the answers on cards of the same color. Color-coding helps support organizing the information on the outline.

- The index cards eventually become a paragraph, the question cards become the topic sentence, while the information cards become the details in the paragraph.

A Poetry Collage

Standards

- Uses a variety of strategies to draft and revise written work
- Uses descriptive language that clarifies and enhances ideas

Materials

- Chart paper
- Markers
- *Poetry Cards* (pages 160–165; poetrycards.pdf)
- *A Poetry Collage Notebook Entry* (page 159; collage.pdf)
- Writer's Notebooks

Mentor Texts

- *Poetry Mentor Texts* (page 166)
- See *Mentor Text List* in Appendix C for other suggestions.

Procedures

Note: Poetry can be taught throughout the year with students building an additional notebook of poetry.

Think About Writing

1. Help students develop an understanding and appreciation for many forms of poetry. Tell students that poetry gives us opportunities to read, write, imagine, think, feel, and share.

Teach

2. Tell students, "Today we will create a collage of poetry. A *collage* is simply a collection or an assortment." Tell students that they will choose what poetry to include in their collages.

3. Select a sample of four or five different types of poems from mentor texts to share with students. Ask students to select the poem that they enjoyed the most. Have students meet in groups based on their selections and discuss what they like most about their selections and what they notice about the poems. Bring students back together and record their responses on chart paper. Discuss the differences between the poems.

4. To review different forms of poetry, distribute the *Poetry Cards* (pages 160–165) to students. You may also use the *Poetry Mentor Texts* (page 166) to select poems, or read some that were studied throughout the year. With each new poem format, review it, model how to write it, discuss examples, and allow time for students to experiment with different poems in their Writer's Notebooks. Students may also revise previously written poems in that form. Repeat this so that students are building their drafts for their poetry collages.

5. Provide students options for presenting their poetry collages and plan a poetry slam to share their work.

A Poetry Collage *(cont.)*

Engage

6. Allow students time to talk in pairs about poems and poetry formats. Gather students to share their ideas.

Apply

7. Remind students to choose and write poetry that will entertain readers. Provide students with *A Poetry Collage Notebook Entry* (page 159) to add to their Writer's Notebook. Have students complete the *Your Turn* section before proceeding to their writing folders.

Write/Conference

8. Observe and assist students needing support throughout the project. Meet with pairs to monitor progress.

Spotlight Strategy

9. Spotlight students who generated good topics for poetry. For example, "You must be proud of the topics you have generated today. Keep moving forward!"

Share

10. Have students share writing with partners, quads, or the class. Vary and include sharing opportunities daily to provide ideas and inspiration to others.

Homework

Have students look around at home and in the real world for possible poetry topics. Ask students to be ready to add their ideas to their notebook entries tomorrow.

A Poetry Collage Notebook Entry

A Poetry Collage

Writers often collect **poems** that touch their emotions with language that creates visual imagery. Poetry gives us opportunities to read, write, imagine, dream, think, learn, feel, and share.

Poetry comes in many forms, some with specific rules. Some forms include:

- Acrostic
- Diamante
- Limerick
- Bio Poem
- 5 Ws Poem
- Quatrain
- Cinquain
- Free Verse
- Triante
- Couplet
- Haiku
- Tercet

Ideas	Ideas are the topics of your poetry.
Organization	What form and type of poetry will you choose?
Voice	Can the reader feel your passion? Silliness? Sadness? Anger?
Sentence Fluency	Sentence fluency is based on the organizational form of poetry. Your poem may flow smoothly, follow a rhythm or meter, or rhyme based on the poetry form you selected.
Word Choice	Do your words express your ideas clearly? Do you use descriptive language, adjectives, metaphors, or similes to create visual images for your reader?
Conventions	Do you use line breaks and punctuation to enhance your poem? Although mishaps in grammar and spelling can be used to enhance some poetry, is the grammar and spelling correct when needed?

Your Turn:

Use what you have learned about poetry to write poems in some of the forms above.

Poetry Cards

Directions: Distribute cards to students in order to review each form of poetry. Then, select one or two forms of poetry to model writing for students.

Acrostic

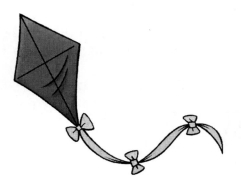

When a word is written vertically down the page and each letter is the beginning sound for a word, phrase, or sentence, it is called an acrostic poem.

Katie's kite

Incredible indigo

Tail waving

Exciting, enjoyable!

Bio Poem

A bio poem is a poem about a person's life—yours or someone else's. Bio poems include colorful and descriptive words and phrases.

First name	Marcus
Who is... (3 words to describe the person)	Who is adventurous, helpful, and brave.
Who is... (the son, daughter, brother, sister of…)	Who is the son of Jim and Barb.
Who loves... (3 people, places, activities, things)	Who loves hunting, fishing, and riding his four-wheeler.
Who feels... (3 feelings and what creates the feelings)	Who feels excited when hunting, calm when fishing, and free as a bird when riding his four-wheeler.
Who needs... (3 needs or hopes)	Who needs family vacations, his brother to leave him alone, and a motorcycle when he turns sixteen.
Who fears... (3 things that frighten the person)	Who fears heights, spiders, and sharks.
Who dreams of one day... (3 wishes or things to accomplish)	Who dreams of one day catching the big one, going to a professional football game, and meeting Travis Pastrana.
Who lives... (where or for what)	Who lives in a beautiful valley surrounded by mountains.
Last name	Smith

Poetry cards (cont.)

Cinquain

A cinquain is a five-line poem that can be used for many different topics including science, social studies, math, fiction, etc.

Line 1: 1 noun; 2 syllables	Dragon
Line 2: 2 descriptive words; 4 syllables	Scary, massive
Line 3: 3 -ing verbs; 6 syllables	Running, flying, landing
Line 4: 4-word phrase; 8 syllables	Glittering scales fiery breath
Line 5: 1-word/synonym for noun; 2 syllables	Monster

Couplet

A couplet is a two-line poem with lines about the same length and with a similar rhythm. Most couplets rhyme the last word of each line.

Squirrels climb and scurry,

Their tails fuzzy and furry.

Poetry Cards (cont.)

Diamante

A diamante is a seven-line poem that is shaped like a diamond.

Line 1: noun	Sahara
Line 2: adjective, adjective	Frigid, harsh
Line 3: three-word sentence	Camels live there
Line 4: four verbs with -ing	Surviving, searching, living, dying,
Line 5: three word sentence	Food is scarce.
Line 6: adjective, adjective	Hot, dry
Line 7: synonym for the noun	Desert

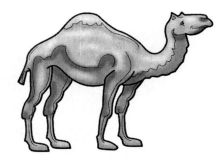

5 Ws Poem

A 5 Ws poem focuses on five questions. Each line of the poem is an answer to a question.

Who?	Children,
What?	Playing outside at recess,
Where?	Under a cherry blossom tree,
When?	After lunch,
Why?	To just have some fun!

#50920—Getting to the Core of Writing—Level 6 © Shell Education

Poetry Cards (cont.)

Free Verse

A free verse poem usually does not have a rhyme scheme or have rhythm. Free verse is a favorite poetic form because there are no rules.

It's what I think.

And I know I'm right,

Even though their eyes look my way and then roll upward.

If only they would listen, just listen.

They would see my side, hear my voice, feel my heart…

Break.

I know I'm right,

It's what I think.

Haiku

A haiku is a traditional form of Japanese poetry. It is a short, descriptive, vivid poem that usually focuses on the beauty of nature. It is usually about nature, uses one of the five senses, and has a "kigo," which is a season word within the poem.

It has exactly 17 syllables.
It is arranged in 3 lines:
  5 syllables
  7 syllables
  5 syllables
	The tree sheds color
	
	only to bare its branches
	
	for a fleeting pause 

Poetry Cards (cont.)

Limerick

A limerick is a poem that is recognized by its rhythm and rhyme scheme. A limerick is a five-line, funny, nonsense poem. Lines 1, 2, and 5 end with a rhyming word, and each line has a specific rhythmic pattern with three accented syllables. Lines 3 and 4 are shorter, end with a rhyming word and typically have two accented syllables.

Line 1: three accented syllables; A	There **once** was a **cow** on the **moon**,
Line 2: three accented syllables; A	Who **traveled** in the **month** of **June**.
Line 3: two accented syllables; B	He **mooed** all **night**,
Line 4: two accented syllables; B	And **looked** such a **sight**,
Line 5: three accented syllables; A	As he **continued** to **moo** his **tune**.

Quatrain

A quatrain is a stanza or verse made up of four lines. A quatrain is the most frequently used poetry pattern. Quatrains can be unrhymed but typically follow two simple poetic patterns. Each pattern consists of two couplets, making an AABB rhyme scheme, which means that Line 1 and Line 2 rhyme while Line 3 and Line 4 rhyme, or an ABBA rhyme scheme, where Line 1 and Line 4 rhyme while Line 2 and Line 3 rhyme. This form is used in many nursery rhymes, such as "Humpty Dumpty."

Line 1: A	Humpty Dumpty sat on a wall,
Line 2: A	Humpty Dumpty had a great fall.
Line 3: B	All the kings horses and all the kings men,
Line 4: B	Couldn't put Humpty together again.

Poetry Cards (cont.)

Triante

A triante is a five-line poem that takes on the shape of a triangle. Typically, a triante includes sensory words and follows a pattern where each line increases by one word.

Line 1: Title (one word)	Ocean
Line 2: Smells (two words)	Clean, Fresh
Line 3: Touch or taste (three words)	Salty, Wet, Cool
Line 4: Sight (four words)	Rolling, White Caps, Splashing
Line 5: Sounds and actions (five words)	Swimming, Diving, Fishing, Sailing, Surfing

Tercet

A tercet is a simple poem that consists of three lines that typically rhyme in an AAA or ABA pattern. When standing alone as a stanza, it may be referred to as a triplet. Most poets use more than one tercet in their poetry.

Line 1: A	Sitting before me, my book,
Line 2: B	Words teasing me to read on,
Line 3: A	Just long enough for a quick look.
Line 4: C	It knows I must sleep and close my eyes,
Line 5: D	But just a page or two will not hurt,
Line 6: C	So I pick it up, it's no surprise.

Poetry Mentor Texts

Bagert, Brod, ed. 1998. *Poetry for Young People: Edgar Allan Poe.* London: Orion Publishing Group.

Bagert, Brod. 2008. *School Fever.* New York: Dial Books for Young Readers.

Bolin, Frances Schoonmaker, ed. 2008. *Poetry for Young People: Carl Sandburg.* New York: Sterling Publishing Company.

————. 2008. *Poetry for Young People: Emily Dickinson.* New York: Sterling Publishing Company.

Driscoll, Michael. 2003. *A Child's Introduction to Poetry.* New York: Black Dog & Leventhal Publishers.

Fletcher, Ralph. 2005. *A Writing Kind of Day: Poems for Young Poets.* Honesdale, PN: Wordsong.

Giggle Poetry. http://www.gigglepoetry.com.

Gookin, Ann. 2005. *Poetry 2005 by 6th Grade Students of Fairfield Middle School.* Fairfield, IA: 1st World Library.

Graves, Donald. 1996. *Baseball, Snakes and Summer Squash: Poems About Growing Up.* Honesdale, PN: Wordsong.

Janeczko, Paul. 2009. *A Kick in the Head: An Everyday Guide to Poetic Forms.* Somerville, MA: Candlewick Press.

Padgett, Ron, ed. 1987. *The Teachers and Writers Handbook of Poetic Forms.* New York: Teachers and Writers Collaborative.

Prelutsky, Jack. 1984. *The New Kid on the Block.* New York: Greenwillow Books.

————. 1993. *It's Raining Pigs & Noodles.* New York: HarperCollins Children's Books.

————. 2004. *If Not for the Cat.* New York: Greenwillow Books.

Roessel, David, ed. 2006. *Poetry for Young People: Langston Hughes.* New York: Sterling Publishing Company.

Schmidt, Gary D., ed. 2008. *Poetry for Young People: Robert Frost.* New York: Sterling Publishing Company.

Silverstein, Shel. 1974. *Where the Sidewalk Ends.* New York: HarperCollins.

————. 1996. *Falling Up.* New York: HarperCollins.

Stevenson, Robert Louis. 2008. *A Children's Garden of Verses.* New York: Star Bright Books.

Word Choice

Show Your Story

The writer's use of rich, descriptive words can show the reader a mental image. By studying word choice, students will learn how to use vivid, colorful, and dynamic words to enrich their writing and make it as precise as possible. The use of amazing words is encouraged; however, everyday words that are used correctly are also celebrated. The mini-lessons assist students in exploring different types of words and the ways they can be used to create interest in writing pieces. Lessons in this section include:

- Lesson 1: Simple to Sophisticated Synonyms (page 169)
- Lesson 2: Using Your Senses to Show, Don't Tell (page 174)
- Lesson 3: Shifting Ideas with Transition Signals (page 177)
- Lesson 4: Building Vocabulary Webs (page 182)
- Lesson 5: Just a Figure of Speech (page 185)
- Lesson 6: The Power of Connotation (page 190)
- Lesson 7: Exploring Etymology (page 195)

The *Wally, Word Choice Detective* poster (page 168) can be displayed in the room to provide a visual reminder for students that word choice is one of the traits of writing. You may wish to introduce this poster during the first lesson on word choice. Then, refer to the poster when teaching other lessons on word choice to refresh students' memories and provide them with questions to help guide them as they make choices for words they use in their writing.

Wally

Word Choice Detective

What words will paint a picture for my reader?

❧ Did I use purposeful words?

❧ Did I use interesting yet appropriate word selections?

❧ Did I use precise nouns, verbs, and adjectives that evoke images?

❧ Did I use figurative language when necessary?

Simple to Sophisticated Synonyms

Standard

Uses descriptive language that clarifies and enhances ideas

Materials

- Chart paper
- Markers
- *Vocabulary Words* (pages 172–173; vocabularywords.pdf)
- *Simple to Sophisticated Synonyms Notebook Entry* (page 171; synonyms.pdf)
- Writer's Notebooks

Mentor Texts

- *Lousy Rotten Stinkin' Grapes* by Margie Palatini
- *The Boy Who Loved Words* by Roni Schotter
- *The Adventures of Tom Sawyer* by Mark Twain
- See *Mentor Text List* in Appendix C for other suggestions.

Procedures

Note: Recognizing the value of using synonyms and more descriptive, challenging words is a valuable tool for young writers. Keep an ongoing chart listing quality examples from read-alouds for students to use as a resource.

Think About Writing

1. Explain to students that one secret to good writing is using the right word in just the right spot. Tell students that they will be working on word choice by learning about synonyms and how they can add meaning to writing.

2. Review mentor texts, if desired, and emphasize how some word choices work better than others.

Teach

3. Tell students, "It is helpful to know and create synonym word lists in order to adjust our vocabulary for our readers. For example, it helps to be able to distinguish between when to use synonyms, such as *big, large, enormous,* and *mammoth.*"

4. Explain to students that authors determine which word clearly and precisely communicates their thoughts and ideas. Tell them that today they will begin building a "Simple to Sophisticated Synonym Word List."

5. On a sheet of chart paper, create a list to show the contrast of words between simple and sophisticated words. Start with a simple word, such as *big.* Ask students to help you add more sophisticated words to the chart.

Simple	Sophisticated
big	bulky
large	enormous
giant	gigantic
huge	mammoth

Simple to Sophisticated Synonyms *(cont.)*

Engage

6. Place students in quads. Give each group three of four simple vocabulary words, either using the *Vocabulary Words* (pages 172–173) or overused words you have observed in student writing. Have students work together to generate simple and sophisticated synonyms and create a chart like the one you modeled for them. Decide if you want students to use a thesaurus or other reference material to help with synonyms.

7. Allow time for collaboration and brainstorming ideas. When students are finished, have them return to the group and have teams share their synonyms.

Apply

8. Provide students with the *Simple to Sophisticated Synonyms Notebook Entry* (page 171) and have them practice completing sentences with different synonyms. Have them complete the *Your Turn* section before proceeding to their writing folders and editing their writing.

Write/Conference

9. Provide time for students to write. Some students may need additional time and repetition of the mini-lesson. Create small guided writing groups for reteaching based on your observations. These sessions should be very focused and to the point.

Spotlight Strategy

10. Spotlight students who are writing sophisticated synonyms. For example, "You are really impressive, writers! You continue to amaze me. Listen to this sentence and pay attention to the sophisticated vocabulary."

Share

11. Have students work in pairs and share some of their best synonyms. Once complete, have students change partners and continue sharing their synonyms.

Homework

Ask students to think of a few simple and easy words and then challenge their family members to come up with more sophisticated synonyms. Have students record their family's ideas and bring them back to the class to share.

Simple to Sophisticated Synonyms

Authors use **synonyms** to make their writing more interesting, vivid, and descriptive. They make sure a synonym matches their intended meaning.

Knowing and understanding how to select synonyms can increase your writing vocabulary. Remember that many words have more than one meaning, so it is important to pay close attention to how the synonym is used in the sentence.

Simple	Sophisticated
big	bulky
large	enormous
giant	gigantic
huge	mammoth
get	gain
buy	procure
shrink	diminish

Your Turn:

Practice using synonyms by completing each sentence with one simple synonym and three sophisticated synonyms. Then, revise your current writing project(s) using sophisticated synonyms.

Those shoes are _____.

Calee's room is _____.

Michael _____ the ball.

The kitten _____ through the house.

Her new dress is _____.

Vocabulary Words

Directions: Cut out the cards. Distribute vocabulary words to students and have them create sophisticated synonyms.

said	fast
ugly	slow
small	nice
good	short

Vocabulary Words (cont.)

bad	**old**
boring	**hot**
hard	**dark**
easy	**loud**

Using Your Senses to Show, Don't Tell

Standard
Uses descriptive language that clarifies and enhances ideas

Materials
- *Using Your Senses to Show, Don't Tell Notebook Entry* (page 176; senses.pdf)
- Writer's Notebooks

Mentor Texts
- *Rumble Fish* by S. E. Hinton
- *Show; Don't Tell! Secrets of Writing* by Josephine Nobisso
- *Canoe Days* by Gary Paulsen
- See *Mentor Text List* in Appendix C for other suggestions.

Procedures

Note: This lesson can be repeated often when focusing on descriptive writing in any genre of text.

Think About Writing

1. Tell students that in order to be successful with descriptive writing, authors must be observant and fully aware of everything around them. Authors pay attention to small details that others may overlook. Explain that this lesson will teach students how to pay attention to small details that they may see, hear, taste, touch, or smell.

2. Review mentor texts, if desired, and discuss how sensory details enhance stories.

Teach

3. Share with students that authors who write stories using the five senses will describe things that help a reader be completely immersed in the story. Today, students will be aware of their senses and what they notice in the world around them.

4. Review the five senses and share the following sentences or create your own: "Kara walked on the sand, looking at the waves and sipping the ice-cold lemonade along the way. The sound of seagulls echoed on the coast and the salty air surrounded her." Ask students, "What visual images did this create in your mind? What senses do you notice?"

5. Share sections of descriptive language from mentor texts. Discuss the sensory words and phrases used by the author to create visual images for the reader.

Using Your Senses to Show, Don't Tell (cont.)

Engage

6. Tell students that good descriptions in writing are sensory yet precise. Conduct an activity called "Showing with Sensory Words." Place students in pairs. Have students close their eyes and take a mental snapshot of a moment in time they want to share. What do they see, hear, taste, feel, and smell? Students will share these observations with partners and have the partners guess what they are describing. Give both students a chance to give descriptions.

Apply

7. Provide students with the *Using Your Senses to Show, Don't Tell Notebook Entry* (page 176) and have them practice creating specific details so that the reader can experience what is being described through their "senses." Have them complete the *Your Turn* section before proceeding to their writing folders.

Write/Conference

8. Provide time for students to write. Make observations in your Conferring Notebook on student work. Plan future instruction based on your records.

Spotlight Strategy

9. Spotlight students who are using sensory words in their writing. For example, "Spotlighting Sara's sensory words. Great work today!"

Share

10. Have students work in small groups to share their interesting sentences with sensory descriptions.

Homework

Have students write about an event using the five senses. It can be a simple event, such as a family dinner or homework time.

Using Your Senses to Show, Don't Tell

Authors know that the best stories unfold like a painting on the page or a movie in your mind. They share stories with their readers by immersing them in **sensory details**. To be successful with descriptive writing, you must be observant and fully aware of everything around you. Use sensory images to describe what you see, hear, touch, smell, and taste to create your story. For example:

Jamey walked down the hallway to greet her bath, sipping the ice-cold diet soda along the way. The sweet melodic music was playing on the radio and beckoned her to unwind.

Kim's thick dark curls were piled high and loose on top of her head. Huge, dangling earrings rocked back and forth as she swung her head, and her ruby red lips curled up in a smile.

A silk shirt framed Jeff's sunburned face. His shirt was tucked into black pleated pants and over his shoulder he casually threw an expensive sport coat.

Your Turn:

Practice writing sensory details using the following as starters. Then, move into writing your own. Make a sketch to show your thinking after you've written your descriptions.

> *Wiry gray hair with metal-rimmed glasses*
>
> *Sidewalk bustling with shoppers*
>
> *Playground filled with screaming children*
>
> *A meadow with a herd of cattle munching on grass*
>
> *A snake twisting and turning in the flower garden*

Shifting Ideas with Transition Signals

Standard

Uses explicit transitional devices

Materials

- Chart paper
- Markers
- *Shifting Ideas with Transition Signals Notebook Entry* (page 179; transitionsignals.pdf)
- Writer's Notebooks
- *Transition Signals* (pages 180–181; signals.pdf)

Mentor Texts

- *Meanwhile* by Jules Feiffer
- *Woe Is I Jr.: The Younger Grammarphobes' Guide* by Patricia O'Conner
- *Thunder Cake* by Patricia Polacco
- *Tornadoes* by Seymour Simon
- *The Patchwork Path: A Quilt Map to Freedom* by Bettye Stroud
- See *Mentor Text List* in Appendix C for other suggestions.

Procedures

Note: Different genres require different transition signals to shift thinking. It is important that students understand the meaning and purpose of a transition word or phrase.

Think About Writing

1. Have students practice using transition signals to indicate a shift in their thinking as they develop informative, opinion/argumentative, and narrative stories, compositions, and essays. Display *Transition Signals* (pages 180–181) for students who need assistance getting started.

2. Review mentor texts, if desired, and note how transitions help the flow of the text. For example, in *Tornadoes* by Seymour Simon, the following transition words and phrases are included:

    The first step, Sometimes, By the time, Fortunately

    Discuss the differences between these words and how they work.

Teach

3. Review how different genres of writing require different transitions based on the purpose of the writing. Then, explain that transition words introduce a thought, show a sequence/order, indicate time, compare or contrast, stress an important point, or summarize.

4. Using chart paper, create a T-chart with the headings *Narrative* and *Informative or Opinion*. Add transition words from the mentor texts and discuss the authors' purpose for using those specific transition words. Use this chart to collect additional transition words in other familiar texts.

Shifting Ideas with Transition Signals *(cont.)*

Engage

5. Divide students into triads and write the following on the board:

   The smell of hot dogs and hamburgers cooking on the grill left my mouth watering in anticipation. Delicious brownies were covered with paper to discourage the flies. The fountain of fireworks had their last fizzle, which signaled the time to feed my rumbling stomach.

   Have groups rewrite the paragraph using transition words to show the best way to let the reader know what's coming next and how to transition smoothly from one idea to the next.

6. As a group, discuss how different transition words may give different meanings to the writing.

Apply

7. Provide students with the *Shifting Ideas with Transition Signals Notebook Entry* (page 179) and have them practice using appropriate transition signals.

Write/Conference

8. Provide time for students to write. For groups that need additional support, provide sample paragraphs or use student writing to show how the use of specific transition words can give different meaning to a text.

Spotlight Strategy

9. Spotlight students who are using transition words in their writing. For example, "You are amazing writers! Listen to the flow and movement of these sentences."

Share

10. Have students return to their groups. Have them share something they learned today.

Homework

Ask students to use at least three or four of the transition words they learned. Have them share with family members the reasons why transition words are necessary for quality writing.

Shifting Ideas with Transition Signals

Authors use **transition words** and phrases to prepare the reader for what will happen next and to link their ideas and thoughts together.

Remember, some transition words are more suited for specific genres, though many can be used in any genre. Transition words may be used to introduce a thought, to show a sequence or order, to indicate time, to compare or contrast, to stress an important point, or to summarize/conclude.

Transition Words for Narrative Writing	Transition Words for Informative or Opinion Writing
• In the beginning, • Before long, • Meanwhile, • Later that day, • It all started when • One morning, • After a while, • Since I was late, • The next morning, • The rest of the time, • While I walked along, • Suddenly, • At that moment, • Previously, • Followed by • Finally,	• In the first place, • On the other hand, • Conversely, • However, • In addition, • Also, • Because • They are different • Similarly, • Uniquely, • Most compelling evidence • Summing up, • In other words, • Consequently, • As a result, • Ultimately,

Your Turn:

Select a piece of writing from your folder, highlight the transition words, and revise by adding transition words that help make the writing connected logically and smoothly.

Transition Signals

Directions: Display transition words and help students select the right phrase to improve essays, reports, research papers, and narrative writing. The list below is not an extensive list, but is intended to support your instruction.

Narrative: To introduce	**Narrative:** To show time	**Narrative:** To summarize and conclude
• Long ago, • One summer night, • One morning, • In a tiny log cabin, • One summer day, • On a splendid day, • Whenever I can, • It was in the summer • Down the street, • The rest of the day	• All at once • In the next moment, • Later in the • Since we are ready, • The next day, • When I awoke, • Later that afternoon, • Meanwhile, • After that,	• As you can see, • Finally, • To this day, • Fortunately, • As it all turned out, • So the next time you • When I think back,
Informative or Opinion: To introduce	**Informative or Opinion:** To compare	**Informative or Opinion:** To contrast
• First, • Initially, • To begin with, • It is a fact that • Scientists say • Experts tell us • Is it true that • In my opinion • It is my belief that • There is no doubt that • I question • Did you know	• On the other hand, • Not to mention • Equally important • Also, • Likewise, • Comparatively, • Similarly, • Identically, • Not only… but also… • Furthermore, • Additionally,	• Although… • In contrast… • On the other hand… • In spite of… • However…. • Conversely…. • Nevertheless… • Otherwise… • Despite… • Instead… • Unlike…

Transition Signals (cont.)

Informative or Opinion:	Informative or Opinion:	Informative or Opinion:
To show time	To stress importance	To summarize/conclude
• Eventually, • At the present time, • In due time, • Immediately, • Formerly, • Instantly, • During, • Presently, • At this point, • Prior to	• In fact, • To put it differently, • In particular, • For this reason • In this case, • It is important to realize • To demonstrate, • To clarify, • As a result,	• After all, • In the final analysis, • As shown above, • In fact, • To summarize, • In conclusion, • To sum up, • All things considered, • Given these ideas,

Building Vocabulary Webs

Standard

Uses a variety of prewriting strategies

Materials

- Chart paper
- Markers
- *Building Vocabulary Webs Notebook Entry* (page 184; vocabularywebs.pdf)
- Writer's Notebooks

Mentor Texts

- *Harriet Tubman: Conductor on the Underground Railroad* by Ann Petry
- *Tornadoes* by Seymour Simon
- *Travels with Charley: In Search of America* by John Steinbeck
- See *Mentor Text List* in Appendix C for other suggestions.

Procedures

Note: Understanding vocabulary that is topic-specific gives students the confidence to write with more sophisticated language. Vocabulary webs also improve spelling and support visual learners.

Think About Writing

1. Tell students that they already know some things about the characteristics and text structure of nonfiction writing. As authors plan and organize information for nonfiction writing, they may develop a vocabulary web to support them plan their writing. Explain that they are going to create vocabulary webs to support their own nonfiction writing.

2. Review mentor texts, if desired, and point out the topic-specific vocabulary used.

Teach

3. Explain that when it comes to writing nonfiction, the more key words a writer knows about a topic, the easier it is to effectively communicate a message. Use a sheet of chart paper to model building a vocabulary web. Write a topic in the center of the page and draw a circle or rectangle around the word. Draw a few lines out from the topic to create a web.

4. Ask students to help you brainstorm words associated with the topic. Read a related text about the focus topic and as you read, have students suggest words to add to your vocabulary web.

5. When you are finished with the web, review it as a group and talk about the words that made the web.

   - What do these words tell us about the topic?

   - How are these words related to each other?

   - If you were writing about this topic, how might you use this web to help you with your writing?

Building Vocabulary Webs (cont.)

Engage

6. Ask students to work in pairs to complete their own vocabulary webs. Provide them with a topic related to something the class is currently studying. Ask pairs to work together to build vocabulary webs using the words they know about the topic that they may want to include in a writing piece.

7. Have students share their work when they are finished and discuss how the webs are similar or different.

Apply

8. Provide students with the *Building Vocabulary Webs Notebook Entry* (page 184) and have them read about vocabulary webs and study a sample web. Then, students can practice creating vocabulary webs to write clear and concise information in a text.

Write/Conference

9. Support students who are having difficulty completing the vocabulary web. Use mentor texts when possible to show how familiar vocabulary is used in nonfiction writing. Keep informative observations in your Conferring Notebook.

Spotlight Strategy

10. Spotlight students who are successfully working on vocabulary webs. For example, "Listen to these words that Hector came up with for his topic. They are such important words to include in any nonfiction writing about this topic!"

Share

11. Have students meet in pairs and share the vocabulary they brainstormed for their own topics of interest. Allow a few minutes to share and then have students switch partners. Repeat this a few times.

Homework

Ask students to play a vocabulary web game with their families. Students can name a topic and see how many words the entire family can name related to that topic.

Building Vocabulary Webs Notebook Entry

Building Vocabulary Webs

As authors plan and organize information for nonfiction writing, they may develop a **vocabulary web** to support them during the writing process, such as the one below.

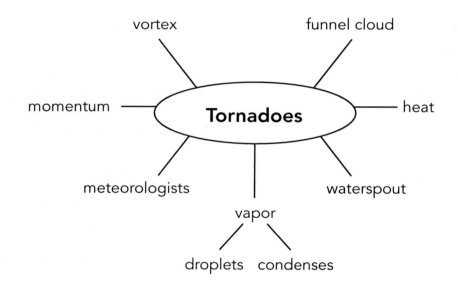

vortex   funnel cloud

momentum   **Tornadoes**   heat

meteorologists   waterspout

vapor

droplets   condenses

Your Turn:

Choose a topic and build a vocabulary web for your next nonfiction writing project.

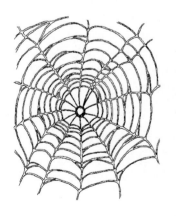

Just a Figure of Speech

Standard

Uses descriptive language that clarifies and enhances ideas

Materials

- Chart paper
- Markers
- *Topic Cards* (pages 188–189; topiccards.pdf)
- *Just a Figure of Speech Notebook Entry* (page 187; figureofspeech.pdf)
- Writer's Notebooks

Mentor Texts

- *Creatures of Earth, Sea, and Sky: Poems* by Georgia Heard
- *Canoe Days* by Gary Paulsen
- *It Figures! Fun Figures of Speech* by Marvin Terban
- See *Mentor Text List* in Appendix C for other suggestions.

Procedures

Note: Add new figures of speech to the class chart created in this lesson as students hear or read them.

Think About Writing

1. Remind students that authors use similes, idioms, hyperboles, alliteration, and onomatopoeia to add descriptive language to their writing. Personification and metaphors are two figures of speech that make interesting comparisons by showing how two different things are similar.

2. Review mentor texts, if desired, and explore the use of figures of speech to tell stories.

Teach

3. Tell students, "Authors use metaphors and personification to stir a reader's imagination. An author could simply write, 'The water was shiny.' Instead, the author may write, 'The sunlight danced across the water, creating a sea of floating diamonds.' Personification gives nonhuman objects human qualities, such as when the 'sunlight danced.'"

4. Explain that a metaphor, like a simile, is a comparison of two things, except without the use of *like* or *as*. Examples of metaphors include *This assignment is a breeze. His room is a pigsty.*

5. Create a chart with the headings *Personification* and *Metaphor*. Add additional examples that students share or read.

Personification	Metaphor
His pencil raced across the page.	Michael is a bolt of lightning once he hits the baseball.
In the forest, the wind sang a soft lullaby.	We could have had pizza leftover, if the kids weren't such pigs.

Just a Figure of Speech (cont.)

Engage

6. Tell students that they will work in quads. Give each group *Topic Cards* (pages 188–189) and direct them to create sentences that contain metaphors and personification.

7. Allow three to four minutes for students to write.

Apply

8. Provide students with the *Just a Figure of Speech Notebook Entry* (page 187) and have them read about different types of figurative language. Encourage them to use the examples as they work on the *Your Turn* section with a partner. Then, have them to read their own writing to see where they may incorporate figurative language.

Write/Conference

9. Have students tell you about their writing and the skills they are working on in their writing. Observe and support their efforts by offering compliments and modeling examples.

Spotlight Strategy

10. Spotlight students who are writing with figurative language. For example, "Listen to this amazing description in Lilah's writing. Smart work!"

Share

11. Have students work in pairs and share their work. Encourage students to be PALS—**P**raise, **A**sk, **L**ook, and **S**uggest. Allow a few minutes for students to share.

Homework

Have students think about personification and metaphors and return to class with at least two examples of each.

Just a Figure of Speech Notebook Entry

Just a Figure of Speech

Authors use **figurative language** to create writing that is more interesting and realistic. It helps the reader visualize and feel the emotions of their stories.

Metaphor: a comparison of two or more unlike things

As summer arrived, the grass became a blanket of green.

Personification: giving nonhuman objects human characteristics

The tall field grass bowed in the gentle breeze.

Simile: a comparison of two or more unlike things using the words *like* or *as*

The grass felt like a carpet under our feet.

Hyperbole: an extreme exaggeration

After the warm rain, the grass grew a foot overnight.

Alliteration: the repetition of the same initial sound or syllable in a phrase or sentence

The cattle grazed on the green grass at Granny Gap.

Your Turn:

Work with a partner and use the starters to create sentences using figurative language.

The tornado…

The morning news…

A flower in the garden…

My computer…

The night sky…

Topic Cards

Directions: Distribute the cards to students and have them create sentences that contain metaphors and personification.

sun	night
water	wolf
tree	leaves
curtains	ocean

#50920—*Getting to the Core of Writing—Level 6* © Shell Education

Topic Cards (cont.)

song	**wind**
hair	**popcorn**
stars	**bear**
car	**moon**

The Power of Connotation

Standard
Uses descriptive language that clarifies and enhances ideas

Materials
- Chart paper
- Markers
- A picture of a rose
- *Word Cards* (pages 193–194; wordcards.pdf)
- *The Power of Connotation Notebook Entry* (page 192; connotation.pdf)
- Writer's Notebooks

Mentor Texts
- "The Gettysburg Address" by Abraham Lincoln
- "I Have a Dream" by Martin Luther King Jr.
- See *Mentor Text List* in Appendix C for other suggestions.

Procedures
Note: Students can learn that connotations are present in many aspects of our culture besides writing. Additional lessons can discuss the connotations in news reporting, entertainment, and advertising.

Think About Writing
1. Tell students that using strong emotional language is characteristic of great authors. They select specific words that may influence and affect their readers' reactions and emotions. Explain that great speeches by Dr. Martin Luther King Jr. and Abraham Lincoln are filled with emotional language.

Teach
2. Tell students, "Today we are going to learn how denotation and connotation can affect the meaning in your writing." Explain that *denotation* refers to the dictionary definition of a word. *Connotation* is an association, usually emotional, that the word brings to mind.

3. On a sheet of chart paper, write the words *Denotation* and *Connotation*. Show students a picture of a rose and then write:

   A rose bloomed on the rose bush.

   The rose he gave her touched her heart.

   Discuss the following questions:

   - How are these sentences similar and different?
   - What does the rose symbolize in each sentence?
   - When might an author want to use one sentence over the other?

   In the first sentence, the denotative meaning of the word *rose* is used—a red flower. In the second sentence, *rose* goes beyond the denotative meaning to the connotative meaning, referring to things associated with roses, such as love and affection.

The Power of Connotation (cont.)

Engage

4. Divide students in quads and have one student in each group be a recorder. Distribute a *Word Card* (pages 193–194) to each group. Have students write the denotative meaning and then create a list of connotations related to their word. Then, have students write one sentence with a positive connotation and one with a negative connotation to share with the class.

Apply

5. Provide students with *The Power of Connotation Notebook Entry* (page 192) and have them read about the powerful effects of emotional (connotative) and dictionary (denotative) meanings of words. This understanding will sharpen their messages in writing and add deeper meaning.

Write/Conference

6. Provide time for students to write. Be available to support students with the different word choices in this lesson. Make anecdotal notes in your Conferring Notebook for future reference.

Spotlight Strategy

7. Spotlight students who recognize the use of connotation and denotation in their own writing. For example, "Spotlight on Chloe. Listen to how she described this topic using words that have positive connotations. Great job!"

Share

8. Have selected students share how they wrote sentences differently when using the concepts of denotation versus connotation.

Homework

Ask students to watch television and write down words they hear that create positive or negative connotations. Have them be ready to share the words when they return to class.

The Power of Connotation Notebook Entry

The Power of Connotation

Authors select specific words that may influence and affect their readers' reactions and emotions.

Denotation is a word's dictionary definition.

> Snake: one of many scaly reptile species
>
> *The _snake_ slithered through the tall grass.*

Connotation is the emotional feelings, images, and memories that accompany a word. It is what comes to mind when you read or hear the word.

> Snake: evil, danger, dishonest, treachery, creepy
>
> *The salesman was like a _snake_ ready to strike.*

Compare each pair of sentences below that have the same denotative meaning but different connotations.

That girl is smart.	The watch is inexpensive.
That girl is brainy.	The watch is cheap.

Your Turn:

For each of these words, write synonyms with positive and negative connotations. For example:

Denotation	Positive Connotation	Negative Connotation
heavy	plump	fat or obese

- short
- stubborn

- child
- politician

- smart
- nice

#50920—Getting to the Core of Writing—Level 6 © Shell Education

Word Cards

Directions: Distribute two or more cards to each group. Then, have students identify the connotative and denotative meanings of the words, create a list of related synonyms, and write a sentence using both a positive and negative connotation.

thin	**house**
walk	**smell**
cheap	**pretty**
smart	**smile**

Word Cards (cont.)

kid	old
restaurant	poor
greedy	dishonest
hot	mom

#50920—Getting to the Core of Writing—Level 6 © Shell Education

Exploring Etymology

Standard

Uses conventions of spelling in written compositions

Materials

- Chart paper
- Markers
- *Etymology Chart* (page 198; etymologychart.pdf)
- *Exploring Etymology Notebook Entry* (page 197; exploringetymology.pdf)
- Writer's Notebooks

Mentor Texts

- *Twilight Comes Twice* by Ralph Fletcher
- See *Mentor Text List* in Appendix C for other suggestions.

Procedures

Note: Explicitly teaching students the meanings of roots and affixes gives them the ability to expand their reading and writing vocabulary. Revisit this lesson during the year to build knowledge of roots and affixes.

Think About Writing

1. Explain to students that successful writers continue to expand their vocabulary to ensure they are including the right words and phrases to describe and tell their stories. Sometimes these words include Greek and Latin roots and affixes.

2. Review mentor texts, if desired, and note the frequency of words that come from Greek and Latin roots and affixes.

Teach

3. Tell students, "We will explore etymology, or the study of word history, to expand our own vocabulary for the purpose of reading and writing." Write the word *Etymology* on the board or a sheet of chart paper and explain that it means to study the origin of a word. Then, create a three-column chart with the headings *Prefix*, *Root Word*, and *Suffix*.

4. Display the *Etymology Chart* (page 198) for additional support and examples. Explain the following:

    A *root word* is a word that may stand by itself. (-*aqua*-, -*meter*-)

    A *prefix* is a word part/syllable connected to the front of a word that can alter the meaning of the root word. (*re*-, *post*-)

    A *suffix* is a word part/syllable connected to the end of a word that may change the tense or meaning of the root word. (-*ment, -tion*)

Ask students to share any additional examples they have and add them to the appropriate location on the class chart.

Exploring Etymology *(cont.)*

Engage

5. Divide students into quads. Post three charts around the room titled *Prefixes*, *Suffixes*, and *Root Words*. Each group will brainstorm words to add to their chart. Give each group a turn to add information and examples to the chart.

6. When the student groups are finished adding affixes and root words to the chart, look at the new additions together and discuss new vocabulary. Use the information to generate spellings of any unknown words.

Apply

7. Provide students with the *Exploring Etymology Notebook Entry* (page 197) and have them add the new vocabulary to their Writer's Notebooks. Challenge students to create additional examples to include in their writing.

Write/Conference

8. Work with students who are in need of further instruction. Confer with students individually or in small groups.

Spotlight Strategy

9. Spotlight students who are writing new vocabulary words with prefixes, roots, or suffixes.

Share

10. Have students meet back in their original groups and share the words they have generated on their own.

Homework

Have students share what they learned with family members and use roots and affixes to make new words. Encourage students to talk about the words as a family and then have students share them at school.

Exploring Etymology Notebook Entry

Exploring Etymology

Successful writers continue to expand their vocabulary to ensure they are including the right words and phrases to describe and tell their stories.

Knowing and understanding different parts of words helps us break them down and understand their meaning.

A **root word** is a word that may stand by itself. (*-aqua-, -meter-*)

A **prefix** is a word part/syllable connected to the front of a word that alters the meaning of the root word. (*re-, post-*)

A **suffix** is a word part/syllable connected to the end of a word that changes the tense or meaning of the root word. (*-ment, -tion*)

Prefixes	Root Words	Suffixes
trans- (across)	*-geo-* (earth)	*-ible* (able to be)
pre- (before)	*-tele-* (from afar)	*-meter* (measure)
re- (again)	*-ject-* (throw)	*-logy* (study of)
dis- (not, opposite of)	*-dem-* (people)	*-ation/-ion* (action or process)
auto- (self, same)	*-port-* (to carry)	*-gram* (written)
co- (together)	*-dict-* (to say)	*-oid* (resembling)

Your Turn:

Use the roots and affixes above to generate new words. As you encounter unfamiliar words in your reading, identify roots, prefixes, or suffixes to understand the meanings of those words. Use your Writer's Notebook as a resource during your writing to find the right words for your story.

Etymology Chart

Directions: Display the chart for students, explaining unfamiliar terms.

Word Part Type	Word Part	Meaning	Origin	Examples
Prefix	auto-	self, same	Greek	autopilot, autobiography, automatic
	co-	together	Latin	coauthor, coworker, cooperate
Root	-dem-	people	Greek	democracy, pandemic
	-port-	to carry	Latin	import, support, deport
Suffix	-meter	measure	Greek	parameter, thermometer, geometry
	-ment	forms nouns from verbs	Latin	amazement, movement, government

#50920—Getting to the Core of Writing—Level 6 © Shell Education

Voice

Expressing Your Feelings

Voice is the most elusive of the traits of quality writing. It is the passion, experiences, and creativity that is brought to the reader's attention through the writer's ability to convey his or her own observations gleaned from experiences. Voice grows as the writer grows. In *Write to Learn*, Donald Murray (2004) describes voice as "the person in the writing." When students are able to put their speech in writing, their personality shines through.

Voice is evident in the stories and literature we share with students every day. It is in those books that we can barely tear ourselves away from, the ones we want to keep reading and can hardly wait to turn the page. Think about the texts you read to your students again and again. You share them because the author's voice connects in some way to you personally. To call attention to voice, collect examples on anchor charts and help students recognize and value its purpose through your read-alouds and student writing. As you model writing, use conventions to show emotions and transfer passion from speech to print.

Voice is what makes writing come alive. Although sometimes difficult to teach, it is recognizable in writing through the personal tone and feeling of the writing piece. This section contains mini-lessons that focus on how students can connect with their readers to compel them to continue reading. Lessons in this section include:

- Lesson 1: I Know How You Feel (page 201)
- Lesson 2: Voice Reflections (page 204)
- Lesson 3: The Voice of R.A.F.T. (page 207)
- Lesson 4: If I Were A... (page 210)
- Lesson 5: A Writer's Toolbox for Voice (page 213)

The *Val and Van, Voice* poster (page 200) can be displayed in the room to provide a visual reminder for students that voice is one of the traits of writing. You may wish to introduce this poster during the first lesson on voice. Then, refer to the poster when teaching other lessons on voice to refresh students' memories and provide them with questions to help guide them as they make an effort to show voice in their writing.

Val and Van
Voice

What is the purpose of my writing?

❤ Did I express myself with my own originality?

❤ Did I convey the purpose of my writing?

❤ Did I recognize and connect with my audience?

❤ Did I sound honest and confident in my position?

I Know How You Feel

Standard

Uses descriptive language that clarifies and enhances ideas

Materials

- Chart paper
- Markers
- *I Know How You Feel Notebook Entry* (page 203; howyoufeel.pdf)
- Writer's Notebooks

Mentor Texts

- *Fly Away Home* by Eve Bunting
- *Old Yeller* by Fred Gipson
- *Shiloh* by Phyllis R. Naylor
- *My Ol' Man* by Patricia Polacco
- *My Rotten Redheaded Older Brother* by Patricia Polacco
- See *Mentor Text List* in Appendix C for other suggestions.

Procedures

Note: Young writers need exposure to voice through a myriad of authors. Read aloud often to your students. Talk about the voice of each author and how emotions or feelings are shared with readers.

Think About Writing

1. Explain that each person has a unique personality and voice in writing. Authors share their voices with readers by expressing their passion for a topic, showing emotions, and selecting words and phrases that represent their characters or themselves. Explain that the voice of a text includes the "mood" in which we write.

2. Review mentor texts, if desired, and emphasize how voice is used to express emotions and feelings.

Teach

3. Tell students that they will explore the trait of voice using descriptive writing to show the "mood" to their readers. Remind students that mood can be expressed through the different emotions, feelings, and attitudes of the narrator or character in the story. Explain that an author does not have to explicitly state everything by writing sentences like "It was embarrassing. I was angry. I loved that dog." Instead, the reader can understand feelings and moods through descriptive writing.

4. Share a section of a mentor text that reflects a mood or feeling. Create a three-column chart with the headings *Text, Mood/Feeling,* and *The Author Showed Voice By....*

Text	Mood/Feeling	The Author Showed Voice By
My Ol' Man (father arriving)	children's excitement and anticipation	using descriptive language, such as "eyes were blazing" and "mother of all stories"
My Ol' Man (selling the car)	Ritchie's desperation	using more descriptive words in place of "said," such as "burst out" and "pleaded"

I Know How You Feel (cont.)

5. Next, think aloud as you record your thoughts about the selection you shared. Continue to read additional sections and ask students to talk in pairs about the author's voice. Then, add responses to the chart.

Engage

6. Tell students that they will work with a partner and choose one or two texts to read and look for evidence of voice in the stories. Explain that you want them to find the emotion or feelings and explain how the author used voice. Tell students to be ready to share.

7. It may be helpful to review different emotions, especially more complicated feelings, such as fear, disappointment, jealousy, and confusion, and discuss examples of situations that may create such feelings.

Apply

8. Challenge students to use descriptive words and phrases in their writing that reflect their voices. Provide students with the *I Know How You Feel Notebook Entry* (page 203) and have them practice writing with a strong voice. Have students complete the *Your Turn* section before proceeding to their writing folders.

Write/Conference

9. Provide time for students to write. Work with students who are showing signs of confusion. Confer with students individually or in small groups.

Spotlight Strategy

10. Spotlight students who are writing with a strong voice. For example, "Your voice really comes through! Class, listen to these words and see what kind of voice you hear from this author."

Share

11. Have students meet in pairs to share their writing. Ask students to listen for voice in the writing and determine which emotions or feelings are conveyed.

Homework

Ask students to think about favorite stories, television shows, and movies. Have them discuss with family members what they have learned about voice and then share what kinds of voices they hear in stories, shows, and movies.

I Know How You Feel Notebook Entry

I Know How You Feel

Authors share their **voice** with readers by expressing their passion for a topic, showing emotions and selecting words and phrases that represent their characters or themselves. Voice includes the mood in which we write. Study the work of other authors and consider how voice is reflected in their writing.

When writing a story, letter, or other form of writing, think about how you want your reader to feel or react. Read it aloud and ask yourself, "What kind of voice am I using? Serious? Hopeful? Silly?" Your reader should be able to understand how you feel about the topic in your writing.

Your Turn:

Use descriptive language to reflect voice in your writing projects. The moods and feelings below may support you in developing voice in your writing projects. Add others to your Writer's Notebook.

- adventurous
- angry
- annoyed
- bossy
- brave
- caring
- curious
- daring
- disappointed

- energetic
- excited
- friendly
- frightened
- funny
- gloomy
- happy
- hopeful
- lonely

- mischievous
- nervous
- quiet
- rude
- sad
- scholarly
- shy
- surprised
- wicked

happy

hopeful

nervous

overwhelmed

surprised

suspicious

Voice Reflections

Standard

Uses descriptive language that clarifies and enhances ideas

Materials

- Chart paper
- Markers
- *Voice Reflections Notebook Entry* (page 206; reflections.pdf)
- Writer's Notebooks

Mentor Texts

- *Petite Rouge* by Mike Artell
- *Three Little Cajun Pigs* by Mike Artell
- *Grannie and the Jumbie: A Caribbean Tale* by Margaret Hurst
- *Smoky Mountain Rose: An Appalachian Cinderella* by Alan Schroeder
- See *Mentor Text List* in Appendix C for other suggestions.

Procedures

Note: Reading familiar stories but changing the language to reflect a different culture helps students respect and understand a culture that is different from their own.

Think About Writing

1. Tell students that authors include a special voice in their writing by creating characters with rich, authentic dialogue. Different characters that experience different things use very different dialogue. The way an author writes dialogue gives the writing a voice that can be identified by the reader. It also tells the reader who the character is as well as more about the character's culture and personality.

2. Review mentor texts, if desired, and explain that writers can add voice by representing language and culture from different communities, such as rural and urban, or from different parts of the country, such as New York, California, Mississippi, etc. Remind students that good writing always avoids stereotyping and negative representations.

Teach

3. Share the vocabulary and sayings from *Smoky Mountain Rose: An Appalachian Cinderella*, a book on Appalachian culture. The dialect reflected is typical of parents and grandparents living in the 1940s and 50s in the mountains of the Carolinas, Virginias, Kentucky, and Tennessee. Ask students to take note of the different sounds of words in the story.

4. Read a few pages from the book. On chart paper, create a T-chart with the headings *I Heard* and *It Means*. Ask students to share words they noticed that sounded familiar but may come from a specific place or region. Share a different excerpt and again ask for observations. Ask students to examine the chart and notice any patterns in the recorded words.

Voice Reflections (cont.)

5. Read and analyze a variety of texts to provide students with multiple examples of vocabulary and dialect.

Engage

6. Tell students that they are going to use what they learned about voice to retell a familiar tale. Provide students with the *Voice Reflections Notebook Entry* (page 206) and have them discuss the retelling of the "The Three Billy Goats Gruff." Ask students to think about how the different dialogue changes the story. Which version do students prefer? Remind students that writing with different dialects celebrates diversity and gives readers an opportunity to consider people from other cultures.

Apply

7. Tell students that they will write a text (or a portion of a text) with dialogue that includes a specific kind of character for the story. Have students choose a favorite tale and rewrite the story from the culture or personality of the chosen character. Remind them to think about the words, phrases, and unique pauses that the character might say in the dialogue. Then, have students think about who is telling the story and how the voice of this particular character reflects a different tone.

Write/Conference

8. Provide time for students to write. Be available to support students with the trait of voice. Make anecdotal notes in your Conferring Notebook for future reference and conferring.

Spotlight Strategy

9. Spotlight students who recognize the use of personality and dialect in student writing. For example, "Spotlight on Ezra. Listen to how he rewrote this story to make the main character the villain. Great job!"

Share

10. Have selected students share how they rewrote dialogue from the perspective of a different character.

Homework

Ask students to notice the use of language and dialect in their favorite stories, movies, and television shows. Have them play a game with a family member in which they act and talk like a familiar character, and a family member has to guess who it is.

Voice Reflections Notebook Entry

Voice Reflections

Different characters who experience different things share very different **dialogue**. The way an author writes dialogue gives the writing a voice that can be identified by the reader. It also tells the reader who the character is, as well as more about culture and personality.

Read this version of "The Three Billy Goats Gruff" told from the perspective of a character living in Appalachia.

The Three Billy Goats Gruff

Now ya'll listen here! There once were three billy goats called "The Gruffs." I reckon' they lived in a barn in the middle of winter, but when spring comes along them goats started a-pining for that lush sweet grass up in the mountains.

On the way to the mountains, those three Billy Goats Gruff had to cross a rushin' river, with just one bridge to the other side. Now ya'll, in under that bridge lived a terrible, ug'le, one-eyed troll.

The three goats went a-rumblin' down that old dirt road. The smallest Billy Goat Gruff was the first to reach the bridge. Trippity trappity, trippity trappity, went the li'l hooves as he moseyed cross that bridge.

"Who's that sashayin' cross my bridge?" grumbled the troll.

"Tiny Billy Goat Gruff," squeaked a small voice. "I'm goin' to the mountain to eat the sweet spring grass."

"Laws-a marcy! No you're not, you mis'rable goat! I'm gonna' eat you for my breakfast!"

Your Turn:

Pick a favorite tale of your own. Choose a character from another place in the world. Retell the tale from the perspective of this new character.

The Voice of R.A.F.T.

Procedures

Note: Learning how to identify and incorporate the trait of voice in writing takes time. Sharing literature with strong voice is the best way to demonstrate this writing trait.

Think About Writing

1. Explain that authors use voice in their writing to make emotional connections with their readers. They want their readers to relate to the message in the text. Tell them they will learn about strategies that writers use to connect with their readers.

Teach

2. Tell students, "We will explore an important strategy many authors use to ensure they are addressing the needs of their readers. It is called R.A.F.T." Explain that authors use R.A.F.T. in prewriting to identify their own roles as writers, the audience they are writing for, the format of the writing projects, and the topics they are writing.

3. Think aloud as you explain how to begin planning a writing piece. Use a chart like the one below to explain what R.A.F.T. means.

    Role of the writer: Who are you as the writer?

    Audience: To whom are you writing?

    Format: In what format are you writing?

    Topic: What are you writing about?

4. Model how to create R.A.F.T. writing options using *The Adventures of Tom Sawyer* by Mark Twain.

Role	Audience	Format	Topic
Huck	Tom	Thank you note	Being a good friend
Tom	Becky	Poem	I want to be more than friends
Tom	Aunt Polly	Letter	Sorry, I'll be good!

The Voice of R.A.F.T. (cont.)

Engage

5. Have students think of other examples to add to the chart. Select one example and model how to turn the idea into a piece of writing.

6. Have students work with a group to create writing projects based on the R.A.F.T. selected. Ask students to think about how voice will play an important role in the writing.

7. Gather groups together as a class and share writing. Discuss how the role, audience, format, and topic affected the voice of the writing.

Apply

8. Tell students to consider the R.A.F.T. strategy as they plan their writing. Provide students with *The Voice of R.A.F.T. Notebook Entry* (page 209). Remind students that a strong and clear voice is what makes their writing unique from any other author's.

Write/Conference

9. Assist groups that require additional support with getting started. Then, support other groups, returning to guide the small group onto the next task. Note observations in your Conferring Notebook for future reference.

Spotlight Strategy

10. Spotlight students who created a piece of writing using the R.A.F.T. strategy. For example, "Incredible! Just listen to the voice in Frank's writing. I know so much about these characters already."

Share

11. Have writers meet in small groups and share sections of their own writing that show voice.

Homework

Ask students to listen to a commercial advertisement or read a story. Ask them to think about R.A.F.T. and how it affects an author's voice.

The Voice of R.A.F.T. Notebook Entry

The Voice of R.A.F.T.

As authors plan and organize their writing, **R.A.F.T.** helps answer the following questions.

Role of the writer: Who are you as the writer?

Audience: To whom are you writing?

Format: In what format are you writing?

Topic: What are you writing about?

Your Turn:

Use the R.A.F.T. chart below to practice organizing and adding voice to your writing.

Role	Audience	Format	Topic
yourself	yourself	letter	your interests
child	grandparents	thank you note	current events
teacher	parents	news article	science
coach	the public	eulogy	social studies
reporter	Earth	speech	stories you have read or topics you have read about
historical figure	the ocean	editorial	
famous person	judge	testimonial	health
police officer	friends	comic	environment
animal	scientists	poem	family
plant	artists	song	"I wonder" questions
nonhuman object	fairy tale character	paragraph	
sibling	president	story	
	pet	brochure	
		instructions	
		want ad	

If I Were A...

Standard

Uses descriptive language that clarifies and enhances ideas

Materials

- *If I Were A… Notebook Entry* (page 212; ifiwerea.pdf)
- Writer's Notebooks

Mentor Texts

- *Voices in the Park* by Anthony Browne
- *I Am the Dog, I Am the Cat* by Donald Hall
- *Sweet Tooth* by Margie Palatini
- *Two Bad Ants* by Chris Van Allsburg
- See *Mentor Text List* in Appendix C for other suggestions.

Procedures

Note: Teach students that voice can be found in all genres of literature. Use familiar stories to discuss voice. Repeat this lesson often with a variety of texts.

Think About Writing

1. Explain to students that voice is the way that an author speaks on paper. Tell students that the voice of a text sometimes depends on the style of the writing. An author can be serious, formal, chatty, or even funny to give the writing different voices. Explain to students that reading favorite authors exposes them to different voices and allows them to try out their techniques.

2. Review mentor texts, if desired, and compare the various uses of voice.

Teach

3. Tell students, "We will explore how voice is developed through a character's point of view, or their perspective." Share the example of *Sweet Tooth* by Margie Palatini, a funny story told from the tooth's perspective, that is filled with voice.

4. Share parts of the text that exemplify voice. Ask students questions to help them identify these elements of the story:

   How did Palatini create a character from a tooth?

   What is the tooth's personality?

   How do we know?

   What problem does the tooth have?

   What are the consequences in the story?

   How does Palatini use words and phrases to create humor and interest?

If I Were A... (cont.)

Engage

5. Tell students that they will be practicing how to incorporate voice in their writing by drafting a short passage from the perspective of an object or animal. Have students work in pairs. Tell students to brainstorm with their partner and think about subjects for their passages. Have pairs discuss the setting, characteristics, problems and solutions, consequences of actions, etc. You may wish to brainstorm a class list of possible subjects for writing.

Apply

6. Have students practice giving their writing personality and voice to keep readers interested and to keep the writing lively. Provide students with the *If I Were A… Notebook Entry* (page 212). Have students complete the *Your Turn* section.

Write/Conference

7. Gather a small group of writers who may need additional support. Assist them with getting started, then rove and support others, returning to move small groups onto the next task. Note observations in your Conferring Notebook for future reference.

Spotlight Strategy

8. Spotlight students who are writing interesting characters with distinctive perspectives and voices.

Share

9. Ask students to find a new partner to share with today. Ask students to try to identify the character from the writing. Encourage them to listen closely to the voice of the story. Is it true to the character?

Homework

Ask students to make observations about interesting subjects for writing. Ask them to consider different points of view, such as a parent's, brother's, sister's, baby's, etc. Have students add their observations to their Writer's Notebooks.

If I Were A... Notebook Entry

If I Were A...

Authors use **voice** to speak to their readers. The characters they choose and the words and phrases they select all contribute to an author's style of writing. An author's voice may be serious, formal, chatty, or even humorous.

A character or narrator may evoke the voice of the author. As readers, we read to find out their perspective or point of view. Use these questions to begin thinking about adding voice to your own writing:

- What is the character's personality?

- What are the character's likes? Dislikes?

- What does the character need or want? Why?

- Is there a problem? How will the character solve the problem? What are the consequences of the problem?

Your Turn:

Choose an animal, plant, or object, and bring it to life! Write a story from the point of view of your choice. Give it a voice. Let your reader understand and feel what it is like to be that animal, plant, or object. For example, if the subject is "shoes," the voice of "flip-flops" is very different from the voice of "hiking boots." Select from the list below or pick your own subject.

• shoe s	• car	• cell phone
• cake	• nature	• school supply
• insect	• shark	• sports equipment
• body part	• food	• candy
• clothing	• baby	• silverware

#50920—*Getting to the Core of Writing—Level 6* © Shell Education

A Writer's Toolbox for Voice

Standard

Uses content, style, and structure appropriate for specific audiences and purposes

Materials

- *A Writer's Toolbox for Voice Notebook Entry* (page 215; toolbox.pdf)
- Writer's Notebooks

Mentor Texts

- *Voices in the Park* by Anthony Browne
- *Marshfield Dreams: When I Was a Kid* by Ralph Fletcher
- *Twilight Comes Twice* by Ralph Fletcher
- *Caves* by Stephen Kramer
- *The Ghost Dance* by Alice McLerran
- See *Mentor Text List* in Appendix C for other suggestions.

Procedures

Note: Although many find voice difficult to teach, exposing students to quality literature gives them opportunities to find the author speaking to them from the page.

Think About Writing

1. Introduce the idea that just as people say things using different words and expressions, so do writers as they develop their own distinct voice. Explain to students that the way they share their messages on paper will bring out their unique voice in writing.

2. Review mentor texts, if desired, and compare the various uses of voice.

Teach

3. Tell students, "Authors use a variety of tools for creating a unique voice in any piece of writing. There are several to choose from, so remember to be selective and only choose those tools you need for that particular piece of writing."

4. Display the voice tools that can be found on the *A Writer's Toolbox for Voice Notebook Entry* (page 215). Discuss usage and examples related to each. Talk about the use of the tools in students' own writing.

   - Which tool would be useful for the writing you are doing?
   - Which tool is the most challenging for you?
   - What book or author is a good example of one of these types of tools?

A Writer's Toolbox for Voice *(cont.)*

Engage

5. Have students talk in pairs about which tool(s) they plan to try in their writing. Listen and observe the student pairs so you can share a few observations with students. Share ideas with the whole class.

Apply

6. Remind students that voice is the personal thumbprint of an author. Provide students with *A Writer's Toolbox for Voice Notebook Entry*. Have students complete the *Your Turn* section. Have students use the toolbox to select strategies for adding voice to their writing.

Write/Conference

7. Gather a small group of writers who may need additional support. Assist them with selecting a tool to try in their own writing. Make observations in your Conferring Notebook.

Spotlight Strategy

8. Spotlight students who are incorporating a tool in their own writing. For example, "Spotlight on Carissa. Listen to how she used this tool to add a clear voice to her writing."

Share

9. Have students share a section of their writing that demonstrates the use of a voice tool. Challenge others to identify the tool or strategy that was used to create voice in the text.

Homework

Ask students to make observations of voice from language used at home. Have them add these observations to their Writer's Notebooks to support future writing projects.

A Writer's Toolbox for Voice Notebook Entry

A Writer's Toolbox for Voice

Authors use a variety of tools to create a unique voice in any piece of writing. There are several to choose from, so remember to be selective and only choose the tools you need for that particular piece of writing. Each of these tools can support you as you begin developing voice in your writing. Remember, your writing should reflect you and your personality.

The Reader Tool: Who is your audience?

Choose a style and voice appropriate for your intended reader. A note to Grandma will sound different from a note to your best friend.

The Topic Tool: What do you love? What are your interests?

Use topics in your writing that you know the most about or topics that you care deeply about, and voice will naturally be a part of your writing.

The Style Tool: What is the purpose and style of your writing?

Will the words and phrases you use reflect a funny story? A persuasive letter? Will your words be serious? Poetic? Scientific? Informative? Sympathetic? Friendly?

The Narrator/Character Tool: What are traits of your narrator and/or character(s)?

Is the character a star athlete? A brave sailor? A historical figure? A person of great wealth? Scared? Bossy? Homeless? Sick and weak? Caring? Jolly?

The Dialogue Tool: What does the narrator/character sound like?

Let the dialogue show the culture, personality, and emotions of your character. Pretend you are that person speaking.

Your Turn:

Use these tools to enhance the voice in your writing. In your Writer's Notebook, keep a continuous record of authors and texts that represent these voice tools.

Conventions
Checking Your Writing

Writing that does not follow standard conventions is difficult to read. The use of correct capitalization, punctuation, spelling, and grammar is what makes writing consistent and easy to read. Students need to have reasonable control over the conventions of writing. This section provides mini-lessons that guide students and help them internalize conventions as they write and check their work for conventions. Lessons in this section include the following:

- Lesson 1: Commonly Misspelled Words (page 219)
- Lesson 2: Punctuation Partners (page 224)
- Lesson 3: The Sensational Six (page 227)
- Lesson 4: Boot Camp Caps Chant (page 231)
- Lesson 5: Presenting SOP Pronouns (page 234)
- Lesson 6: The CUPS Challenge (page 237)
- Lesson 7: What's the Difference? (page 241)
- Lesson 8: Time to Edit! (page 244)

The *Callie, Super Conventions Checker* poster (page 218) can be displayed in the room to provide a visual reminder for students that conventions is one of the traits of writing. You may wish to introduce this poster during the first lesson on conventions. Then, refer to the poster when teaching other lessons on conventions to refresh students' memories and provide questions to help guide them as they make an effort to use correct conventions in their writing.

Callie
Super Conventions Checker

How do I edit my paper?

❞ Did I check for capitalization and punctuation?

❞ Did I use the correct grammar?

❞ Did I spell words conventionally?

❞ Did I reread for accuracy?

❞ Is my draft ready for publishing?

Commonly Misspelled Words

Standard

Uses conventions of spelling in written compositions

Materials

- Chart paper
- Markers
- *Commonly Misspelled Words* (pages 222–223; misspelled.pdf)
- *Commonly Misspelled Words Notebook Entry* (page 221; commonlymisspelled.pdf)
- Writer's Notebooks

Mentor Texts

- *Woe Is I Jr.: The Younger Grammarphobe's Guide to Better English in Plain English* by Patricia O'Conner
- See *Mentor Text List* in Appendix C for other suggestions.

Procedures

Note: Consult *Teaching Kids to Spell* as an additional teaching resource as you discuss spelling strategies (Gentry and Gillet 1993). Help students learn spelling strategies by keeping a list of commonly misspelled words to use during instruction.

Think About Writing

1. Explain that correctly spelling words helps readers understand what they are reading. The rules of spelling help people know they are communicating about the same things. Tell students that authors who pay close attention to spelling are not hindered in their writing process but are instead more effective in conveying their messages.

2. Review mentor texts, if desired, and emphasize how proper spelling makes the writing and reading process more enjoyable.

Teach

3. Tell students, "Today we will explore a strategy for reading and understanding commonly misspelled words. It is called *Analyze, Visualize, and Spell.*"

4. Choose a few words from the *Commonly Misspelled Words* (pages 222–223), write them on chart paper, and model the strategy:

   Analyze

   Step 1: Say the word in syllables.

   Step 2: What sounds, chunks, or patterns do you see and hear? Is the word related to another word that you know how to spell?

   Step 3: Listen for and notice prefixes and suffixes.

   Visualize

   Step 1: Have you read or seen the word before? Is it spelled like another word you know?

   Step 2: How are the letters arranged? What does it look like?

commonly Misspelled Words *(cont.)*

Spell

Step 1: Write the word.

Step 2: Check it using available reference resources, such as spell checker, a dictionary, or the Internet.

Engage

5. Divide the class into small groups. Tell students that they are going to work together in their groups to practice using the new strategy of *Analyze, Visualize,* and *Spell*.

   Display the following sentence:

   We viseted the Navy Peir and perchased a few comik books.

   If necessary, assist students in identifying the misspelled words. Then, monitor and support groups as they practice the spelling strategy. Allow students to share results and discuss how the new strategy assisted in their spelling.

Apply

6. Tell students that they will analyze misspelled words to improve their own writing. Provide students with the *Commonly Misspelled Words Notebook Entry* (page 221) and have them practice using the *Analyze, Visualize,* and *Spell* strategy. Students can also examine their writing projects for spelling revisions.

Write/Conference

7. Have students begin to practice this strategy in their own writing. Support students needing further assistance with more explicit instruction.

Spotlight Strategy

8. Spotlight one or two writers who are working hard and paying attention to letter patterns in challenging vocabulary words.

Share

9. Ask students to turn to the person sitting closest and discuss a difficult word that they spelled correctly and how they did it.

Homework

Ask students to teach someone at home this new strategy for spelling. Then, students can locate a text that has been written by a family member and edit it for spelling.

Commonly Misspelled Words Notebook Entry

Commonly Misspelled Words

Learning to identify and revise misspelled words is a valuable strategy in writing. Be aware of the words you write, and increase your vocabulary to make your writing more interesting.

Analyze

> Step 1: Say the word in syllables.
>
> Step 2: What sounds, chunks, or patterns do you see and hear? Is the word related to another word that you know how to spell?
>
> Step 3: Listen for and notice prefixes and suffixes.

Visualize

> Step 1: Have you read or seen the word before? Is it spelled like another word you know?
>
> Step 2: How are the letters arranged? What does it look like?

Spell

> Step 1: Write the word.
>
> Step 2: Check it using available reference resources, such as spell checker, a dictionary, or the Internet.

Your Turn:

Use *Analyze*, *Visualize*, and *Spell* with the following commonly misspelled words. Examine your writing and edit for spelling.

- selebrat
- speshal
- beutiful
- becuz
- muzeeum
- garintee

Commonly Misspelled Words

Directions: Model how to spell the words below using the *Analyze, Visualize,* and *Spell* strategy.

actually	especially	really
a lot	everything	receive
already	excellent	separate
apologize	excitement	successfully
attitude	favorite	surprise
basically	finally	they
beautiful	friend	through
because	grammar	tomorrow

#50920—*Getting to the Core of Writing—Level 6* © Shell Education

Commonly Misspelled Words (cont.)

believe	doesn't	necessary
calendar	guaranteed	probably
canceled	instead	realistic
college	library	until
courageous	lying	usually
decision	mischievous	vegetable
different	museum	Wednesday

Punctuation Partners

Standard
Uses conventions of punctuation in written compositions

Materials
- Chart paper
- Markers
- Language arts textbooks or other classroom texts
- *Punctuation Partners Notebook Entry* (page 226; punctuation.pdf)
- Writer's Notebooks

Mentor Texts
- *Those Shoes* by Maribeth Boelts
- *Home Run* by Robert Burleigh
- *The Book of "Unnecessary" Quotation Marks: A Celebration of Creative Punctuation* by Bethany Keeley
- *Eats, Shoots & Leaves: Why, Commas Really Do Make a Difference!* by Lynne Truss
- *Freedom Summer* by Deborah Wiles
- See *Mentor Text List* in Appendix C for other suggestions.

Procedures
Note: It is important to review commas, parentheses, and dashes as some students may not have mastery of previous conventions.

Think About Writing
1. Explain that authors work hard to use punctuation correctly, but they also want to include punctuation to emphasize and clarify their stories.

2. Review mentor texts, if desired, and emphasize how punctuation clarifies and focuses ideas.

Teach
3. Tell students, "Today we will review some rules of punctuation and then focus on other appropriate conventions—commas, dashes, and parentheses." Explain that authors use different punctuation marks in their writing for specific purposes.

4. Using a sheet of chart paper, quickly review ending punctuation, quotation marks, ellipses, colons, and semicolons. Then, introduce commas, dashes, and parentheses using the following information and showing examples from familiar texts and mentor texts:

   - *Commas* are used to set off a parenthetical element, to separate items in a series or after an introductory phrase, and to show separation of two independent clauses.

   - *Dashes* are used to indicate a brief interruption, a change of thought, the adding of additional information, or a parenthetical statement.

   - *Parentheses* are used to clarify information or add a personal thought.

Punctuation Partners *(cont.)*

Engage

5. In triads, have students review the uses of commas, dashes, and parentheses. Each student in the group will select a type of punctuation, state its purpose, and give an example of how it might be used in a sentence.

6. Have the triads work together to browse texts (a language arts textbook or other texts). Ask them to look for ways in which authors have used commas, dashes, or parentheses. When students are finished, gather their examples and record them on chart paper.

Apply

7. Tell students that they will practice using punctuation correctly to improve their own writing. Provide students with the *Punctuation Partners Notebook Entry* (page 226) and have them write sentences using commas, dashes, and parentheses.

Write/Conference

8. Provide time for students to examine their own writing projects for punctuation revisions. Monitor editing work.

Spotlight Strategy

9. Spotlight students that are identifying and using different types of punctuation correctly. For example, "You have found excellent examples of our three punctuation marks for today."

Share

10. Have students meet in pairs and work as peer editors. Students can read each other's writing and comment on the use of punctuation.

Homework

Ask students to look for examples of commas, dashes, and parentheses in newspapers, magazines, on the Internet, or in any other available print. Have students record why they think the authors used the punctuation.

Punctuation Partners Notebook Entry

Punctuation Partners

Authors use **punctuation** to emphasize and clarify their writing. They carefully select and place **commas**, **dashes**, and **parentheses** to add tone and style.

Use punctuation like commas, dashes, and parentheses carefully in your writing. They alert readers to details and thoughts important to your message. When used too frequently, they lose meaningful emphasis. They can also confuse readers. For example, think about the use of commas in these two sentences:

Let's eat Grandma.   OR   Let's eat, Grandma.

Commas
A break in a sentence: *Mrs. Dale, my former principal, moved to the beach.*
A list of items: *In my flower basket, I requested roses, lilies, and mums.*
An introductory phrase: *Before he left for dinner, John called to make reservations.*
Independent clauses: *Michael went to Chicago, but he forgot his suitcase.*

Dashes
A dramatic pause to emphasize information: *I begged him to tell me something—anything.*
Don't think about it—just leave!

Parentheses
Set off useful information that is not essential to the meaning of the sentence:
You will need to bring a beach towel and sunscreen (the higher the SPF the better!).

Your Turn:
Refer to the examples above and write your own sentences using commas, dashes, and parentheses.

#50920—Getting to the Core of Writing—Level 6 © Shell Education

The Sensational Six

Standard
Uses conventions of spelling in written compositions

Materials
- Chart paper
- Markers
- *Six Syllable Rules Cards* (page 230; sixcards.pdf)
- *The Sensational Six Notebook Entry* (page 229; sensationalsix.pdf)
- Writer's Notebooks

Mentor Texts
- *100 Words to Make You Sound Smart* by the editors of the American Heritage Dictionaries
- *100 Words Every Middle Schooler Should Know* by the editors of the American Heritage Dictionaries
- See *Mentor Text List* in Appendix C for other suggestions.

Procedures
Note: Many students struggle to read and write multisyllabic words. Post the six syllable rules on chart paper. Have students collect different words with syllable patterns, and analyze and add them to the chart throughout the year.

Think About Writing
1. Explain to students that authors use vivid and colorful language to clarify and expand ideas. Tell them that too often young writers use only short words that they know how to spell, thus limiting their use of rich, scholarly, descriptive language. Share with them that this lesson will help them develop the skills to spell and write multisyllabic words.

2. Review mentor texts, if desired, and note the use of multisyllabic words.

Teach
3. Tell students "Today we will review the six syllable rules." Then, explain that they will learn to use a strategy for spelling multisyllabic words. The strategy includes saying each word slowly, repeating each syllable in a soft voice, and writing the word out syllable by syllable.

4. Using chart paper, model writing each selected word below, syllable by syllable. Work as a group to check for accuracy.

CVC: closed syllable	**riv**/er, **fas**/ci/na/tion
CV: open syllable	**hi**/ber/**na**/tion
CVCe: long vowel/silent e	in/com/p**lete**
Vr-controlled: vowel + r	in/**fir**m/a/ry
V teams: ee, oa, ai, ea	en/ter/**tai**n
C/le: consonant + le	in/op/er/a/**ble**

The Sensational Six *(cont.)*

Engage

5. Have students work in pairs to review the six syllable rules using the *Six Syllable Rules Cards* (page 230) as a resource tool. Ask students to recite the rule and provide an example for each rule.

Apply

6. Provide students with *The Sensational Six Notebook Entry* (page 229) to add to their Writer's Notebook. Have students work on the *Your Turn* section before proceeding to their writing folders.

Write/Conference

7. Pull a small intervention group and provide additional practice using the notebook entry.

Spotlight Strategy

8. Spotlight students who are correctly incorporating the rules in their writing. For example, "May I call attention to those students who have followed the instructions and are working on spelling multisyllabic words? Smart spelling work!"

Share

9. Have students circulate around the room and look at others' work.

Homework

Ask students to make a list of words that can be added to their Writer's Notebooks to increase the level of their vocabulary. Students can ask family members to recommend words.

The Sensational Six Notebook Entry

The Sensational Six

Authors use strategies like the Six Syllable Rules to spell new words they want to use in their writing.

Rule 1: CVC/closed syllable Syllable ends with a consonant, vowel is short hat rab/bit	**Rule 2: CV/open syllable** Syllable ends with a vowel, the vowel is long me ta/ble
Rule 3: CVCe Syllable has one vowel, one consonant, and *e*, the vowel sound is long home com/plete	**Rule 4: VR/r-controlled** Syllable has vowels or vowel digraphs followed by *r*, the vowel sound is changed by "r": ar, er, ir, or, ur, air, eer, ear chair or/der
Rule 5: Vowel teams Syllable has two vowels, the vowel is usually the long sound of the first letter: ee, ea, ai, oa ex/plain re/deem	**Rule 6: Consonant -le** Syllable has a consonant followed by "le" peo/ple gen/tle

Spelling Procedure

Say the word at least two times (*unreliable*).

Say each syllable. Listen to the first syllable. (*un/re/li/a/ble*)

Write the first syllable (*un*).

Slide your finger through the syllable and read it.

Repeat with each syllable in the word.

Loop your finger under each syllable and blend.

Say the word.

Your Turn:

Practice the spelling procedure using the following words: *superabundant, translation, reproductive, department, turpentine, microscope, correlate.*

Six Syllable Rules Cards

Directions: Cut out the cards. Distribute the cards to students and have them create additional examples for each rule.

CVC/closed syllable

Syllable ends with a consonant, vowel is short

hat	ri/ver
run	let/ter
bet	re/spect

CVCe

Syllable has one vowel, one consonant, and e, the vowel sound is long

take	com/pete
came	des/pite
vine	ig/nite

CV/open syllable

Syllable ends with a vowel, the vowel is long

he	ta/ble
so	ce/dar
she	ci/der

VR/r-controlled

Syllable has vowels or vowel digraphs followed by *r*, the vowel sound is changed by "r": ar, er, ir, or, ur, air, eer, ear

or	or/der
ar	far/mer
ur	fur/nish
air	chair
er	dress/er
ir	sou/ve/nir
ear	near
eer	pi/o/neer

Vowel teams

Syllable has two vowels, the vowel is usually the long sound of the first letter: ee, ea, ai, oa

ee	wheel/chair
ea	pea/nut
ai	com/plain
oa	road/side

Consonant -le

Syllable has a consonant followed by "le"

peo/ple
tem/ple
re/spon/si/ble
gen/tle
sta/ble

Boot Camp Caps Chant

Standard
Uses conventions of capitalization in written compositions

Materials
- Chart paper
- Markers
- *Boot Camp Caps Chant Notebook Entry* (page 233; capschant.pdf)
- Writer's Notebooks

Mentor Texts
- *A Swiftly Tilting Planet* by Madeleine L'Engle
- *Missing May* by Cynthia Rylant
- See *Mentor Text List* in Appendix C for other suggestions.

Procedures
Note: Using chants, raps, and music helps bring engagement, motivation, and joy to classroom learning.

Think About Writing
1. Remind students that certain rules of capitalization must be followed. Knowing which words require capital letters makes writing look clean and polished.
2. Review mentor texts, if desired, and emphasize the use of proper capitalization.

Teach
3. Tell students that they will learn a chant today. Explain that a chant is a song with repeated phrases. Tell them you will be the leader and they will repeat everything you say. Share the real-world example of a boot camp chant in which military personnel repeat the phrases from a person of authority.
4. Ask students to listen for the rules of capitalization in the chant. Think aloud about why an author would want to use capital letters correctly when writing.

Engage
5. Use the chant on the *Boot Camp Caps Chant Notebook Entry* (page 233) and ask students to repeat each line back. Then, use chart paper to make a list of rules and examples from the chant.

Capitalization Rules	Examples
First word in a sentence and all proper nouns	**L**ast week, **J**oey and **I** made an apple pie.
Days of the week and months of the year	Every **T**uesday in **J**une I play basketball.
Names of cities, states, and countries	I live in **S**an **A**ntonio, **T**exas.
Important words in titles	*The Adventures of Tom Sawyer.*
Places and holidays	On **M**emorial **D**ay, we are going to **D**isney **W**orld.

Boot Camp Caps Chant *(cont.)*

Apply

6. Provide students with the *Boot Camp Caps Chant Notebook Entry* to add to their Writer's Notebook. Have students work on the *Your Turn* section before proceeding to their writing folders. Have them follow the rules of capitalization in their own writing.

Write/Conference

7. Work with a small group and focus on one or two rules only. Find the skills that are easily confused or forgotten and focus on those skills.

Spotlight Strategy

8. Find and spotlight one or two students who correctly edited for capitalization.

Share

9. Ask students to share their writing in pairs and go over their changes. Encourage students to discuss, reflect, and question the use of capital letters.

Homework

Ask students to share the Boot Camp Caps Chant with family members. Have them also share the important rules that they learned from the chant.

Boot Camp Caps Chant Notebook Entry

Boot Camp Caps Chant

(Repeat each line.)

I don't know but I've been told.

Sixth grade writers are really bold.

We know the rules of the capital game.

That's why writing will bring us fame.

The beginning of a sentence and the pronoun "I,"

ALWAYS need a capital, don't deny!

Days of the week and months of the year,

Names and titles need capitals, dear!

Capitalize names of special places,

Cities and states need upper cases.

We're gonna do our very best,

To capitalize words on every test!

C. A. P. I. T. A. L.

These Capital Rules will serve us well!

Your Turn:

Use the capitalization rules to make any necessary corrections in your Writer's Notebook. Then, edit for capitalization in your writing folder.

Presenting SOP Pronouns

Standard

Uses pronouns in written compositions

Materials

- Chart paper
- Markers
- *Presenting SOP Pronouns Notebook Entry* (page 236; pronouns.pdf)
- Writer's Notebooks
- Index cards

Mentor Texts

- *I and You and Don't Forget Who: What Is a Pronoun?* by Brian Cleary
- *Mine, All Mine* by Ruth Heller
- *If You Were a Pronoun* by Nancy Loewen
- *Woe Is I, Jr.: The Younger Grammarphobes' Guide to Better English in Plain English* by Patricia O'Conner
- See *Mentor Text List* in Appendix C for other suggestions.

Procedures

Note: Correcting incorrect speech patterns requires effort and repetition. Revisit, repeat, and reflect on this lesson often. Model the mini-lesson for specific pronoun usage.

Think About Writing

1. Tell students that pronouns are words that people sometimes use incorrectly. Explain that pronouns make speaking and writing more efficient. An author can use the word *he* instead of repeatedly writing *Jimmy's best friend's neighbor's dad*. Tell students that they are going to practice how to use pronouns.

2. Review mentor texts, if desired, and emphasize the efficiency of using pronouns in place of longer nouns.

Teach

3. Tell students that there are several different types of pronouns in our language, but today they will focus on three types of personal pronouns: **S**ubjective, **O**bjective, and **P**ossessive—SOP. Explain that SOP is an acronym they can use to remember personal pronouns and their antecedents

4. Remind students that an antecedent is the noun being replaced with a pronoun. Remind them that pronouns must match the antecedent in both number (singular/plural) and gender.

5. Provide examples of the three types of personal pronouns. Write SOP on chart paper and share information about personal pronouns and record notes on the chart paper:

   - *Subjective pronouns* serve as the subject of the sentence and replace a noun, the antecedent. These include *I, she, he, we, you, they, it,* and *who*.

   - *Objective pronouns* receive the effect of the action and usually follow a verb or a preposition. These include *me, you, him, her, it, us, them,* and *whom*.

Presenting SOP Pronouns *(cont.)*

- *Possessive pronouns* show ownership of a person/people or thing/things, the antecedents. These include *my, your, his, her, its, our, their* (used before a noun); and *mine, yours, his, hers, ours, yours,* and *theirs* (used alone).

Engage

6. Ask students to work in pairs and review the acronym SOP to recall the three types of personal nouns. Have pairs go back and forth to see how many pronouns can be shared that represent each type.

Apply

7. Provide students with the *Presenting SOP Pronouns Notebook Entry* (page 236) to add to their Writer's Notebook. Have students work on the *Your Turn* section before proceeding to their writing folders. Have them incorporate pronouns in their own writing.

Write/Conference

8. Select groups of students who may need reinforcement of the skills introduced in this lesson. Create index cards that have SOP pronouns written on each card. Have students create accurate sentences using the pronouns on the cards.

Spotlight Strategy

9. Spotlight students who are accurately using pronouns. For example, "You used that pronoun correctly! I knew exactly who you were referring to in your sentence."

Share

10. Have students work in triads to share examples of how they incorporated personal pronouns in their writing.

Homework

Ask students to share what they have learned with parents and to write three sentences with one subjective, one objective, and one possessive pronoun. Have them bring the sentences to class to share with the group.

Presenting SOP Pronouns Notebook Entry

Presenting SOP Pronouns

Authors use **pronouns** in their writing to reduce monotonous repetition and add clarity. Remember, there are several different types of pronouns in our language, but focus on three types of personal pronouns: *Subjective*, *Objective*, and *Possessive*. Remember them with the acronym SOP!

Subjective pronouns serve as the subject of the sentence and replace a noun, the antecedent. These include *I*, *she*, *he*, *we*, *you*, *they*, *it*, and *who*.

Jackie and <u>I</u> plan to attend the conference in 2013.

Objective pronouns receive the effect of the action and usually follow a verb or a preposition. These include *me*, *you*, *him*, *her*, *it*, *us*, *them*, and *whom*.

The accident frightened <u>her</u> because the deer was injured.

Possessive pronouns show ownership of a person/people or thing/things, the antecedents. These include *my*, *your*, *his*, *her*, *its*, *our*, *their* (used before a noun); and *mine*, *yours*, *his*, *hers*, *ours*, *yours*, and *theirs* (used alone).

Jessie borrowed <u>my</u> baseball cleats for practice.

Those gym shoes are <u>mine</u>.

Remember, an **antecedent** is the noun being replaced with a pronoun.

Your Turn:

Use the sentences above as models to create your own SOP sentences in your Writer's Notebook. Look at your current writing and edit for correct usage of personal pronouns.

The CUPS Challenge

Standard

Uses conventions of spelling, capitalization, and punctuation in written compositions

Materials

- Chart paper
- Markers
- *The CUPS Challenge Writing Sample* (page 240; cupssample.pdf)
- Colored pencils (green, orange, red, blue)
- *The CUPS Challenge Notebook Entry* (page 239; cupschallenge.pdf)
- Writer's Notebooks

Mentor Texts

- CCSS and literature from Core Reading Program
- See *Mentor Text List* in Appendix C for other suggestions.

Procedures

Note: This lesson needs repetition to build automaticity in finding errors in capitalization, grammar, usage, punctuation, and spelling. Challenge students to edit their work before turning it in.

Think About Writing

1. Explain to students that they have reviewed and learned rules for using correct capitalization, punctuation, grammar, and spelling. Tell them that as beginning authors, it is important to have expectations and procedures for editing work before it is available for readers. Although the content of their writing may be interesting and engaging, numerous incorrect conventions can prevent a reader from enjoying the message.

Teach

2. Explain to students that they will review using editing skills to help correct errors in their writing. Write the acronym CUPS down the side of a sheet of chart paper. Review the following and record notes for students to review:

    C: Capital Letters. "Boot Camp Caps Chant" refers to rules of capitalization.

    U: Usage of Grammar. Grammar rules include subject/verb agreement and using correct pronouns.

    P: Punctuation. "Punctuation Partners" refers to basic punctuation, such as commas, parentheses, and dashes.

    S: Spelling. "The Sensational Six" helps us read and write multisyllabic words.

The CUPS Challenge (cont.)

3. Tell students that they will follow a procedure for editing a writing sample.

   Green: Circle the first letter in each sentence, proper nouns, and any other word(s) that need capitals.

   Orange: Underline incorrect grammar usage.

   Red: Place a red circle around incorrect punctuation: periods, question marks, exclamation points, quotation marks, commas, parentheses, or dashes.

   Blue: Circle any misspelled words and make corrections above the misspelled words.

   Model how to use these colors and methods to mark a writing sample and make edits.

Engage

4. Divide students into quads. Each student will receive a copy of the *CUPS Challenge Writing Sample* (page 240) and a colored pencil. Tell students that the color of pencil dictates their job in the group. Encourage students to use the class chart for support. When they are finished, work together as a group and compile all corrections onto a final sample.

Apply

5. The CUPS checklist can be used to publish any writing that will be viewed in public. Provide students with *The CUPS Challenge Notebook Entry* (page 239) to add to their Writer's Notebook. Have them use the list to help them edit their own writing.

Write/Conference

6. Provide time for students to review writing and make changes. Circulate around the room and help students who need it.

Spotlight Strategy

7. Spotlight everyone for working hard to learn editing skills. For example, "Good for you for making those changes. These edits will make your writing easier to read and understand!"

Share

8. Select a few students to share excerpts from edited writing samples.

Homework

Have students choose drafts from their writing folders to take home. Ask them to each work with a sibling or parent to edit a writing sample so that it is completely free of errors.

The CUPS Challenge Notebook Entry

The CUPS Challenge

It is important to have expectations and procedures for editing your writing before it is available for readers. Authors know that incorrect conventions can affect their readers' opinion of their writing, even if the content is engaging and interesting. Use the CUPS Challenge when editing your writing.

C: Capitalization

Green: Circle the first letter in each sentence, proper nouns, and any other word(s) needing capitals.

U: Usage of Grammar

Orange: Underline incorrect grammar usage.

P: Punctuation Guidelines

Red: Place a red circle around incorrect punctuation: periods, question marks, exclamation points, quotation marks, commas, parentheses, or dashes.

S: Spelling

Blue: Circle any misspelled words, and make corrections above the misspelled word.

Your Turn:

Select writing from your folder. Practice editing using the CUPS Challenge. Challenge a partner and exchange papers for editing.

Name: _____ Date: _____

The CUPS Challenge Writing Sample

Directions: Read the paper below. Analyze it! With your group, check for accuracy in capitalization, usage of grammar, punctuation, and spelling. After editing for capitalization, place a check next to the letter it represents. Continue to edit for usage of grammar, punctuation, and spelling and check off the appropriate letters.

The perfekt summer day

can you gues how I spended a perfekt summer day. I am picnic with my famile and frends at the park? we wach fireworks and wear speshal blinking necklases and braslets. when the sun dips behind the horizon the blinking necklases and baslets glow in the dark.

kids jump up and down on a trampoleen while the adults cook hambergers on the grill. The smell of smoke from the grill tickles our noses and make us hunger for the food   At the picnic table the food is cover with cloths to keep flies from gathring on the potato salid sliced tomatos and onions are ready to load on the hamberger buns

the smell of bug sprae permeats the air and mosquitoes are disapearing Into the ground. at last, mom shout, foods on the table. Come and git It   all the kids rush to the table and sat quietle weighting for the adults to have a silent moment. then the excited chatter begin   soon the meal would be over and the firewerks would began the darknes begin to wrap arms aroud us and the fontain display exploded into the air. with a sense of awe and exhawstion our perfekt summer day end with a sigh and sense of expectation for our fuchure perfekt summer day.

C _____

U _____

P _____

S _____

#50920—*Getting to the Core of Writing—Level 6* © Shell Education

What's the Difference?

Standard

Uses conventions of spelling in written compositions

Materials

- Chart paper
- Markers
- *What's the Difference? Notebook Entry* (page 243; difference.pdf)
- Writer's Notebooks

Mentor Texts

- *Grammar Girl's 101 Misused Words You'll Never Confuse Again* by Mignon Fogarty
- *If You Were a Homonym or a Homophone* by Nancy Loewen
- *A Dictionary of Homophones* by Leslie Presson
- See *Mentor Text List* in Appendix C for other suggestions.

Procedures

Note: Keep an ongoing list of homophones and other words that are often misused. Add to the list as students find other words that are confusing or closely related to other vocabulary.

Think About Writing

1. Tell students that writers of all ages often confuse words that sound alike but have different meanings. Explain that they will learn how to distinguish between similar words.

Teach

2. Tell students, "We will become familiar with words commonly misused by writers." Explain to students that some of these words are homophones, which are words that sound the same, but are spelled differently and have different meanings.

3. Select a pair of homophones. Using chart paper, show students how to fold a sheet of paper into four equal sections. In the first section of the paper, write the first homophone and a brief definition with a sketch that shows the definition. In the section below, write a sentence that uses the word appropriately. Then, do the same for the other homophone in the other two sections. Model completing this paper for students. Talk about how they can compare the words by looking at the definitions, sketches, and sentences.

What's the Difference? *(cont.)*

Engage

4. Tell students that they will be working in quads. Each group will pick a misused word from the *What's the Difference? Notebook Entry* (page 243). As a group, students will use the homophone pair and complete the four-sectioned paper by having each student complete one section. Students will write the word, provide a definition, sketch a visual representation, and use the word in a sentence. When students are finished, have them share their work with the group.

5. If technology is available, allow students to create and print using clip art and photos as visual representations.

Apply

6. Provide students with the *What's the Difference? Notebook Entry* to add to their Writer's Notebook. Have them recognize words that are commonly misused in writing. Encourage students to add an entry to the notebook to support their writing in the future.

Write/Conference

7. Provide time for students to review their work. Give them time and assistance to understand new and unfamiliar word definitions.

Spotlight Strategy

8. Spotlight students who are able to distinguish between two similar words and then use the words correctly in their own writing.

Share

9. Have students share out with the whole group the ways in which they are able to distinguish between two similar words and how they used a word appropriately in their own writing.

Homework

Ask students to share with their parents how they are able to choose appropriate words for their writing and avoid picking the wrong misused word.

What's the Difference? Notebook Entry

What's the Difference?

Authors are aware of commonly misused words in their writing. If used incorrectly, these words cause confusion for the reader.

Being aware of these words increases your word knowledge and your writing fluency. Remember, some of these words are **homophones**. Homophones are words that sound the same, but are spelled differently and have different meanings.

accept—to receive	except—to leave out
affect—to influence	effect—the result of someting
among—surrounded by	between—in the middle
principal—main; leader of school	principle—attitude or belief
its—belonging to	it's—contraction for "it is"
there—a place or location	their—belonging to someone
than—word used to compare	then—next in order
less—smaller in amount/degree	fewer—smaller in number
bad—adjective; describes noun	badly—adverb; modifies verb
your—belonging to you	you're—contraction for "you are"
farther—a greater distance	further—a greater extent/degree

Your Turn:

Select a word pair from the list below. Write the words, give brief definitions, sketch visual representations, and use the words in a sentence.

past/passed	brake/break	stationary/stationery
threw/through/though	sore/soar	all together/altogether
elicit/illicit	lay/lie	right/write
road/rode/rowed	weather/whether	to/too/two

Time to Edit!

Standard

Uses a variety of strategies to edit written work

Materials

- *Time to Edit! Notebook Entry* (page 246; timetoedit.pdf)
- *Time to Edit! Writing Sample for Editing* (page 247; sampleediting.pdf)
- Writer's Notebooks

Mentor Texts

- *Twilight Comes Twice* by Ralph Fletcher
- *Woe Is I Jr.: The Younger Grammarphobe's Guide to Better English in Plain English* by Patricia O'Conner
- *Twenty-Odd Ducks: Why, Every Punctuation Mark Counts!* by Lynne Truss
- See *Mentor Text List* in Appendix C for other suggestions.

Procedures

Note: Learning to edit takes time and practice. Provide multiple opportunities for students to work in groups, in pairs, and independently to polish and refine writing drafts.

Think About Writing

1. Tell students that all writers make mistakes, but editing makes writing stronger and more focused for readers. Explain to students that they are going to work on building their editing skills.

2. Review mentor texts, if desired, and emphasize the use of correct conventions.

Teach

3. Tell students, "Authors, editors, journalists, and young writers often use a list of universal editing marks for proofreading. You will get to practice using this list." Explain to students that editing written work before publishing it requires time and careful thought.

4. Display the editing symbol chart on the *Time to Edit! Notebook Entry* (page 246). Use the *Time to Edit! Writing Sample* (page 247) or another unedited writing sample to model editing the text. Review each editing mark and how each mark is used to indicate changes to a text. Begin to edit the writing sample, but leave some of it unedited for students to complete.

Time to Edit! *(cont.)*

Engage

5. Provide students with *Time to Edit! Writing Sample for Editing*. Allow them to work in pairs and give them approximately 10 minutes to complete the editing process with a partner. Then, have students come back as a whole group and debrief and reflect. Make notes on your copy of the writing sample as they share out their editing comments.

Apply

6. Provide students with the *Time to Edit! Notebook Entry* to add to their Writer's Notebook. Ask students to select writing samples from their folders and use their notebook entries to support the editing work.

Write/Conference

7. Provide time for students to edit their work. Conduct individual or small-group conferences and support students with the editing process.

Spotlight Strategy

8. Spotlight students who are editing their writing. For example, "You are making this text much more clear and meaningful by editing it."

Share

9. Have students share out with the whole group the kinds of edits they are making based on the list of editing marks. Continue to share this information as students work on editing over the next few days.

Homework

Ask students to share with their parents how authors edit to make writing more powerful. Have students tell their parents how they are editing their own work. Have students get suggestions from their parents about how to improve their writing.

Time to Edit! Notebook Entry

Time to Edit!

Authors and editors use a set of universal editing marks when proofreading writing. Using the same marks helps everyone involved in a project understand the suggested editing needed in the writing.

Editing Mark	Meaning	Example
☰	Capitalize	david gobbled up the grapes.
/	Change to lower case	My mother hugged Me when I Came Home.
⊙	Insert a period	The clouds danced in the sky ⊙
sp ◯	Check spelling	I (laffed) at the story.
∿	Transpose words or letters	How you are?
∧	Add a word or letter	Would you please pass the pizza?
∧,	Insert a comma	I have two cats, two dogs and a goldfish.
˅ ˅	Insert quotation marks	That's amazing, she shouted.
℘	Delete	Will you call call me on the phone tonight?
¶	New paragraph	… in the tree. ¶ After lunch, I spent the day…

#50920—Getting to the Core of Writing—Level 6 © Shell Education

Name:_____ Date:_____

Time to Edit! Writing Sample for Editing

Directions: Read the text below. With your partner, check for accuracy in capitalization, usage of grammar, punctuation, and spelling. Use the correct editing marks as you edit.

what is hot, sandy and tons of fun. you guest it! A summer day at myrtle beach. every

summer my Famile spends a week at our beach Condo, wich is on second row, one block from

the ocean with a spectacular veiw of sailboats and charter fishing boats?

The whitecaps just off the shore crash in the beach bringing driffwood and seeweed to the

coastline. Conch oyster and clam shells, poleshed by the sand and water in many diferent

sizes and shapes warsh up on the shore ice cream carts with melodious tinkling bells pushed

by tan youthful lads and ladies move down the sandy beach!

certainly you can see a hot summer day provides the perfect landscape for a day at the Beach.

join me under an umbrella on the beach

Essential Materials

Create a toolkit of items you can carry around with you as you conference with students. The toolkit can be a shoebox, a plastic tote, or anything you are comfortable carrying around from student to student. Any supplies that will help make your conference run smoothly are appropriate to put in the tote. Suggested items are listed below:

- Teacher Conferring Notebook
- Mentor text(s) used for daily writing lesson (changes regularly)
- Highlighters or highlighting tape (to draw attention to words)
- Scissors, glue, tape, or a small stapler for revision, cutting, pasting, and moving around
- Sticky notes for making suggestions
- Colored pens for editing (green, red, blue, black, orange)
    - Green—capitalization
    - Red—punctuation
    - Blue—spelling
    - Black—inserting
    - Orange—grammar usage
- Whiteboard or magnetic board with markers for modeling
- Correction tape or correction fluid
- Assorted paper

Conferring Notebook
Getting to the Core of Writing

Mini-Lesson Log

Date	Mini-Lesson Instructional Focus

Conference Log

P: Praise—What strategies did I notice the student using independently?

TP: Teaching Point—What teaching point will move this student forward in his or her development as a writer?

Name: Date: P: TP:	Name: Date: P: TP:	Name: Date: P: TP:	Name: Date: P: TP:
Name: Date: P: TP:	Name: Date: P: TP:	Name: Date: P: TP:	Name: Date: P: TP:
Name: Date: P: TP:	Name: Date: P: TP:	Name: Date: P: TP:	Name: Date: P: TP:

Conference Countdown

10 Conversation—The conversation should feel like a friendly chat with the student doing the most talking. Keep in mind, the person doing the most talking is doing the most learning.

9 It's about the WRITER, not the Writing—Teach the strategy that will support the writer after he or she is finished with this particular piece of writing. For example, do not just spell a word for a student, but teach him or her to segment the sounds to spell many words.

8 Focus on the Content—You are not there to simply fix up the conventions of a writing piece. When possible, have the student read the piece aloud before you even look at it and focus purely on the content. It's a challenge!

7 Observe, Praise, Guide, Connect—Establish a routine to become effective and efficient.

6 Begin with Praise!—Everyone likes a compliment. Beginning with a compliment gives students a sense of joy and pride in their work as well as recognizes developing writing skills.

5 Talk Like a Writer to a Writer—Use the language and vocabulary of a writer and respect the student's developmental level of writing.

4 Connect or not to Connect?—When conferring, only make connections to your daily mini-lesson when appropriate for the student's piece of writing.

3 Record and Reflect—Use your Conferring Notebook to monitor the progress of writing in your classroom and individual students. The information is valuable in defining your focus for writing instruction.

2 Variety—Incorporate a variety of activities that meet the multiple learning modalities of your students like varying your conferring group sizes.

1 Be There!—Your face and eyes tell it all. Let students know you truly care about the writing they are sharing with you.

Conferring Step-by-Step

The four phases of a conference structure are:

1. Observe
2. Praise
3. Guide
4. Connect

Observe—Use observation as a chance to build your background knowledge of the writer. During this element of the conference, you will determine what the writer knows and can do independently, and what the writer can do with support, called the zone of proximal development (Vygotsky 1978). Begin by asking yourself:

- What do I already know about this student's developmental level of writing and past writing from my conference notes and previous observations?

- What can I learn from the student's current writing piece and writing behaviors?

- What can I learn through questioning and listening to the writer?

When asking students about their writing work, open-ended questions provide guidance and support for students to begin reflecting on their writing. A closed-ended question, such as, "Is this you in the story?" elicits a simple one- or two-word response. An open-ended question, such as, "What can you tell me about your story?" offers opportunities for the writer to explain and describe ideas, motives, and feelings about his or her work, ultimately gaining clarity and developing a deeper understanding of his or her writing. You might ask the writer:

- So, what are you working on in your writing today?

- What can you tell me about your important writing work?

Through your observation, you should determine a successful writing point and one teaching point that will help this student become a more independent writer. Selecting a teaching point can be daunting as we analyze a young writer's work. Teachers often ask, "How do you know what to work on when there are so many things?" The truth is there is no right answer. Here are some ideas to guide you as you select teaching points:

- Use what you know about the growth of this writer. Where is this writer developmentally?

- Consider what the student is working on at this time. What is the student's focus in his or her writing?

- Use the current writing curriculum and the Common Core State Standards.

- Use what is being taught in mini-lessons and whole-group instruction.

Where we ourselves are as writers, as well as where we are as teachers of writing, greatly affects our decisions. As you become more knowledgeable about the developmental phases of writers and the understanding of quality writing instruction, your decisions become more sophisticated. The more you confer with your writers, the more effective you become at making decisions during conferring. Most importantly, select one teaching point that will support each writer during your conference. Calkins, Hartman, and White (2003) remind us to teach to the writer and not to the writing.

Conferring Step-by-Step *(cont.)*

Praise—Recognize the writer for work well done. Always begin a conference with a positive comment. This praise provides positive feedback intended to identify what the student is doing correctly and to encourage the writer to repeat that accomplishment in future writing. Isolate and identify the successful writing strategy in the student's writing piece. When praises are authentic and specific, they become a teachable moment. Below are some examples of powerful praise:

- "Something I really like that you've done is how you shared the setting with your reader. That's exactly what good writers do!"

- "I see here in your writing you chose to use sophisticated words to give your reader more details in your story. Wonderful words!"

- "Just like the authors we have been studying, you have included descriptive details that help your reader visualize exactly what is happening in your story."

- "I am so impressed with the way you just got right to work and accomplished so much writing in such a short amount of time."

Guide—Personalize and scaffold instruction to meet the writer's needs. The instruction includes sharing the writing strategy you will teach the writer, demonstrating the strategy, and then guiding the writer through practicing the process. Teach the writer a personalized strategy based on your earlier decisions. When the decision is based on a previously taught mini-lesson, writers make additional connections and greater achievement is gained. As part of the routine of the mini-lesson, you must explicitly state what you will teach the student.

- Mentor texts and writing samples are excellent resources to weave into your conference instruction. Writers can visualize the craft you are teaching when they are exposed to concrete examples, particularly from real literature.

- Initial teaching remarks may include, "Let me show you something that good writers do…" and, "Sometimes in my writing, I try to…"

By offering support while the student practices the strategy, you increase the chances of success. Any time you engage students in the application of new strategies, you enhance the probability they will recall that strategy in future writing. Once the writer is engaged in practice, you may move on to confer with another writer. However, leave the writer with expectations until you return, such as, "When I get back, I want to see …" Upon your return, provide specific feedback relative to your expectations. For example, "Well done! Now I really have a picture in my mind of your character."

Conferring Step-by-Step *(cont.)*

Connect—Make connections between teaching and future writing. First, clearly restate what the writer learned and practiced. Then, remind and encourage the writer to use the strategy in future writing. As students become familiar with the conference structure, you may ask the student to share the new learning to get a sense of his or her understanding of your teaching. Making connections may begin as follows:

- "Remember, good writers always…"

- "Tell me what you just learned as a writer."

Writer's Workshop conferences will vary in length and type based on the time of year and the needs of your class. Conferences are most successful when routines and expectations have been established and adolescent writers can manage their own writing time. At the beginning of the year, while establishing routines, drop-by conferences provide a quick glimpse into what each student is working on and what kind of help is needed. Once routines are established, meet with students in individual and/or small-group conferences that are focused around specific needs. You may also include peer conferences, but this requires modeling, experience, and practice. Initially, we use *Compliment and Question*. The compliment should be more than a general statement, such as, "I like your story." It should be specific to the writing, such as, "I like the way you ask a question to begin your story." A question should be something the peer would like to know more about or something that needs clarification.

The conference should be brief and reflect the student's age and development. Small group conferences may be as long as 8–10 minutes as you will be checking in with each student. Hold the conference wherever you prefer. Some teachers prefer moving desk to desk or table to table while others prefer that students join them at a small conference table. Remember these two points:

- *Have a seat!* Wherever you decide to hold your conferences, it is important that students know you are committed to giving them your attention. By sitting down, you are sending the message that you are there with them at that moment.

- *Be prepared!* Have materials readily available to you during the conference. You may wish to compile a Conferring Toolkit of essential materials (see page 248 of Appendix A) that can be carried with you or placed in your conference area.

Continuing to provide meaningful and relevant conferences requires some form of keeping notes during your writing conferences. A simple but thorough conference summary can identify areas of writing deficiencies and strengths as you plan future mini-lessons, select students for small-group conferences, and report student progress to parents. To support you as you make conferring a priority in Writer's Workshop, pages for the *Conferring Notebook* are included on pages 249–252.

Benchmark Assessment Overview

Administering a Benchmark (page 257) is a guide to assist you as you begin giving benchmarks. It is important that the prompt is uniform across classrooms when measuring growth at a school level. Sixth grade benchmark prompts should be simple and attainable. For example:

- What if you were to explore your favorite place and find something extraordinary? What if it were a magic lamp? What would you do? Write an interesting story and tell about the experience.

- The local Board of Education is considering approval of gardening projects on school sites to provide fresh fruit and vegetables for school breakfasts and lunches. Make a claim to the board members about school gardening and support your claim with details and evidence.

- Your family members have many life experiences. Use your interview notes* to write an informative piece about specific information from past memories and experiences. Provide details, facts, and examples to support your writing.

The Writing Rubric (pages 258–259; writingrubric.pdf) is a tool to analyze student writing skills.

The Writing Report (page 260; writingreport.pdf) serves as a summative report of a student's writing benchmarks. The completed form along with the beginning-, middle-, and end-of-year benchmarks are placed in the student's record folder at the end of the year.

The Grouping Mat (page 261; groupingmat.pdf) is an at-a-glance chart showing which students in your classroom have attained particular benchmarks. Simply circle the current benchmark period, and complete the chart by recording the students' names in the boxes. Your goal is to see the students' names progressively move upward on the rubric report.

The core of writing instruction is the desire to support writers as they explore, discover, and learn the writing process. It also involves determining what knowledge and skills writers have developed over a period of time. Assessment is a continuous process and, when used properly, benefits teachers as well as students.

* Students were asked to interview family members prior to the benchmark.

Administering a Benchmark

Writing Benchmarks are usually administered at the beginning, middle, and end of the school year to measure improvements and determine the writer's strengths and deficits in writing development. To get started, follow these guidelines:

- Administer the Writing Benchmark Prompt to the entire class. This may be timed or untimed based on the local benchmark expectations.

- It is important not to practice the prompt prior to the writing benchmark session.

- Do not provide teacher support. Your goal is to determine what students are able to do independently. If a student demonstrates frustration, redirect the student to the prompt and pose questions for clarity.

- Allow students to use classroom displays, such as word walls. Note words copied from the word wall.

- Distribute paper to each student. Use paper familiar to students. Students should write their names and the date on the back so that it is not seen prior to scoring the writing. This will help you to stay objective as you grade the writing piece .

- Supply pencils when necessary.

- Explain to your class that this process will show how much they have grown as writers and that a prompt will be given at the beginning, middle, and end of the year.

- Read the prompt to your students. Paraphrase the prompt when necessary to clarify understanding. You may wish to display the prompt or provide individual copies.

- Create a procedure and an environment similar to your standardized writing assessment, including the use of a computer for word-processing software as applicable.

Sixth Grade Writing Rubric

	Ideas	Sentence Fluency	Organization	Word Choice
3 Advanced	• Maintains main idea; narrowed and focused topic • Supports main idea with descriptive details, anecdotes, examples, evidence, and facts	• Writes sentences that are smooth with effective flow and rhythm • Includes a variety of sentence lengths: simple, compound, complex • Includes variety of sentence types: declarative, interrogative, exclamatory, imperative • Includes varied sentence beginnings	• Writes in a logical and purposeful sequence • Includes an inviting introduction • Uses transition words to connect ideas • Includes a conclusion that satisfies the reader • Includes paragraph breaks that are purposefully organized	• Uses descriptive, colorful language to evoke strong visual images, including figurative language • Includes vocabulary that is varied yet purposeful to topic and audience
2 Proficient	• Expresses main idea; fairly broad topic • Uses some descriptive details and anecdotes with limited examples, evidence, and facts	• Writes sentences that are mostly smooth • Includes some sentence variety in length and type • Includes some variation in sentence beginnings	• Shows some evidence of logical sequence • Shows some evidence of an introduction • Uses some transition words • Includes a conclusion • Shows some evidence of paragraph breaks	• Makes some attempts at descriptive language • Uses some variation in vocabulary; mostly common words and phrases
1 Basic	• Attempts to present main idea; unclear topic • Develops few, if any, details; somewhat random	• Writes sentences that are difficult to follow or read aloud • Includes choppy, basic, simple sentences, sentence fragments, and/or run-on sentences • Lacks variety in sentence type • Repeats sentence beginnings	• Lacks evidence of logical sequence; random string of thoughts • Lacks inviting beginning • Lacks use of transition words to connect ideas • Lacks satisfying conclusion • Shows little evidence of paragraph breaks	• Lacks descriptive language • Uses limited vocabulary; monotonous and repetitious
0 Below Basic	Student attempts to write, but result is off-topic, illegible, insufficient, or otherwise fails to meet criteria for a score of 1			

Sixth Grade Writing Rubric (cont.)

		Voice	Conventions
3 **Advanced**		• Shows originality, excitement, and commitment to topic • Speaks to and connects with audience and purpose; engages reader	• Little, if any, need for editing • Capitalization is correct, errors may be minor • Consistently correct usage of grammar • Effective and correct use of punctuation • Few errors in spelling
2 **Proficient**		• Shows some originality, excitement, and commitment to topic • Writes with some sense of the audience	• Some need for editing • Capitalization may be inconsistent • Correct grammar usage is fairly consistent • Inconsistent use of punctuation • Most common words spelled correctly
1 **Basic**		• Shows little of writer's personality or commitment to topic • Reads rather dull and mechanical; connecting to no particular audience	• Extensive editing necessary • Capitalization appears random; sparse • Grammar and usage interfere with readability • Little use of correct punctuation • Frequent spelling errors
0 **Below Basic**		Student attempts to write, but result is off-topic, illegible, insufficient, or otherwise fails to meet criteria for a score of 1	

Sixth Grade Writing Report

Student Writing: _____ **Teacher:** _____ **Year:** _____

Beginning of the Year Writing Benchmark 1 Date:				Total	Summary
Ideas	Sentence Fluency	Organization	Word Choice		Advanced: 15–18
3 2 1 0	3 2 1 0	3 2 1 0	3 2 1 0		Proficient: 11–14
Voice		Conventions			Basic: 6–10
3 2 1 0		3 2 1 0			Below Basic: 0–5

Notes: _____

_____

Middle of the Year Writing Benchmark 2 Date:				Total	Summary
Ideas	Sentence Fluency	Organization	Word Choice		Advanced: 15–18
3 2 1 0	3 2 1 0	3 2 1 0	3 2 1 0		Proficient: 11–14
Voice		Conventions			Basic: 6–10
3 2 1 0		3 2 1 0			Below Basic: 0–5

Notes: _____

_____

End of the Year Writing Benchmark 3 Date:				Total	Summary
Ideas	Sentence Fluency	Organization	Word Choice		Advanced: 15–18
3 2 1 0	3 2 1 0	3 2 1 0	3 2 1 0		Proficient: 11–14
Voice		Conventions			Basic: 6–10
3 2 1 0		3 2 1 0			Below Basic: 0–5

Notes: _____

_____

Sixth Grade Grouping Mat

	Ideas	Sentence Fluency	Organization	Word Choice	Voice	Conventions
3 Advanced						
2 Proficient						
1 Basic						
0 Below Basic						

Sixth Grade Benchmark Writing Samples

Beginning of the Year

Prompt: What if you were to explore your favorite place and find something extraordinary? What if it were a magic lamp? What would you do? Write an interesting story and tell about the experience.

One day, not too long ago, there was a girl named Salena. Her family had been the poorest in the land. Salena's older brother, Dan, was fourteen years old, and had a job working for a local farmer. The pay wasn't the best, but the farmer sometimes gave them free produce. Salena liked the farmer and visited him almost every day. She also liked his farm animals, and gave them all names. Ginger, the pig, was her favorite though.

Salena's parents were delightful. Her mom was a housewife, but she was very kind. Her father sold most of the crops from their garden, beans, wheat, and corn were the main things he would sell. What her dad couldn't sell, Salena's mother would cook. Her mother was a fine cook, with the little she had to cook with, and she did please the family. When they all came home, they came to a delicious meal, even though there was little to eat.

Salena was a wonderful girl, but she was one to go looking for trouble. When she was looking for trouble, eventually, it found her. Salena loved to go exploring through the forest. When it was sunny was the best time to be there. Knowing that it was sunny, she wanted to go exploring today. She went to her mother to ask if it was alright for her to go.

"Mother?" Salena asked. "May I go to the forest to explore?" Salena waited for a response. Her mother looked at her with a smile.

"Yes, you may, dear," her mother replied, "but be careful!"

Salena was exploring through the unearthly forest, loving her surroundings, when she came to a cave.

"Wow," Salena muttered, "all the times I've been through here, I have never seen that!" She found the courage to walk closer to it. Finally, when she was up to the bloodcurdling cave, she slowly walked inside.

Salena wondered around in the cave, until it came to an end. "What's this?" she asked herself as she reached for what looked like a small button. WOOSH! The wall in front of her was gone!

"Wow," she exclaimed.

She walked inside, step by step. She was amazed, for all around her were mountains of jewels and gold! Salena explored through the land of jewels, when she spotted a plaque. It said, "Take only what ye shall need!" She looked at the plaque a minute, and then saw something else written on the plaque. It said, "but if ye are not the chosen one, leave the lamp!"

"Leave the lamp?" Salena mimicked.

"What lamp?" Salena looked around for this lamp, but found nothing.

"WHO DARES TO WAKE ME?" a deep frightening voice asked. "Uh…uh…uh…" Salena stuttered. "S-S-Salena." The voice paused for a few seconds. "Salena?" he asked in a calmer voice. Salena was still frightened. "Y-yes sir!" Salena answered shocked.

Sixth Grade Benchmark Writing Samples (cont.)

Beginning of the Year (cont.)

"The chosen one!" the voice replied.

"Here, I will show you to the lamp, Miss Salena," the voice informed her. Salena was confused when the voice showed itself for he was but a small lizard! "Come, " the lizard told her. "I will show you the way."

He led her through tunnels until he came to a stop. "Here we are," he said. The walls glittered with diamonds and the floor shimmered with peices of gold! She looked up and on the top of a mountain of jewels was a glow. Salena started to climb the mountain, but she slipped! She caught herself quickly. It would have been terrible if she had fallen. After climbing a while she found herself at the top. There in front of her eyes was the lamp! She observed that the lamp was very dusty, so she took her sleve and was cleaning it off when WOOSH! She was so startled that she almost fell. There before her eyes was a giant floating man! Your wish is my command," it promised her.

Salena had a smile on her face when she heard this, so without a breath she made wishes. Her first wish was that her family wasn't poor. Second was that she and her brother could go to school. The last wish! She had to think hard, so she wished for her family to always be happy. "As you wish," the genie said.

So, as it all turned out, Salena's life was never unhappy, or troubling again

Beginning of the Year Writing Benchmark 1: Narrative Date:				Total	Summary
Ideas	Sentence Fluency	Organization	Word Choice	17 Advanced	Advanced: 15–18 Proficient: 11–14 Basic: 6–10 Below Basic: 0–5
③ 2 1 0	③ 2 1 0	③ 2 1 0	③ 2 1 0		
Voice		Conventions			
3 ② 1 0		③ 2 1 0			

Notes:

- Supports main ideas with descriptive details and anecdotes (Ideas)
- Includes sentence variety in length and type (Sentence Fluency)
- Includes variation in sentence beginnings (Sentence Fluency)
- Writes in a logical and purposeful sequence (Organization)
- Paragraph breaks are purposefully organized (Organization)
- Uses descriptive, colorful language (Word Choice)
- Writes with some sense of audience (Voice)
- Little need for editing (Conventions)

Sixth Grade Benchmark Writing Samples (cont.)

Middle of the Year

Prompt: The local Board of Education is considering approval of gardening projects on school sites to provide fresh fruit and vegetables for school breakfasts and lunches. Make a claim to the board members about school gardening and support your claim with details and evidence.

Dear Board Members,

I believe every school should have a garden! If students in our school system would grow their own garden, they would be eating healthier by cutting down on processed foods. Having a garden at every school would strengthen children's work ethic as well as increase marketing opportunities between the children and their communities. Gardening at school would also reduce the travel time between harvesting the crop and bringing to the consumer. This would result in cutting costs and healthier eating habits.

In fact, if schools were planting a garden, every child should know there are many responsibilities. Start by plowing and cultivating the area where you plan to put your garden. Next, you make neat rows to place seeds or plants into the ground. Fertilize plants and seeds to help them grow. Finally, be sure to cover plants when it frosts so they will not freeze.

In a school garden plot, the plants would require care from students and the environment to grow. As with most plants, the garden will need plenty of water and sunlight. It will be the responsibility of the students to weed the garden so that plants can thrive. To protect plants from bugs, the garden should be sprayed with insecticide. Small animals, such as rabbits and birds can eat the plants, so remember to protect the garden from them.

I believe school gardening can teach children many life lessons. Children will learn the importance of hard work and how it can pay off in the end. Teamwork will be needed to grow a successful garden. Children can work early morning and late evenings after school. Gardening can also teach children patience as plants do not grow overnight.

Harvesting the garden is a very busy time. When the vegetables are ready, you must pick them from your garden and clean them well. You must decide how many to cook now and what to save for later. If you can or freeze, you can save the leftovers for winter.

To sum up, gardening at school teaches children many lessons, responsibilities, and teamwork. Children are also eating better by eating less processed foods. In many cases, children eat more vegetables, knowing they grew them themselves. Schools profit not only by cutting costs but by also forming bonds between the children by teamwork.

I believe this makes schools healthier and more enjoyable to the children. As a student, I believe this is a smart choice for schools, children and parents. Will you support this choice for our county schools? With this idea, I believe children have nothing to lose and everything to gain.

Sixth Grade Benchmark Writing Samples (cont.)

Middle of the Year (cont.)

Middle of the Year Writing Benchmark 2: Opinion Date:				Total	Summary
Ideas	Sentence Fluency	Organization	Word Choice	16 Advanced	Advanced: 15–18
3 ② 1 0	3 ② 1 0	③ 2 1 0	③ 2 1 0		Proficient: 11–14
Voice		Conventions			Basic: 6–10
③ 2 1 0		③ 2 1 0			Below Basic: 0–5

Notes:

- Some evidence of details, anecdotes, examples, evidence, and facts (Ideas)
- Writes sentences that are mostly smooth (Sentence Fluency)
- Evidence of paragraph breaks with transition words to connect ideas (Organization)
- Vocabulary purposeful to topic (Word Choice)
- Shows commitment to topic and audience (Voice)
- Little need for editing (Conventions)

Sixth Grade Benchmark Writing Samples

End of the Year

Prompt: Your family members have many life experiences. Use your interview notes* to write an informative piece about specific information from past memories and experiences. Provide details, facts, and examples to support your writing.

Back in Time

The Stulting Family owned land near the small town of Hillsboro, West Virginia. Stulting was the family name of the famous Pearl S. Buck, author of many books. When the opportunity became available, the Stultings sold their home to George Edgar, a productive farmer and a wonderful community citizen. He purchased the house and the land in the early 1940's. He also owned 800 to 1,000 acres that joined the Pearl S. Buck property, in addition to leasing adjoining land. This property also included the property belonging to George Edgar's grandfather.

In the winter, Mr. Edgar lived in the Pearl S. Buck home, which was closer to town. Heavy snowfall and icy roads limited access to the family farm. In the summer, he lived in his grandfather's slightly elevated 18 room house, which was built of homemade bricks made by slaves. He enjoyed the pristine view as well as the opportunity to look out over the livestock as they grazed in the fields below.

On the farm, they cultivated all 800 acres. They grew corn, wheat, barley, rye, soybeans, and oats. The corn, oats and soybeans was made into silage to feed the steers and sheep. The remainder of the corn, not ground into silage, was used to feed the hogs. By purchasing the Pearl S. Buck property, George Edgar was able to keep 400 head of cattle, 60 brood sows, (females that had piglets) along with 1,100 head of sheep. Sixty "brood sows," would produce approximately 600 piglets, raised for market and to feed the many hired hands.

As a result, 6 full time workers were employed on the farm and during the summer months as many as 16 school boys would help with the harvest. The extra help was used to build haystacks in the fields and to hoist hay into the barn mow with a fork and pulley pulled by a team of horses. With so many hired hands to feed, the workers would butcher approximately 25 hogs each year. A cook was hired to prepare daily noontime meals and the butchered hogs were used to feed hungry hired hands.

Animals were not the only things raised on the farm. Mr. Edgar also raised vegetables, including potatoes, tomatoes, beans and lettuce. All of this fresh produce was used to feed the hired summer help.

* Students were asked to interview family members prior to the benchmark.

Sixth Grade Benchmark Writing Samples (cont.)

End of the Year (cont.)

My Grandpa Starks was one of the many hired hands to work on the George Edgar Farm. He worked there between the years of 1952–1957. Although working on a farm is hard work, he enjoyed it. At 6:30, he milked the cows and separated the cream from the milk using a separator. He drove the tractor to the fields to plow, cultivate, plant and seed. Although tired, he continued to work in the field. He especially enjoyed taking time out from work to talk with the other hired hands around a table that was 5' wide and 12' long.

The time that my Grandpa Starks worked on the farm was truly a learning experience. In fact, he used his knowledge from the Stulting Family farm later to operate his own farm.

End of the Year Writing Benchmark 3: Informative Date:				Total	Summary
Ideas	Sentence Fluency	Organization	Word Choice	16 Advanced	Advanced: 15–18 Proficient: 11–14 Basic: 6–10 Below Basic: 0–5
③ 2 1 0	③ 2 1 0	3 ② 1 0	③ 2 1 0		
Voice		Conventions			
3 ② 1 0		③ 2 1 0			

Notes:

- Supports interview with evidence of details, anecdotes, examples, and facts (Ideas)
- Sentences are smooth with rhythm and flow (Sentence Fluency)
- Shows some evidence of introduction and conclusion (Organization)
- Vocabulary is purposeful to topic (Word Choice)
- Shows some originality and excitement (Voice)
- Little need for editing (Conventions)

Mentor Text List

Managing Writer's Workshop

DiSalvo, DyAnne. 2008. *The Sloppy Copy Slipup.* New York: Holiday House.

Fletcher, Ralph. 1996. *A Writer's Notebook: Unlocking the Writer Within You.* New York: HarperCollins.

———. 2005. *Marshfield Dreams: When I Was a Kid.* New York: Henry Holt and Co.

Leedy, Loreen. 2005. *Look at My Book: How Kids Can Write & Illustrate Terrific Books.* New York: Holiday House.

Lionni, Leo. 1973. *Swimmy.* New York: Dragonfly Books.

Moss, Marissa. 1995. *Amelia's Notebook.* New York: Simon & Schuster.

Schotter, Roni. 1999. *Nothing Ever Happens on 90th Street.* New York: Orchard Books.

Ideas

Allen, Susan. 2003. *Read Anything Good Lately?* Minneapolis, MN: Millbrook Press.

———. 2006. *Written Anything Good Lately?* Minneapolis, MN: Millbrook Press.

Armstrong, Jennifer. 2006. *The American Story: 100 True Tales from American History.* New York: Knopf Books for Young Readers.

Ash, Caroline. 2011. *Top 10 of Everything 2012: More Than Just the No. 1.* New York: Sterling.

Baylor, Byrd. 1985. *Everybody Needs a Rock.* New York: Aladdin.

———. 1995. *I'm in Charge of Celebrations.* New York: Aladdin.

———. 1998. *The Table Where Rich People Sit.* New York: Aladdin.

Boelts, Maribeth. 2009. *Those Shoes.* Somerville, MA: Candlewick.

Bolotin, Norman. 2002. *Civil War A to Z: A Young Reader's Guide to Over 100 People, Places, and Points of Importance.* New York: Dutton Children's Books.

Brinckloe, Julie. 1986. *Fireflies.* New York: Aladdin.

Bunting, Eve. 1990. *The Wall.* New York: Clarion Books.

———. 2000. *The Memory String.* New York: Clarion Books.

Cleary, Beverly. 2000. *Dear Mr. Henshaw.* New York: HarperCollins.

Clement, Rod. 1999. *Grandpa's Teeth.* New York: HarperCollins.

Crews, Donald. 1992. *Shortcut.* New York: Greenwillow Books.

Cronin, Doreen. 2003. *Diary of a Worm.* New York: HarperCollins.

Cutler, Nellie Gonzalez, and Jonathan Rosenbloom, eds. 2011. *TIME for Kids Big Book of How.* New York: Time for Kids Books.

Mentor Text List (cont.)

Ideas (cont.)

Denenberg, Dennis, and Lorraine Roscoe. 2006. *50 American Heroes Every Kid Should Meet*. Minneapolis, MN: Millbrook Press.

Ewald, Wendy. 2002. *The Best Part of Me: Children Talk About Their Bodies in Pictures and Words*. New York: Brown Books for Young Readers.

Fletcher, Ralph. 1996. *A Writer's Notebook: Unlocking the Writer Within You*. New York: HarperCollins.

———. 2005. *Marshfield Dreams: When I Was a Kid*. New York: Henry Holt and Co.

Freedman, Russell. 2001. *Give Me Liberty! The Story of the Declaration of Independence*. New York: Holiday House.

Harris, Caroline. 2008. *I Wonder Why Whales Sing and Other Questions About Sea Life*. Boston: Kingfisher.

Huliska-Beith, Laura. 2000. *The Book of Bad Ideas*. New York: Little, Brown Young Readers.

Humphrey, Sandra McLeod. 2005. *Dare to Dream! 25 Extraordinary Lives*. Amherst, NY: Prometheus Books.

Janeczko, Paul B. 2005. *A Poke in the I: A Collection of Concrete Poems*. Somerville, MA: Candlewick Press.

Jenkins, Steve. 2006. *Almost Gone: The World's Rarest Animals*. New York: HarperCollins.

Kalman, Bobbie. 1997. *How a Plant Grows*. New York: Crabtree Publishing Company.

———. 2008. *The ABCs of Habitats*. New York: Crabtree Publishing Company.

King, David. 2003. *Children's Encyclopedia of American History*. New York: DK Publishing, Inc.

MacLachlan, Patricia. 1994. *All the Places to Love*. New York: HarperCollins.

———. 1995. *What You Know First*. New York: HarperCollins.

McNulty, Faith. 1979. *How to Dig a Hole to the Other Side of the World*. New York: HarperCollins.

Moss, Marissa. 1995. *Amelia's Notebook*. New York: Simon & Schuster.

———. 2003. *Amelia's 5th-Grade Notebook*. New York: Simon & Schuster.

———. 2005. *Amelia's 6th-Grade Notebook*. New York: Simon & Schuster.

Murphy, Jim. 2000. *Blizzard*. New York: Scholastic.

Muth, Jon. 2002. *The Three Questions (Based on a story by Leo Tolstoy)*. New York: Scholastic.

Orr, Wendy. 1996. *Peeling the Onion*. New York: Bantam Doubleday Dell Books for Young Readers.

Paul, Ann Whitford. 2009. *Writing Picture Books: A Hands-On Guide from Story Creation to Publication*. Cincinnati, OH: Writer's Digest Books.

Paulsen, Gary. 1987. *Hatchet*. New York: Simon & Schuster.

Polacco, Patricia. 1998. *My Rotten Redheaded Older Brother*. New York: Aladdin.

Mentor Text List (cont.)

Ideas (cont.)

Polacco, Patricia. 1998. *Thank You, Mr. Falker*. New York: Philomel Books.

———. 1999. *My Ol' Man*. New York: Penguin.

Rosenthal, Amy Krouse. 2006. *One of Those Days*. New York: G. P. Putnam's Sons.

Rylant, Cynthia. 1982. *When I Was Young in the Mountains*. New York: Puffin.

Schotter, Roni. 1999. *Nothing Ever Happens on 90th Street*. New York: Scholastic.

Schwartz, David M. 1998. *G is for Googol: A Math Alphabet Book*. New York: Tricycle Press.

Simon, Seymour. 1992. *Our Solar System*. New York: HarperCollins.

———. 1999. *Tornadoes*. New York: HarperCollins.

Wells, Robert E. 1996. *How Do You Lift a Lion?* Morton Grove, IL: Albert Whitman & Company.

Wiesner, David. 1991. *Tuesday*. New York: Houghton Mifflin Harcourt.

———. 2006. *Flotsam*. New York: Clarion Books.

Wong, Janet S. 2002. *You Have to Write*. New York: Margaret K. McElderry Books.

Yolen, Jane. 1987. *Owl Moon*. New York: Philomel Books.

Sentence Fluency

Alcott, Louisa May. 1855 (2012). *Little Women*. Hollywood, FL: Simon & Brown.

Baylor, Byrd. 1998. *The Table Where Rich People Sit*. New York: Aladdin.

Berkes, Marianne. 2010. *Going Home: The Mystery of Animal Migration*. Nevada City, CA: Dawn Publications.

Brooks, Bruce. 1987. *The Moves Make the Man*. New York: Harper Trophy.

Bunting, Eve. 1991. *Fly Away Home*. New York: Clarion Books.

———. 2000. *The Memory String*. New York: Clarion Books.

———. 2003. *Whales Passing*. New York: Clarion Books.

Cleary, Brian P. 2001. *To Root, to Toot, to Parachute: What Is a Verb?* Minneapolis, MN: Carolrhoda Books.

Crossingham, John. 2000. *Football in Action*. New York: Crabtree Publishing Company.

Dahl, Roald. 1980. *The Twits*. New York: Puffin Books.

Dr. Seuss. 1960. *Oh, the Places You'll Go*. New York: Random House Children's Books.

Fletcher, Ralph. 1997. *Twilight Comes Twice*. New York: Clarion Books.

Giovanni, Nikki. 2007. *Rosa*. New York: Square Fish.

Golenbock, Peter. 1992. *Teammates*. New York: Houghton Mifflin Harcourt.

Mentor Text List *(cont.)*

Sentence Fluency *(cont.)*

Hiscock, Bruce. 2008. *Ookpik: The Travels of a Snowy Owl.* Honesdale, PA: Boyds Mills Press.

Hopkinson, Deborah. 2005. *Under the Quilt of Night.* New York: Aladdin.

———. 2012. *Sky Boys: How They Built the Empire State Building.* New York: Dragonfly Books.

Lauber, Patricia. 1993. *Volcano: The Eruption and Healing of Mount St. Helens.* New York: Aladdin.

Lee, Dennis. 2006. *Alligator Pie.* Toronto: Key Porter Books.

Lester, Julius. 2007. *Day of Tears.* New York: Hyperion Books.

MacLachlan, Patricia. 1994. *All the Places to Love.* New York: HarperCollins.

McCloskey, Robert. 1943. *Homer Price.* New York: Viking.

McLerran, Alice. 1995. *The Ghost Dance.* New York: Clarion Books.

Palatini, Margie. 2000. *Bedhead.* New York: Simon & Schuster.

———. 2009. *Lousy Rotten Stinkin' Grapes.* New York: Simon & Schuster.

Paterson, Katherine. 1987. *The Bridge to Terabithia.* New York: HarperCollins.

Paulsen, Gary. 1995. *Dogteam.* New York: Bantam Doubleday Dell Books for Young Readers.

Pearsall, Shelley. 2003. *Trouble Don't Last.* New York: Yearling.

Petry, Ann. 1995. *Harriet Tubman: Conductor on the Underground Railroad.* New York: HarperCollins.

Polacco, Patricia. 1998. *Thank You, Mr. Falker.* New York: Philomel Books.

Ryan, Pam Muñoz. 2000. *Esperanza Rising.* New York: Scholastic.

Rylant, Cynthia. 1992. *An Angel for Solomon Singer.* New York: Orchard Books.

Taylor, Mildred D. 1997. *Roll of Thunder, Hear My Cry.* New York: Puffin Books.

Walton, Rick. 2007. *Just Me and 6,000 Rats: A Tale of Conjunctions.* Layton, UT: Gibbs Smith.

Wick, Walter. 1997. *A Drop of Water: A Book of Science and Wonder.* New York: Scholastic Press.

Yep, Laurence. 1975. *Dragonwings.* New York: HarperCollins Children's Books.

Yolen, Jane. 1987. *Owl Moon.* New York: Philomel Books.

Organization

Ada, Alma Flor. 1997. *Dear Peter Rabbit.* New York: Aladdin.

Arnosky, Jim. 2009. *Slither and Crawl: Eye to Eye with Reptiles.* New York: Sterling.

Bagert, Brod. 2005. *Giant Children.* New York: Puffin.

———. 2008. *School Fever.* New York: Dial Books for Young Readers.

Mentor Text List *(cont.)*

Organization *(cont.)*

Bishop, Nic. 2008. *Frogs.* New York: Scholastic Nonfiction.

Blackburn, Ken, and Jeff Lammers. 1996. *Kids' Paper Airplane Book.* New York: Workman Publishing Company.

Borden, Louise. 2001. *A. Lincoln and Me.* New York: Scholastic.

Bridges, Ruby. 1999. *Through My Eyes: Ruby Bridges.* New York: Scholastic.

Brinckloe, Julie. 1986. *Fireflies.* New York: Aladdin.

Bunting, Eve. 1991. *Fly Away Home.* New York: Clarion Books.

Clark, Roy, and Christopher Scanlan. 2005. *America's Best Newspaper Writing.* New York: Bedford/St. Martin's.

Clements, Andrew. 2007. *Dogku.* New York: Simon & Schuster.

Cobb, Vicki. 2003. *I Face the Wind.* New York: HarperCollins.

Cohen, Sasha. 2005. *Fire on Ice: Autobiography of a Champion Figure Skater.* New York: HarperCollins.

Cooney, Caroline B. 1996. *Driver's Ed.* New York: Bantam Doubleday Dell Books for Young Readers.

Crews, Donald. 1992. *Shortcut.* New York: Greenwillow Books.

Dahl, Roald. 2009. *Boy: Tales of Childhood.* New York: Puffin.

De Young, C. Coco. 2000. *A Letter to Mrs. Roosevelt.* New York: Yearling.

DiSalvo, DyAnne. 2008. *The Sloppy Copy Slipup.* New York: Holiday House.

Fletcher, Ralph. 2005. *Marshfield Dreams: When I Was a Kid.* New York: Henry Holt and Co.

———. 2007. *How to Write Your Life Story.* New York: HarperCollins.

Frazee, Marla. 2003. *Roller Coaster.* Orlando, FL: Harcourt.

Gantos, Jack. 2004. *Hole in My Life.* New York: Farrar, Straus and Giroux.

Greenfield, Eloise. 1978. *Honey, I Love and Other Love Poems.* New York: HarperCollins.

Hobbs, Will. 2004. *Bearstone.* New York: Aladdin.

Houston, Gloria. 1992. *My Great-Aunt Arizona.* New York: HarperCollins.

Huliska-Beith, Laura. 2000. *The Book of Bad Ideas.* New York: Little, Brown Young Readers.

Janeczko, Paul B. 2009. *A Kick in the Head: An Everyday Guide to Poetic Forms.* Somerville, MA: Candlewick Press.

Keller, Helen, and Candace Ward. 1996. *Helen Keller: The Story of My Life.* New York: Dover Publications.

Kloske, Geoffrey. 2005. *Once upon a time, the End (asleep in 60 seconds).* New York: Atheneum Books for Young Readers.

Mentor Text List *(cont.)*

Organization *(cont.)*

Laden, Nina. 1994. *The Night I Followed the Dog.* San Francisco: Chronicle Books.

Laminack, Lester. 2010. *Snow Day!* Atlanta, GA: Peachtree Publishers.

Leedy, Loreen. 1990. *The Furry News: How to Make a Newspaper.* New York: Holiday House.

Lester, Julius. 1999. *John Henry.* New York: Puffin.

———. 2000. *To Be a Slave.* New York: Puffin.

Levin, Mark. 2004. *Kids in Print: Publishing a School Newspaper.* Columbus, NC: Mind-Stretch Publishing.

Lollis, Sylvia, and Joyce Hogan. 2002. *Should We Have Pets? A Persuasive Text.* New York: Mondo Publishing.

Lowry, Lois. 2000. *Looking Back: A Book of Memories.* New York: Delacorte Press.

MacLachlan, Patricia. 1995. *Baby.* New York: Bantam Doubleday Dell Books for Young Readers.

Marshall, James. 1993. *Red Riding Hood.* New York: Puffin Books.

Mazer, Anne. 1994. *The Salamander Room.* New York: Dragonfly Books.

Moss, Marissa. 1995. *Amelia's Notebook.* New York: Simon & Schuster.

Orloff, Karen Kaufman. 2010. *I Wanna New Room.* New York: Putnam Juvenile.

Pallotta, Jerry. 1993. *The Extinct Alphabet Book.* Watertown, MA: Charlesbridge Publishing.

Parks, Rosa, and Jim Haskins. 1999. *Rosa Parks: My Story.* New York: Puffin Books.

Pilkey, Dav. 1999. *The Paperboy.* New York: Orchard Books.

Prelutsky, Jack. 2004. *If Not for the Cat.* New York: Greenwillow Books.

———. 2008. *Pizza, Pigs, and Poetry: How to Write a Poem.* New York: Greenwillow Books.

Ryan, Pam Muñoz. 2000. *Esperanza Rising.* New York: Scholastic.

———. 2002. *When Marian Sang.* New York: Scholastic.

Rylant, Cynthia. 1993. *The Relatives Came.* New York: Atheneum Books for Young Readers.

———. 2006. *The Journey: Stories of Migration.* New York: The Blue Sky Press.

Schroeder, Alan. 2000. *Smoky Mountain Rose: An Appalachian Cinderella.* New York: Puffin Books.

Scieszka, Jon. 2008. *Knucklehead: Tall Tales and Almost True Stories of Growing Up.* New York: Viking Juvenile.

Silverstein, Shel. 1996. *Falling Up.* New York: HarperCollins.

———. 2004. *Where the Sidewalk Ends.* New York: HarperCollins.

Simon, Seymour. 1999. *Tornadoes.* New York: HarperCollins.

Mentor Text List (cont.)

Organization (cont.)

Simon, Seymour. 2003. *Hurricanes*. New York: HarperCollins.

Stine, R. L. 1998. *It Came From Ohio: My Life as a Writer*. New York: Scholastic.

Taylor, Mildred D. 1997. *Roll of Thunder, Hear My Cry*. New York: Puffin Books.

Teague, Mark. 2002. *Dear Mrs. LaRue: Letters from Obedience School*. New York: Scholastic Press.

Tebow, Tim. 2011. *Through My Eyes: A Quarterback's Journey*. Zondervan.

Toft, Kim Michelle. 2005. *The World That We Want*. Watertown, MA: Charlesbridge Publishing.

Van Allsburg, Chris. 1988. *Two Bad Ants*. Boston: Houghton Mifflin.

Wardlaw, Lee. 2011. *Won Ton: A Cat Tale Told in Haiku*. New York: Henry Holt and Co.

Winter, Jeanette. 2011. *The Watcher: Jane Goodall's Life with the Chimps*. New York: Schwartz & Wade.

Wyeth, Sharon Dennis. 1998. *Something Beautiful*. New York: Dragonfly Books.

Yolen, Jane. 1987. *Owl Moon*. New York: Philomel Books.

Young, Ed. 1996. *Lon Po Po: A Red-Riding Hood Story from China*. New York: Penguin Putnam Books for Young Readers.

Word Choice

Arnold, Tedd. 2007. *Even More Parts*. New York: Puffin.

Bloch, Serge. 2008. *Butterflies in My Stomach and Other School Hazards*. New York: Sterling.

Brennan-Nelson, Denise. 2004. *My Teacher Likes to Say*. Chelsea, MI: Sleeping Bear Press.

Cannon, Janell. 1997. *Verdi*. Orlando, FL: Harcourt Brace & Company.

Cleary, Brian P. 1999. *A Mink, a Fink, a Skating Rink: What Is a Noun?* Minneapolis, MN: Carolrhoda Books.

———. 2000. *Hairy, Scary, Ordinary: What Is an Adjective?* Minneapolis, MN: Lerner Publishing Group.

———. 2003. *Dearly, Nearly, Insincerely: What Is an Adverb?* Minneapolis, MN: Millbrook Press.

———. 2005. *Pitch and Throw, Grasp and Know: What Is a Synonym?* Minneapolis, MN: Millbrook Press.

Cook, Julia. 2008. *It's Hard to be a Verb!* Chattanooga, TN: National Center for Youth Issues.

Dahl, Michael. 2007. *If You Were a Synonym*. Mankato, MN: Picture Window Books.

———. 2007. *If You Were an Adverb*. Mankato, MN: Picture Window Books.

Dahl, Roald. 1980. *The Twits*. New York: Puffin Books.

Edwards, Pamela Duncan. 1996. *Some Smug Slug*. New York: Katherine Tegen Books.

Feiffer, Jules. 1997. *Meanwhile....* New York: HarperCollins.

Mentor Text List (cont.)

Word Choice (cont.)

Fletcher, Ralph. 1997. *Twilight Comes Twice*. New York: Clarion Books.

Guiberson, Brenda Z. 1996. *Into the Sea*. New York: Henry Holt and Co.

Haseley, Dennis. 2002. *A Story for Bear*. Orlando, FL: Harcourt Children's Books.

Heard, Georgia. 1997. *Creatures of Earth, Sea, and Sky: Poems*. Honesdale, PA: Boyds Mills Press.

Heller, Ruth. 1988. *Kites Sail High: A Book About Verbs*. New York: Puffin Books.

———. 1989. *Many Luscious Lollipops: A Book About Adjectives*. New York: Puffin Books.

———. 1990. *Merry-Go-Round: A Book About Nouns*. New York: Puffin Books.

———. 1991. *Up, Up and Away: A Book About Adverbs*. New York: Puffin Books.

Hinton, S. E. 1989. *Rumble Fish*. New York: Dell Laurel-Leaf.

Johnson, David A. 2006. *Snow Sounds: An Onomatopoeic Story*. Boston: Houghton Mifflin.

Kellogg, Steven. 1985. *Chicken Little*. New York: HarperCollins.

King, Martin Luther Jr. 1997. *I Have a Dream*. New York: Scholastic.

Laminack, Lester. 2004. *Saturdays and Teacakes*. Atlanta, GA: Peachtree Publishing.

Leedy, Loreen. 2003. *There's a Frog in My Throat! 440 Animal Sayings a Little Bird Told Me*. New York: Holiday House.

———. 2009. *Crazy Like a Fox: A Simile Story*. New York: Holiday House.

Lincoln, Abraham. 2010. *The Gettysburg Address*. New York: Penguin Books.

Loewen, Nancy. 2011. *Stubborn as a Mule and Other Silly Similes*. Mankato, MN: Picture Window Books.

MacLachlan, Patricia. 1994. *All the Places to Love*. New York: HarperCollins.

Marshall, James. 1998. *Goldilocks and the Three Bears*. New York: Picture Puffin Books.

Martin, Ann M. 2004. *A Corner of the Universe*. New York: Scholastic.

Nobisso, Josephine. 2004. *Show; Don't Tell! Secrets of Writing*. Westhampton Beach, NY: Gingerbread House.

Noble, Trinka Hakes. 1992. *Meanwhile Back at the Ranch*. New York: Puffin Books.

O'Conner, Patricia T. 2007. *Woe Is I Jr.: The Younger Grammarphobe's Guide to Better English in Plain English*. New York: G. P. Putnam's Sons.

Palatini, Margie. 2009. *Lousy Rotten Stinkin' Grapes*. New York: Simon & Schuster.

Paulsen, Gary. 2001. *Canoe Days*. New York: Dragonfly Books.

Petry, Ann. 1995. *Harriet Tubman: Conductor on the Underground Railroad*. New York: HarperCollins.

Polacco, Patricia. 1997. *Thunder Cake*. New York: Penguin Group.

Mentor Text List (cont.)

Word Choice (cont.)

Polacco, Patricia. 1998. *Chicken Sunday*. New York: Puffin Books.

Rylant, Cynthia. 1992. *An Angel for Solomon Singer*. New York: Orchard Books.

Say, Allen. 1993. *Grandfather's Journey*. Boston: Houghton Mifflin.

Schotter, Roni. 2006. *The Boy Who Loved Words*. New York: Random House.

Shaskan, Trisha Speed. 2008. *If You Were Onomatopoeia*. Mankato, MN: Picture Window Books.

Simon, Seymour. 1999. *Tornadoes*. New York: HarperCollins.

Steig, William. 1986. *Brave Irene*. New York: Farrar, Straus and Giroux.

———. 1990. *Shrek!* New York: Farrar, Straus and Giroux.

Steinbeck, John. 1997. *Travels with Charley: In Search of America*. New York: Penguin Books.

Stroud, Bettye. 2007. *The Patchwork Path: A Quilt Map to Freedom*. Somerville, MA: Candlewick Press.

Terban, Marvin. 1983. *In a Pickle and Other Funny Idioms*. New York: Clarion Books.

———. 1993. *It Figures! Fun Figures of Speech*. New York: Clarion Books.

Twain, Mark. 1998. *The Adventures of Tom Sawyer*. New York: Dover Publications.

Van Allsburg, Chris. 1988. *Two Bad Ants*. Boston: Houghton Mifflin Books for Children.

Walton, Rick. 2004. *Suddenly Alligator: Adventures in Adverbs*. Layton, UT: Gibbs Smith.

Williams, Charlie. 2005. *Flush! An Ode to Toilets*. Seattle, WA: Sound Safari Theater.

Wood, Audrey. 2006. *The Bunyans*. New York: Scholastic.

Yolen, Jane. 1987. *Owl Moon*. New York: Philomel Books.

Voice

Ada, Alma Flor. 2001. *Yours Truly, Goldilocks*. New York: Aladdin.

Aliki. 1984. *Feelings*. New York: Greenwillow Books.

Artell, Mike. 2001. *Petite Rouge: A Cajun Red Riding Hoof*. New York: Dial Books.

———. 2006. *Three Little Cajun Pigs*. New York: Dial Books.

———. 2010. *Jacques and de Beanstalk: A Cajun Tale*. New York: Dial Books.

Baylor, Byrd. 1985. *Everybody Needs a Rock*. New York: Aladdin.

Bridges, Ruby. 1999. *Through My Eyes: Ruby Bridges*. New York: Scholastic.

Browne, Anthony. 2001. *Voices in the Park*. New York: DK Publishing.

Bunting, Eve. 1990. *The Wall*. New York: Clarion Books.

Mentor Text List (cont.)

Voice (cont.)

Bunting, Eve. 1991. *Fly Away Home*. New York: Clarion Books.

———. 1996. *Train to Somewhere*. New York: Clarion Books.

———. 2000. *Dreaming of America: An Ellis Island Story*. Mahwah, NJ: Troll Communications.

———. 2000. *The Memory String*. New York: Clarion Books.

Cain, Janan. 2000. *The Way I Feel*. Seattle, WA: Parenting Press.

Cronin, Doreen. 2003. *Diary of a Worm*. New York: HarperCollins.

Fletcher, Ralph. 1997. *Twilight Comes Twice*. New York: Clarion Books.

———. 2005. *Marshfield Dreams: When I Was a Kid*. New York: Henry Holt and Co.

Forward, Toby. 2005. *Wolf's Story: What Really Happened to Little Red Riding Hood*. Somerville, MA: Candlewick Press.

Frame, Jeron Ashford. 2008. *Yesterday I Had the Blues*. Berkeley, CA: Tricycle Press.

Gipson, Fred. 2001. *Old Yeller*. New York: HarperCollins.

Hall, Donald. 1956 (2001). *I Am the Dog, I Am the Cat*. New York: Dial Books.

Hurst, Margaret. 2001. *Grannie and the Jumbie: A Caribbean Tale*. New York: HarperCollins.

Ketteman, Helen. 1997. *Bubba, The Cowboy Prince: A Fractured Texas Tale*. New York: Scholastic.

Kinney, Jeff. 2008. *Diary of a Wimpy Kid: Roderick Rules*. New York: Amulet Books.

Kotzwinkle, William, and Glenn Murray. 2001. *Walter the Farting Dog*. Berkeley, CA: Frog Children's Books.

Kramer, Stephen. 1995. *Caves*. Minneapolis, MN: Carolrhoda Books.

Laminack, Lester. 2004. *Saturdays and Teacakes*. Atlanta, GA: Peachtree Publishing.

McKissack, Patricia. 1986. *Flossie & the Fox*. New York: Dial Books.

McLerran, Alice. 2001. *The Ghost Dance*. Boston: Sandpiper.

Moss, Marissa. 1995. *Amelia's Notebook*. New York: Simon & Schuster.

———. 2005. *Amelia's Most Unforgettable Embarrassing Moments*. New York: Simon & Schuster.

Naylor, Phyllis Reynolds. 2000. *Shiloh*. New York: Aladdin.

O'Malley, Kevin. 2003. *Straight to the Pole*. New York: Walker & Company.

Palatini, Margie. 2000. *Bedhead*. New York: Simon & Schuster Books for Young Readers.

———. 2004. *Sweet Tooth*. New York: Simon & Schuster Books for Young Readers.

Polacco, Patricia. 1998. *Thank You, Mr. Falker*. New York: Philomel Books.

Mentor Text List (cont.)

Voice (cont.)

Polacco, Patricia. 1998. *My Rotten Redheaded Older Brother*. New York: Aladdin.

———. 1999. *My Ol' Man*. New York: Penguin Putnam Books for Young Readers.

———. 2012. *The Art of Miss Chew*. New York: Putnam Juvenile.

Ryder, Joanne. 1996. *Earthdance*. New York: Henry Holt and Co.

Schroeder, Alan. 2000. *Smoky Mountain Rose: An Appalachian Cinderella*. New York: Puffin.

Scieszka, Jon. 1992. *The Stinky Cheese Man and Other Fairly Stupid Tales*. New York. Viking Press.

———. 1996. *The True Story of The Three Little Pigs!* New York: Puffin.

Sullivan, Sarah. 2011. *Passing the Music Down*. Somerville, MA: Candlewick Press.

Trivizas, Eugene. 1993. *The Three Little Wolves and the Big Bad Pig*. New York: Aladdin.

Twain, Mark. 1998. *The Adventures of Tom Sawyer*. New York: Dover Publications.

Van Allsburg, Chris. 1988. *Two Bad Ants*. Boston: Houghton Mifflin.

Ware, Cheryl. 1999. *Flea Circus Summer*. New York: Scholastic.

Conventions

Baylor, Byrd. 1995. *I'm in Charge of Celebrations*. New York: Aladdin.

Boelts, Maribeth. 2009. *Those Shoes*. Somerville, MA: Candlewick Press.

Brinckloe, Julie. 1986. *Fireflies*. New York: Aladdin.

Bunting, Eve. 1996. *Train to Somewhere*. New York: Clarion Books.

Burleigh, Robert. 2003. *Home Run*. New York: Voyager Books.

Cleary, Brian. 2004. *I and You and Don't Forget Who: What Is a Pronoun?* Minneapolis, MN: Millbrook Press.

Editors of the American Heritage Dictionaries. 2006. *100 Words To Make You Sound Smart*. Boston: Houghton Mifflin.

———. 2010. *100 Words Every Middle Schooler Should Know*. Boston: Houghton Mifflin.

Fletcher, Ralph. 1997. *Twilight Comes Twice*. New York: Clarion Books.

Fogarty, Mignon. 2011. *Grammar Girl's 101 Misused Words You'll Never Confuse Again*. New York: St. Martin's Press.

Gray, Libba M. 1999. *My Mama Had a Dancing Heart*. New York: Orchard Books.

Heller, Ruth. 1997. *Mine, All Mine. A Book About Pronouns*. New York: Puffin.

Howard, Elizabeth F. 1991. *Aunt Flossie's Hats (and Crab Cakes Later)*. New York: Clarion Books.

Mentor Text List *(cont.)*

Conventions *(cont.)*

Keeley, Bethany. 2010. *The Book of "Unnecessary" Quotation Marks: A Celebration of Creative Punctuation*. San Francisco: Chronicle Books.

L'Engle, Madeleine. 2007. *A Swiftly Tilting Planet*. New York: Square Fish.

Loewen, Nancy. 2007. *If You Were a Homonym or a Homophone*. Mankato, MN: Picture Window Books.

———. 2007. *If You Were a Pronoun*. Mankato, MN: Picture Window Books.

Moss, Marissa. 1995. *Amelia's Notebook*. New York: Simon & Schuster.

Muth, Jon. 2002. *The Three Questions (Based on a story by Leo Tolstoy)*. New York: Scholastic.

Nixon, Joan Lowery. 1995. *If You Were a Writer*. New York: Aladdin.

O'Conner, Patricia. 2007. *Woe Is I Jr.: The Younger Grammarphobe's Guide to Better English in Plain English*. New York: G. P. Putnam's Sons.

Paulsen, Gary. 1996. *Brian's Winter*. New York: Delacorte Press.

Polacco, Patricia. 1998. *Thank You, Mr. Falker*. New York: Philomel Books.

Presson, Leslie. 1997. *A Dictionary of Homophones*. New York: Barron's Educational Series.

Rylant, Cynthia. 1992. *Missing May*. New York: Scholastic.

Shulevitz, Uri. 1998. *Snow*. New York: Farrar, Straus and Giroux.

Truss, Lynne. 2006. *Eats, Shoots & Leaves: Why, Commas Really Do Make a Difference!* New York: G. P. Putnam's Sons.

———. 2007. *The Girl's Like Spaghetti: Why, You Can't Manage without Apostrophes!* New York: G. P. Putnam's Sons.

———. 2008. *Twenty-Odd Ducks: Why, Every Punctuation Mark Counts!* New York: G. P Putnam's Sons.

Turner, Priscilla. 1996. *The War Between the Vowels and the Consonants*. New York: Farrar, Straus and Giroux.

Van Allsburg, Chris. 1988. *Two Bad Ants*. Boston: Houghton Mifflin.

Walker, Sally M. 2008. *The Vowel Family: A Tale of Lost Letters*. Minneapolis, MN: Carolrhoda Books.

Wiles, Deborah. 2005. *Freedom Summer*. New York: Aladdin.

Yolen, Jane. 1987. *Owl Moon*. New York: Philomel Books.

Sample Home Connections Letter

Dear Parents,

One of our first writing projects is to decorate our Writer's Notebook. The notebook is a very important part of our writing time together. In the notebook, students will practice the many skills learned during Writer's Workshop. The notebook serves as an ongoing resource as your child becomes a writer.

Over the weekend, students are asked to decorate the cover of their Writer's Notebook in the form of a collage and return them to school on Monday. The notebook decorations should reflect your child's interests. Here is a list of possible items to include on the notebook:

- photographs
- magazine clippings
- stickers
- scrapbooking items

- shapes and letters
- printed clipart
- construction paper
- illustrations and drawings

Attached is a copy of the cover of the notebook that I made last year. Some of the items that I have on it are pictures of my close family members and my pet, music notes, a picture of an mp3 player (because I love music), a picture of a book by my favorite author, roses (because that is my middle name), airplanes and sandals (because I like to travel), and credit cards (because I love to shop). I also used some various scrapbooking items to decorate.

Remember these ideas should reflect your child's interests, hobbies, family, favorites, etc. Take the next step! Share stories and memories and record a list of writing ideas to give your child a jump start.

Please contact me if you have any questions or concerns about the notebook project.

Thank you in advance for your support!

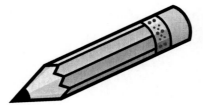

Sincerely,

Ms. Olivito

Supporting with Technology

Whether communicating via cell phones, texts, blogs, tweets, Facebook, or email, or gathering information via Internet, Google, and eBooks, today's students will live in a world increasingly shaped by technology. For this reason, Common Core State Standards highlight the effective use of technology-integrated instruction across the curriculum. Incorporating technology into instruction increases opportunities for students to be active learners, rather than passive receivers of information, and offers new ways of learning and sharing information.

The challenge for most teachers is how to seamlessly integrate technology use so that it does not take time away from writing instruction but enhances that instruction and increases students' interest and involvement. While uses of technology are seemingly limitless and constantly being updated, here are seven important ways teachers are successfully integrating technology into Writer's Workshop:

1. Digital and flip cameras can add excitement to any writing project. Student projects that capture pictures of the life cycle of a chick or a class field trip instantly invite students into a writing project. Digital photos can be used to generate a photo album of writing ideas, organize storyboards, promote language and vocabulary, illustrate student writing, and even be included in slide show presentations.

2. Document cameras are easily integrated in writing lessons and activities by both teachers and students. The benefits of using mentor texts for modeling are sometimes lost on students who may not be close enough to see the specific texts. Whether presenting photographs to gather writing ideas, sharing multiple beginnings from mentor texts, or displaying leaves and fossils to model descriptive language, the document camera offers a myriad of opportunities for modeling writing instruction for all students to see. Using the document camera allows you to zoom in on specific text features and details in illustrations. Students frequently volunteer to display their writing with the document camera and gather feedback from classmates on revising and editing. Teachers and students also enjoy presenting examples of good writing work and highlighting quality features in writing using the document camera.

3. Interactive whiteboards can serve a number of purposes for writing instruction. They provide the opportunity for student engagement and involvement of almost any materials or activity that can be viewed on a computer screen. Consider using the interactive whiteboard to teach whole group keyboarding skills, revising word choice by highlighting verbs or adjectives, using editing marks, building story webs, or reinforcing skills by accessing interactive websites. Of course, whiteboards are an excellent source to demonstrate and model lessons, give presentations, and create class books and word banks.

Supporting with Technology *(cont.)*

4. Publishing tools abound in the technology realm. Students may be involved in illustrating their writing with Microsoft® Paint or a software program like KidPix®. Through word processing, students can create letters, essays, brochures, and even class newsletters. Many teachers use Microsoft® PowerPoint for publishing individual, team, or class writing projects, which can easily be printed and bound into classroom books or saved as eBooks. Podcasts are used to record students as they read their writing. This can support the revising and editing process as they listen carefully to their writing and add a special touch to a final published project. Technology enhances the writer's options for publishing their work. For example, parents and students enjoy viewing and listening to final projects on the school website.

5. Research has never been easier. Though writing teachers must be cognizant of Internet safety, misuse, and plagiarism and follow district policies, they know technology allows for new and purposeful ways to gather and synthesize research. Writing teachers demonstrate technology-driven research procedures and help students locate and bookmark trusted websites. Collaborating with colleagues about their student research websites can make research easy and accessible.

6. URLs (Uniform Resource Locators) are great to include in your classroom newsletter. Offer links for students to practice skills, view presentations, or learn about future topics like Arbor Day. And don't forget the authors! With activities like Ralph Fletcher's *Tips for Young Writers*, Patricia Pollacco's *Who Am I*, or *Poetry Writing with Jack Prelutsky*, author websites are filled with an assortment of information and activities to engage and motivate student writing. Visit author sites while teaching students how to create their own Author's Page. The possibilities are limitless.

7. Collaborative writing projects like ePals and virtual field trips open classroom boundaries to endless learning opportunities. EPals is a modern pen pal project in which students can collaborate on academic and cultural projects as well as establish everlasting friendships in other districts, states, or countries. Virtual field trips (VFTs) offer learning opportunities that might otherwise be limited by distance and funding. Writing projects may be further enhanced by a virtual visit to the San Diego Zoo to learn about animal characteristics and habitats or to the National Aeronautics and Space Administration (NASA) to interview an astronaut.

Terminology Used

In order to adequately implement the lessons included in *Getting to the Core of Writing*, it is necessary to understand the terminology used throughout the resources.

Analytics—In order to be consistent with National Assessment of Educational Progress (NAEP) standards, the following analytics are used when describing writing proficiency:

- **Below Basic/Score 0**—Writing demonstrates an attempt to write, but the result is illegible, insufficient, or otherwise fails to meet the criteria for a score of 1.

- **Basic/Score 1**—Writing demonstrates little or marginal skill in responding to the writing benchmark tasks. Few traits of quality writing are present.

- **Proficient/Score 2**—Writing demonstrates developing skills in responding to the writing benchmark tasks. Most traits of quality writing are evident.

- **Advanced/Score 3**—Writing demonstrates effective skills in responding to the writing benchmark tasks. All traits of quality writing are obvious.

Anchor Charts—Anchor charts are used to track student thinking. In this resource, anchor charts are created cooperatively by the teacher and students. The charts are used to scaffold learning and chart key concepts of writing such as ideas for writing, vocabulary words, and examples of sentence structure. Anchor charts are displayed throughout the room to support a print-rich environment that promotes literacy acquisition.

Anecdotal Observations—Throughout Writer's Workshop, teachers practice the art of becoming astute observers of student writing behaviors. The teacher's Conferring Notebook is an excellent resource to store observations for the entire year of instruction (see Appendix A). As you observe, remember to present a statement of praise and develop a teaching point as this will guide future instructional decisions.

Author's Chair—Students are selected to share their writing with classmates. Usually students sit in a designated chair/stool. Classmates provide feedback to authors in the form of a question or a compliment.

Author's Tea/Author's Luncheon—An author's tea can be held anytime to support student writing efforts. Students invite parents and special loved ones to join them, sometimes with refreshments, to celebrate accomplishments in writing. Each student writes, illustrates, publishes, and presents a favorite piece of writing from the past year. It is important that every student has someone to listen to his or her especially planned presentation. You might invite the principal, cafeteria cook, librarian, or teacher specialists as part of the celebration.

Benchmark Assessments—The beginning-of-the-year benchmark serves as baseline information about a student's writing. Middle-of-the-year and end-of-the-year benchmarks represent a student's progress toward state, district, and/or school benchmark goals.

Terminology Used *(cont.)*

Mentor Texts—A mentor text is a book that offers multiple learning opportunities as both teacher and student develop writing skills. Mentor texts contain explicit and strong examples of the author's craft and are visited repeatedly to explore the traits of quality writing. Your favorite books to share often make the best mentor texts. You may wish to use the recommended mentor text as a read-aloud during your reading block with spirited discussions or quickly review it during Writer's Workshop. During writing block, focus on small samples of text that match the mini-lesson skill. A recommended list of mentor texts is provided as part of each lesson and additional titles are provided in Appendix C.

Notebook Entry—Notebook entries are pages that students will cut out and glue into their Writer´s Notebook. They reinforce the lesson with the key points for students to remember. At the bottom of most notebook entries is a *Your Turn* section where students can practice the skill taught in the lesson.

Turn and Talk—*Turn and Talk* is a management tool for giving opportunities to students to have partner conversations. This procedure may take place at the meeting area or at desks. Students make eye contact, lean toward their partner, talk quietly, or listen attentively.

Triads and Quads—These are terms used to quickly divide the class into groups of three or four.

References

Anderson, Carl. 2000. *How's It Going? A Practical Guide to Conferring with Student Writers*. Portsmouth, NH: Heinemann.

Bjorklund, David F. 1999. *Children's Thinking: Developmental Function and Individual Differences*. New York: Brooks/Cole Publishing Company.

Buckner, Aimee. 2005. *Notebook Know How: Strategies for the Writer's Notebook*. Portland, ME: Stenhouse Publishers.

Calkins, Lucy McCormick. 1994. *The Art of Teaching Writing* (New ed.). Portsmouth, NH: Heinemann.

Calkins, Lucy McCormick, Amanda Hartman, and Zoe White. 2003. *The Conferring Handbook*. Portsmouth, NH: Heinemann.

———. 2005. *One to One: The Art of Conferring with Young Writers*. Portsmouth, NH: Heinemann.

Culham, Ruth. 2003. *6 + 1 Traits of Writing: The Complete Guide (Grades 3 and Up)*. New York: Scholastic.

———. 2008. *6 + 1 Traits of Writing: The Complete Guide for the Primary Grades*. New York: Scholastic.

———. 2008. *Using Picture Books to Teach Writing With the Traits K–2*. New York: Scholastic.

Cunningham, Patricia M. and James W. Cunningham. 2009. *What Really Matters in Writing: Research-Based Practices Across the Curriculum*. Boston, MA: Allyn & Bacon/Pearson.

Davis, Judy, and Sharon Hill. 2003. *The No-Nonsense Guide to Teaching Writing: Strategies, Structures, Solutions*. Portsmouth, NH: Heinemann.

Dolch, Edward W. 1941. *Teaching Primary Reading*. Champaign, IL: The Garrard Press.

Dorn, Linda J., and Carla Soffos. 2001. *Scaffolding Young Writers: A Writer's Workshop Approach*. Portland, ME: Stenhouse Publishers.

Ehri, Linnea C. 1997. "Learning to Read and Write Are One and the Same, Almost." in *Learning to Spell: Research, Theory, and Practice Across Languages*. Edited by Charles A. Perfetti, Laurence Rieben, and Michael Fayol. London: Lawrence Erlbaum Associates.

Erlauer, Laura. 2003. *The Brain-Compatible Classroom: Using What We Know About Learning to Improve Teaching*. Alexandria, VA: Association for Supervison and Curriculum Development.

Fletcher, Ralph. 1996. *A Writer's Notebook: Unlocking the Writer Within You*. New York: HarperCollins.

———. 1999. *Live Writing: Breathing Life Into Your Words*. New York: HarperCollins.

———. 2000. "Craft Lessons to Improve the Quality of Student Writing." Presentation at the 28th Annual Conference of The Maryland International Reading Association. Baltimore, MD.

———. 2002. *Poetry Matters: Writing a Poem From the Inside Out*. New York: HarperCollins.

Fletcher, Ralph, and JoAnn Portalupi. 1998. *Craft Lessons: Teaching Writing K–8*. Portland, ME: Stenhouse Publishers.

———. 2001. *Writing Workshop: The Essential Guide*. Portsmouth, NH: Heinemann.

Frayer, Dorothy, Wayne Frederick, and Herbert Klausmeier. 1969. *A Schema for Testing the Level of Cognitive Mastery*. Madison, WI: Wisconsin Center for Education Research.

References (cont.)

Freeman, Marcia S. 1998. *Teaching the Youngest Writers: A Practical Guide*. Gainesville, FL: Maupin House Publishing, Inc.

———. 2001. *Non-Fiction Writing Strategies: Using Science Big Books as Models*. Gainesville, FL: Maupin House Publising.

Gentry, J. Richard. 2000. *The Literacy Map: Guiding Children to Where They Need to Be (K–3)*. New York: Mondo Publishing.

———. 2002. *The Literacy Map: Guiding Children to Where They Need to Be (4–6)*. New York: Mondo Publishing.

———. 2004. *The Science of Spelling: The Explicit Specifics That Make Greater Readers and Writers (and Spellers!)*. Portsmouth, NH: Heinemann.

———. 2006. *Breaking the Code: New Science of Beginning Reading and Writing*. Portsmouth, NH: Heinemann.

———. 2007. *Breakthrough in Beginning Reading and Writing*. New York: Scholastic.

———. 2008. *Step-by-Step: Assessment Guide to Code Breaking*. New York: Scholastic.

———. 2010. *Raising Confident Readers: How to Teach Your Child to Read and Write—from Baby to Age 7*. Cambridge, MA: Da Capo Lifelong Books.

Gentry, J. Richard, and Jean Wallace Gillet. 1993. *Teaching Kids to Spell*. Portsmouth, NH: Heinemann.

Ginott, Hiam G. 1972. *Teacher & Child: A Book for Parents and Teachers*. New York: Macmillan Publishing Company.

Gould, Judith. 1999. *Four Square Writing Method: A Unique Approach to Teach Basic Writing Skills for Grades 1–3*. Carthage, IL: Teaching and Learning Company.

Graham, Steve, and Michael Hebert. 2010. *Writing to Read: Evidence for How Writing Can Improve Reading. A Carnegie Corporation Time to Act Report*. Washington, DC: Alliance for Excellent Education.

Graham, Steve, Virginia Berninger, and Robert Abbott. 2012. "Are Attitudes Toward Writing and Reading Separable Constructs? A Study with Primary Grade Children." *Reading & Writing Quarterly* 28 (1): 51–69.

Graves, Donald H. 1994. *A Fresh Look at Writing*. Portsmouth, NH: Heinemann.

———. 2003. *Writing: Teachers & Children at Work 20th Anniversary Edition*. Portsmouth, NH: Heinemann.

Jensen, Eric. 2009. *Different Brains, Different Learners: How to Reach the Hard to Reach* (Second ed.). Thousand Oaks, CA: Corwin Press.

Mann, Jean. 2002. "Writing in Grades Four, Five, and Six." In *The Literacy Map: Guiding Children to Where They Need to Be (4–6)*. New York: Mondo Publishing.

McKenna, Michael C., and Dennis J. Kear. 1990. "Measuring attitude toward reading: A new tool for teachers." *The Reading Teacher* 43 (9): 626–639.

References *(cont.)*

McMahon, Carolyn, and Peggy Warrick. 2005. *Wee Can Write: Using 6 + 1 Trait Writing Strategies with Renowned Children's Literature*. Portland, OR: Northwest Regional Educational Laboratory.

Murray, Donald M. 2004. *Write to Learn*. Independence, KY: Cengage Learning.

National Governors Association Center for Best Practices and Council of Chief State School Officers. 2011. *Common Core State Standards Initiative: The Standards*. Retrieved June 2011, from Common Core State Standards Initiative: http://www.corestandards.org

Pearson, P. David, and Margaret C. Gallagher. 1983. "The instruction of reading comprehension." *Contemporary Educational Psychology* 8: 317–344

Ray, Katie Wood. 2001. *The Writing Workshop: Working Through the Hard Parts (And They're All Hard Parts)*. Urbana, IL: National Council Of Teachers of English.

Ray, Katie Wood, and Lisa B. Cleaveland. 2004. *About the Authors: Writing Workshop with Our Youngest Writers*. Portsmouth, NH: Heinemann.

Rog, Lori Jamison, and Pauk Kropp. 2004. *The Write Genre: Classroom Activities and Mini-Lessons That Promote Writing with Clarity, Style, and Flashes of Brilliance*. Ontario, Canada: Pembroke Publishers.

Routman, Regie. 1999. *Conversations: Strategies for Teaching, Learning and Evaluating*. Portsmouth, NH: Heinemann.

———. 2000. *Kids' poems: Teaching Third & Fourth Graders to Love Writing Poetry*. New York: Scholastic Teaching Resources.

———. 2005. *Writing Essentials: Raising Expectations and Results While Simplifying Teaching*. Portsmouth, NH: Heinemann.

Shanahan, T. (In Press). *College and Career Readiness Standards for Reading, Writing, and Speaking and Listening-Draft for Review and Comment*.

Spandel, Vicki. 2001. *Books, Lessons, Ideas for Teaching the Six Traits: Writing in the Elementary and Middle Grades*. Wilmington, MA: Great Source Education Group.

———. 2005. *Seeing with New Eyes: A Guidebook on Teaching and Assessing Beginning Writers Using the Six-Trait Writing Model* (6th Edition.) Portland, OR: Northwest Regional Educational Laboratory.

———. 2008. *Creating Young Writers: Using the Six Traits to Enrich Writing Process in Primary Classrooms* (2nd Edition.). New York: Allyn & Bacon.

Sprenger, Marilee B. 2007. *Becoming a "Wiz" at Brain-Based Teaching: How to Make Every Year Your Best Year*. Thousand Oaks, CA: Corwin Press.

Tate, Marcia L. 2004. *"Sit & Get" Won't Grow Dendrites: 20 Professional Learning Strategies That Engage the Adult Brain*. Thousand Oaks, California: Corwin Press.

Vygotsky, Lev S. 1978. *Mind in Society: The Development of Higher Psychological Processes*. Edited by Michael Cole, Vera John-Steiner, Sylvia Scribner, and Ellen Souberman. Cambridge, MA: Harvard University Press.

Yates, Elizabeth. 1995. *Someday You'll Write: Secrets of a Story Maker*. Greenville, SC: Bob Jones University Press.

Contents of the Teacher Resource CD

Teacher Resources

Page Number	Title	Filename
N/A	The Traits Team	traitsteam.pdf
N/A	Student Writing Samples	samples.doc
N/A	Year-at-a-Glance	yearataglance.pdf
12–13	Suggested Pacing Guide	pacingguide.pdf
24–30	Correlation to Standards	standards.pdf
249	Conferring Notebook Cover	cover.pdf
250	Mini-Lesson Log	minilessonlog.pdf
251	Conference Log	conferencelog.pdf
252	Conference Countdown	conferencecountdown.pdf
258–259	Sixth Grade Writing Rubric	writingrubric.pdf
260	Sixth Grade Writing Report	writingreport.pdf
261	Sixth Grade Grouping Mat	groupingmat.pdf
268–279	Mentor Text List	mentortextlist.pdf
280	Sample Home Connections Letter	samplehomeletter.pdf

Managing Writer's Workshop

Page Number	Title	Filename
37	Components of Writer's Workshop Anchor Chart	writersworkshop.pdf
40	Sample Looks Like, Sounds Like, Feels Like Anchor Chart	lookssoundsfeelschart.pdf
43	Student Mini-Lesson Log	minilessonlog2.pdf
44–45	Fry Sight Word List	frywordlist.pdf
46–47	Short and Long Vowel Charts	shortlongvowelcharts.pdf
48–49	Vowel Teams Chart	vowelteamschart.pdf
54	Traits of Writing Notebook Entry	traitswriting.pdf
55–57	Traits Team Mini Posters	traitsteamposters.pdf
60	Sharing Notebook Entry	sharing.pdf
61	Compliment and Comment Cards	complicommentcards.pdf
64	Turn and Talk Notebook Entry	turntalk.pdf
67	Guidelines for Writer's Workshop Notebook Entry	guidelineswritersws.pdf
70	Peer Conference Notebook Entry	peerconference.pdf
73	The Five-Step Writing Process Notebook Entry	fivestepprocess.pdf

Contents of the Teacher Resource CD (cont.)

Ideas

Page Number	Title	Filename
76	Ida, Idea Creator	ida.pdf
79	My Top Ten Ideas Notebook Entry	topten.pdf
82	Stinky Tennis Shoes Trip Notebook Entry	stinkyshoes.pdf
85	Idea Cache Notebook Entry	ideacache.pdf
88	Ideas from A to Z Notebook Entry	atoz.pdf
91	I Saw It in a Book Notebook Entry	sawit.pdf
94	My Declarations Notebook Entry	mydeclarations.pdf
97	It's My Choice Notebook Entry	mychoice.pdf
100	I Question, Question, Question Notebook Entry	question.pdf

Sentence Fluency

Page Number	Title	Filename
102	Simon, Sentence Builder	simon.pdf
105	Playing with Sentence Patterns Notebook Entry	sentencepatterns.pdf
106	Sentence Fragments	sentencefragments.pdf
109	Double Trouble with Compound Elements Notebook Entry	doubletrouble.pdf
112	The Long and Short of It Notebook Entry	longandshort.pdf
115	Sentence Stretch and Scramble Notebook Entry	sentencestretch.pdf
118	SOS! Semicolons Offer Style Notebook Entry	sosstyle.pdf
121	Adding Details Notebook Entry	addingdetails.pdf
124	Let's Make It Clear! Notebook Entry	makeitclear.pdf

Contents of the Teacher Resource CD *(cont.)*

Organization

Page Number	Title	Filename
126	Owen, Organization Conductor	owen.pdf
129	Playing with Poetry Notebook Entry	playingpoetry.pdf
132	The Stacker Paragraph Notebook Entry	stackerparagraph.pdf
133	Sample Stacker Paragraph	samplestacker.pdf
136	Prewriting with the Knuckle Planner Notebook Entry	prewritingknuckle.pdf
139	Drafting with the Knuckle Planner Notebook Entry	draftingknuckle.pdf
142	Reeling In and Wrapping Up Notebook Entry	reelingin.pdf
145	It's Newsworthy Notebook Entry	newsworthy.pdf
146	Prewriting Organizer	organizer.pdf
149	It's All About Me! Notebook Entry	allaboutme.pdf
152	Organizing Thinking for Expository Writing Notebook Entry	expository.pdf
155	Research from A to D Notebook Entry	researchatod.pdf
156	Narrowing the Topic	narrowtopic.pdf
159	A Poetry Collage Notebook Entry	collage.pdf
160–165	Poetry Cards	poetrycards.pdf

Word Choice

Page Number	Title	Filename
168	Wally, Word Choice Detective	wally.pdf
171	Simple to Sophisticated Synonyms Notebook Entry	synonyms.pdf
172–173	Vocabulary Words	vocabularywords.pdf
176	Using Your Senses to Show, Don't Tell Notebook Entry	senses.pdf
179	Shifting Ideas with Transition Signals Notebook Entry	transitionsignals.pdf
180–181	Transition Signals	signals.pdf
184	Building Vocabulary Webs Notebook Entry	vocabularywebs.pdf
187	Just a Figure of Speech Notebook Entry	figureofspeech.pdf
188–189	Topic Cards	topiccards.pdf
192	The Power of Connotation Notebook Entry	connotation.pdf
193–194	Word Cards	wordcards.pdf
197	Exploring Etymology Notebook Entry	exploringetymology.pdf
198	Etymology Chart	etymologychart.pdf

Contents of the Teacher Resource CD *(cont.)*

Voice

Page Number	Title	Filename
200	Val and Van, Voice	valvan.pdf
203	I Know How You Feel Notebook Entry	howyoufeel.pdf
206	Voice Reflections Notebook Entry	reflections.pdf
209	The Voice of R.A.F.T. Notebook Entry	raft.pdf
212	If I Were A… Notebook Entry	ifiwerea.pdf
215	A Writer's Toolbox for Voice Notebook Entry	toolbox.pdf

Conventions

Page Number	Title	Filename
218	Callie, Super Conventions Checker	callie.pdf
221	Commonly Misspelled Words Notebook Entry	commonlymisspelled.pdf
222–223	Commonly Misspelled Words	misspelled.pdf
226	Punctuation Partners Notebook Entry	punctuation.pdf
229	The Sensational Six Notebook Entry	sensationalsix.pdf
230	Six Syllable Rules Cards	sixcards.pdf
233	Book Camp Caps Chant Notebook Entry	capschant.pdf
236	Presenting SOP Pronouns Notebook Entry	pronouns.pdf
239	The CUPS Challenge Notebook Entry	cupschallenge.pdf
240	The CUPS Challenge Writing Sample	cupssample.pdf
243	What's the Difference? Notebook Entry	difference.pdf
246	Time to Edit! Notebook Entry	timetoedit.pdf
247	Time to Edit! Writing Sample for Editing	sampleediting.pdf